Institutional Change in American Politics

INSTITUTIONAL CHANGE
in American Politics

THE CASE OF TERM LIMITS

Edited by
Karl T. Kurtz, Bruce Cain,
& Richard G. Niemi

The University of Michigan Press   *Ann Arbor*

Copyright © by the University of Michigan 2007
All rights reserved
Published in the United States of America by
The University of Michigan Press
Manufactured in the United States of America
⊗ Printed on acid-free paper

2010   2009   2008   2007   4   3   2   1

A CIP catalog record for this book is available from the British Library.

Library of Congress Cataloging-in-Publication Data

Institutional change in American politics : the case of term limits /
    edited by Karl T. Kurtz, Bruce Cain, and Richard G. Niemi.
        p.   cm.
    Includes bibliographical references and index.
    ISBN-13: 978-0-472-09994-8 (cloth : alk. paper)
    ISBN-10: 0-472-09994-9 (cloth : alk. paper)
    ISBN-13: 978-0-472-06994-1 (pbk. : alk. paper)
    ISBN-10: 0-472-06994-2 (pbk. : alk. paper)
        1. Term limits (Public office)—United States—States.
    2. Legislators—Term of office—United States—States.   I. Kurtz,
Karl T., 1945–   II. Cain, Bruce E.   III. Niemi, Richard G.

JK2488.I57   2007
328.73'073—dc22   2007001724

Foreword

IN THE FALL of 2000, Professor Alan Rosenthal of Rutgers University convened a conference of legislative scholars and users of legislative research at the Eagleton Institute of Politics on the Rutgers campus. The purpose of the conference, entitled "Using Legislative Research," was twofold: (1) to identify topics for legislative research that would be beneficial to the user community and (2) to seek ways to make political science research more useful to legislators and legislative staff. The user group was made up primarily of representatives of three national organizations of state officials: the National Conference of State Legislatures (NCSL), the Council of State Governments (CSG), and the State Legislative Leaders Foundation (SLLF).

There was a strong consensus among attendees at this conference that the impact of term limits was the most important topic for collaborative research between scholars and the user community. At the time of the conference, nineteen states had enacted term limits beginning in 1991, and those limits were just beginning to take effect in the states. By necessity, previous studies of term limits had been either single-state studies or speculative, forward-looking analyses. The participants agreed that the time was ripe for a national, comparative study of the impacts of term limits on the legislative institution.

As a result of the conference, a smaller team was formed for the Joint Project on Term Limits (JPTL). The JPTL team met in January 2001 in the Denver office of the NCSL to design the project that resulted in this edited volume. After funding was obtained, the project team began research in the fall of 2001 and continued through 2004.

Because legislatures play such an important role in our democracy, we believe that it is critical that citizens and policymakers understand the effects of term limits and make adjustments to ensure that legislatures remain effective institutions of representative democracy. The JPTL study examined the impact of term limits on legislatures' capacity for policy-making, the types of members elected, internal legislative operations, and relationships among the branches of government. The goal of the project was not to revisit the debate over whether or not there should be term limits but, rather, to aid citizens in understanding term limit effects and to help legislatures to mitigate the negative influences of term limit reform while building on its positive impacts.

This joint project among three national organizations of state legislators and a group of legislative scholars was a unique collaborative effort. Not only was it the first time the three national organizations had undertaken a joint project, but it was also the first time that legislative scholars and the users of legislative research had joined together to identify a priority research topic and collaborate on carrying it out. We hope that this project is a model for future mutually beneficial research.

The project team was managed by Jennifer Drage Bowser, Rich Jones, and Karl Kurtz of NCSL. The team thanks Matthew Jarvis—then a graduate student at the Institute of Governmental Studies at the University of California, Berkeley—for research assistance and data analysis. For assistance in preparing the manuscript for this book, the team thanks Amy Barse of NCSL.

Dan Sprague, *Executive Director,*
Council of State Governments

William Pound, *Executive Director,*
National Conference of State Legislatures

Stephen G. Lakis, *President,*
State Legislative Leaders Foundation

Contents

Illustrations

Figures

Tables

Introduction

Karl T. Kurtz, Richard G. Niemi, & Bruce Cain

TERM LIMITS ARE the most significant institutional change in American legislatures since the legislative modernization movement of the late 1960s and early 1970s. Indeed, it is difficult to think of a comparable change in the rules of the game in any American democratic institution in the last generation. Term limits, mostly adopted by voter initiatives in the 1990s, are in effect today in fifteen states. The legislatures in these fifteen states have now or soon will have experienced a complete turnover in their membership. More than a thousand experienced legislators have been prevented from running for reelection. New legislators face the prospect of learning their jobs in a very short space of time and completing whatever they hope to accomplish in as few as six years. Under term limits, it is not uncommon for legislators to chair important committees in their first term in office or to serve as Speaker of the House of Representatives after two or three years of service. Legislative organization, culture, and leadership inside the legislatures, as well as significant outside actors, such as lobbyists and governors, have had to adjust to the quickened timetable of short, finite terms in office.

Because term limits are new, there is little evidence about their effects. Three works relating to term limits were published soon after term limits were enacted in the early 1990s (Malbin and Benjamin 1992; Cain 1996; Grofman 1996). Because they were written before term limits took effect, their analyses were necessarily speculative, but they have served as a source of hypotheses for later research. The first comprehensive, comparative study (Carey, Niemi, and Powell 2000) was carried out in 1995, before any legislators were actually turned out of office. Once term limits began to take effect long enough for both electoral and institutional effects to be felt, their consequences could be gauged more fully. Most recent studies, however, have been based on one or two legislatures. Farmer, Rausch, and Green published a useful book of case studies in 2003. Other noteworthy recent single-state case studies are on Maine (Moen, Palmer, and Powell 2004) and Michigan (Sarbaugh-Thompson et al. 2004). A second comparative study, Thad Kousser's *Term Limits and the Dismantling of State Legislative Professionalism* (2005), relies on research in six states and includes comparisons to all 50 states. (See chap. 1 in this volume for a more thorough discussion of the literature on term limits.)

The present volume expands on the nation's first comparative study of term limits since they have taken effect. Our goal in this book is to shed light on the process of institutional change in American politics through an integrated, comparative, thematic analysis of the effects of term limits on state legislatures. This book is based on the premise that institutional design and incentives have a significant impact on individual behavior and policy outcomes. The adoption of term limits is, in a sense, a wonderful natural experiment that allows us to test propositions about how a specified maximum number of years in office changes legislative modes of organization and activity.

Our study takes advantage of the remarkable institutional variation of American legislatures across the fifty states. The universe of state legislatures includes

- 7,382 diverse, elected members and approximately thirty-five thousand legislative staff;
- ninety-nine legislative chambers that vary in size from twenty members to four hundred;
- hundreds of legislative leaders who have different powers and responsibilities from state to state;
- ninety-nine committee systems that differ greatly in how they are appointed and operate;
- traditional part-time "citizen" organizations; full-time, highly professionalized bodies that look more like Congress than the legislatures of other states; and many variations in between.

Now, some of these legislatures have term limits. Yet even term limits are not a single institution, as they vary in the length of service they permit, whether the limits apply to each chamber of the legislature or to both chambers combined, and how long legislators must sit out before running again, if they are allowed to at all. One of our key findings in this book is that the impact of term limits on legislatures is greatly affected by two factors: the degree of professionalization of the legislature and the restrictiveness of the term limit.

This book is organized around substantive topics related to legislative composition and organization. While benefiting from intense scrutiny of the legislatures of a number of states, this is not a collection of state studies. Rather, it focuses on how legislatures have been affected by and have adapted to the presence of term limits. Most of the discussion and debate at the time term limits were adopted in the 1990s was about the presumed effects of turnover on the kinds of individuals who would be elected—including demographics, degree of political experience, and partisanship. But what has proved to be most interesting and of the greatest long-run impact are effects on the organization and operation of the legislatures. Most obviously, the role of seniority has declined sharply, affecting committee appointments and operations and the selection and activity of leaders. The absence of long-term relationships among legislators themselves and between legislators and lobbyists and bureaucrats has disrupted previous patterns of behavior, with consequences not only for their relative power but also for the legislative culture itself. The legislatures have not been passive in all of this, as they have helped inexperienced legislators get up to speed more quickly and have adapted their procedures to meet the altered rules of the game.

This book is the product of the Joint Project on Term Limits (JPTL), a unique three-year cooperative venture between a team of academic political scientists and staff members of the National Conference of State Legislatures, the Council of State Governments, and the State Legislative Leaders Foundation. Twenty-three political scientists and practitioners on the staffs of the three national organizations participated in the project. The project team met at the outset of the project to develop a research design and on two other occasions to discuss progress and share results.

Early on in the process of research design, the project team recognized that the variability of institutional practices among state legislatures presents major challenges to research on term limits, especially as we study change over time. During the fifteen years since term limits were first imposed, legislatures were undergoing other significant demographic, societal, and political changes. The presence of these other influences means that teasing out which institutional effects are due to term limits and which are due to other factors is no easy task. For example, is the growth in the numbers and influence of Latino legislators in Arizona and California a result of term limits or of the dramatic growth in the number of Latino voters in these states over the same period of time? Are changes in the roles of lobbyists particular to the term-limited states, or is a more widespread proliferation of interest groups with registered lobbyists affecting most states? Are changes in the attitudes of legislators toward government and the legislative institution due to term limits or to the "Republican revolution" of 1994? To deal with these complexities, the project team decided to use multiple research methods that allow for comparison between term-limited and non-term-limited states. The multiple research methods also reflect the diversity of experience, training, and research orientation on the project team.

The project team and the authors of this book used a common set of data for our analysis:

1. *A fifty-state survey of all legislators in 2002.* This survey allows for comparisons between the attitudes of legislators from term-limited and non-term-limited states. It updates and expands Carey, Niemi, and Powell's 1995 survey, which asked many of the same questions. Questionnaires were mailed to 7,430 state legislators in February 2002, with follow-up letters sent in March and May of the same year. We received responses from 2,982 legislators (40.1 percent). The results of this survey, which have also been published elsewhere (Carey et al. 2006) are reported, as appropriate, throughout the chapters of this book and particularly in chapter 3. In the text, this survey is generally referred to as the 2002 National Survey of State Legislators. The survey instrument is included in the appendix to this book.

2. *Demographic and electoral data on legislators in all fifty states in 2002.* NCSL's database of state legislators contains the names, party affiliations, dates of service, and district numbers of all lawmakers. These data were supplemented by age, occupation, and education data from Capitol Advantage and merged with data from the national survey of all legislators.

3. *Legislative membership turnover data for 1982–2002.* We collected data on turnover rates from election to election for each of the ninety-nine chambers of the state legislatures. These data have been previously

published (Moncrief, Niemi, and Powell 2004); are reported in detail in chapter 2 of the present volume, which discusses the composition of state legislatures; and are referenced throughout this book.

4. *Interviews and aggregate data on legislative procedures from six term-limited states (Arizona, Arkansas, California, Colorado, Maine, and Ohio) and three non-term-limited control states (Illinois, Indiana, and Kansas) for 2002–4.* The use of control states is particularly important to our effort to separate term limit effects from other changes influencing legislatures during the same period. The selection of case study states was based on obtaining a mix of professionalized, hybrid, and citizen legislatures; the presence (or absence) of other term limit studies; and the agreement of legislative leaders that their state be included in the project. In each state, a pair of investigators consisting of an academic political scientist and a practitioner from one of the national organizations conducted interviews and gathered data based on common procedures and agreed-on key issues for investigation. Condensed versions of these case studies have been published in an edited volume by Rick Farmer, Christopher Z. Mooney, Richard J. Powell, and John C. Green, *Legislating without Experience: Case Studies in State Legislative Term Limits* (forthcoming). Complete versions of the case studies are available at http://www.ncsl.org/jptl/casestudies/CaseContents.htm. The following chapters draw on these case studies as appropriate.

5. *A Survey of Knowledgeable Observers in the nine case study states in 2003.* To supplement the personal interviews in the case study states, the case study investigators identified legislative staff, former legislators, executive agency staff, lobbyists, and reporters who had participated in or observed the state's legislature for at least ten years (i.e., before and after term limits). The knowledgeable observers were asked a series of questions that compared the legislature of today with that of a decade earlier. A total of 551 responses to the survey were received (113 from non-term-limited states and 438 from term-limited states). We interpret the results of this survey with caution for two reasons. First, there is considerable variation in the number of surveys sent out and responses received from state to state (see appendix). Second, the survey depends on the observers' recollection of how today's legislature compares to that of a decade ago. This survey was thus subject to the complications of nostalgia for the "good old days" or the tendency for conventional wisdom to set in. In the chapters that follow, this survey is generally

referred to as the 2003 Survey of Knowledgeable Observers. The complete results of the survey by state are included in the appendix, and particularly significant findings are called out in relevant chapters.

Each of our research tools—surveys, aggregate data, and case study interviews—by themselves have flaws. Combining multiple methods allows us to check clues found using one tool against the findings based on the other tools. It also allows us to take advantage of the differing skills and experiences of our project team.

Authors of individual chapters of this book collected other data that were specific to their chapters but were not generally relied on by everyone. These specific data sets are described in the appropriate chapters. Notably absent from this list of data sources is election data. Because the focus of this book is on the institution of the legislature, the project team deliberately decided not to investigate the electoral effects of term limits, such as open seats, primary and general election competition and contesting, candidate characteristics, or campaign finance.

This book integrates the findings from the five main data sources already described and explores them in eleven comparative, thematic chapters, with a conclusion by the editors. In chapter 1, Jennie Drage Bowser and Gary Moncrief provide a brief overview of the term limits movement, emphasizing not only the rapid gains made by reformers in the 1990s but also the setbacks that occurred in the courts and in the legislatures themselves. In describing the current state of affairs, they note the wide variance in term limit provisions regarding length of service and whether the limit is on consecutive terms or is a lifetime ban. They also document the number of legislators who have been removed from legislative service. Finally, they provide a foundation for the later chapters by reviewing arguments made by both sides in the debate over term limits.

Chapter 2 deals with the effect of term limits on who serves. Quite obviously, as Gary Moncrief, Lynda Powell, and Tim Storey note, term limits dramatically increased turnover upon implementation. However, the rate of future turnover is much less clear, as prospective legislators may choose to wait for open seats rather than challenging short-term incumbents. In addition, term limits have had a very limited impact on the demographics of legislative members, and they have not turned term-limited legislatures into citizen bodies, as all chambers continue to be dominated by persons with career interests in politics.

The orientation of legislators toward their jobs—especially the balance they strike between the interests of their constituents, their own beliefs, and statewide concerns—is the subject of chapter 3, by Lynda Powell, Richard Niemi, and Michael Smith. They conclude that term limits have indeed weakened the link between representatives and individual districts. However, the corresponding hope of the reformers—that legislators would be more attentive to statewide needs—has not been realized, as term-limited legislators tend to be less informed about policies and interests and spend no more time on the task of legislating.

In chapter 4, Thomas Little and Rick Farmer report that leadership selection and tenure have been altered in predictable, dramatic ways: leadership turnover is up, experience is down, and selection is based less on seniority. Leaders' activities and responsibilities have also changed, with leaders in term-limited states playing a bigger role in member education and training and in candidate recruitment and fund-raising. Ultimately, leaders in term-limited states are not as powerful as their non-term-limited predecessors or their counterparts in non-term-limited states, though Little and Farmer emphasize that the effects vary depending on institutional characteristics and history.

Bruce Cain and Gerald Wright argue in chapter 5 that there have been declines in all three major roles of committees: obtaining information independent of the executive branch and lobbyists, serving as a forum for deliberation, and regulating the flow of bills to the legislature (gatekeeping). The evidence also points to enhanced leadership influence over committees. Like Little and Farmer in chapter 4, the authors of chapter 5 note variations in effects. Senates generally differ from Houses because they have more experienced members, and the effects of term limits may be stronger where the limits are shortest and where reentry provisions are most restrictive.

In chapter 6, on legislative staff, Brian Weberg and Karl Kurtz find no evidence that term limits have affected the number of staff working in legislatures. They summarize research indicating that, contrary to the expectations of staff themselves, staff have not gained influence where term limits have been implemented. Term limits have pushed nonpartisan staff to emphasize their role in educating members on the legislative process, whereas partisan staff have expanded their roles as policy and political advisers. The addition of partisan staff to state legislatures has been an important trend over the past few decades. Term limits may accelerate this shift in situations where both types of staff are in place when term limits take effect.

In chapter 7, David Berman argues that some of the biggest changes brought about by term limits are in the way legislators behave toward one another. By reducing legislative experience, changing legislative incentives, and weakening the control of legislative leaders, term limits have made legislators more hurried and aggressive. They have become less respectful of the process.

Christopher Mooney observes in chapter 8 that the impact of term limits on interest group influence on state policy-making is not yet clear but that term limits have had a considerable effect on the number and behavior of lobbyists. Because long-standing personal ties are broken and because new legislators tend to be suspicious of lobbyists while needing them more, the number of lobbyists has grown, and they work harder than before. They have more influence in the legislative process, but this power is more evenly distributed among them.

Richard Powell, in chapter 9, and Thad Kousser and John Straayer, in chapter 10, note the weakening of legislators relative to executives, especially with respect to budgetary matters and legislative oversight. Kousser and Straayer, though noting an overall decline in legislative power, also echo chapters 4 and 5 in emphasizing the importance of institutional structures and histories. In some states, budgeting authority has been increasingly concentrated in the hands of a few members since the implementation of term limits; in several other states, power has become more diffused. Powell argues that the effects of shifting power were not intended by term limit reformers but are nonetheless dramatic. The three authors agree that the sharply limited experience of term-limited legislators makes it more difficult for the legislators to deal effectively with the governor and the careerist bureaucracy.

In chapter 11, Alan Rosenthal argues that the high turnover and short tenures associated with term limits make it imperative to provide training for new legislators. While almost all states make an effort to train new members, he notes that term-limited legislatures have to work especially hard to get their members up to speed quickly. He enumerates a number of standards that ought to apply to all states, illustrating how one state—non-term-limited Georgia—provides a good model for running such a program.

In the conclusion in chapter 12, the editors return to the arguments for and against term limits set forth in chapter 1 and assess them against our empirical data, as a way of summarizing the book. We also speculate about the future of term limits in the states, including both currently observable adaptations and prospective ones. The authors of this book take term limits to be a fact of legislative life today. While we use the arguments of the proponents and opponents of term limits as a foil—or at least an organizing device—for our analysis, we do not wish to enter the debate over the arguments for and against limiting the terms of state legislators. Instead, our goal is to document and analyze the effects of this institutional change on the behavior of lawmakers and the work of legislatures and to uncover how these democratic institutions have adapted to term limits. Our focus is more on how term limits actually work than on what is right or wrong with them.

How one interprets our findings—that is, whether term limits are viewed as good or bad—depends on how our readers view the role of legislatures. Because we find that term limits have weakened legislatures, especially in relation to the executive branch, institutional defenders who place value on the ability of legislatures to balance the power of the executive will find reasons in this book to further critique term limits. Those readers who seek to limit government, who distrust elected officials and their institutions, or who aim to weaken legislatures will find ammunition for an argument that term limits are at least partially achieving their goal.

CHAPTER I

Term Limits in State Legislatures

Jennie Drage Bowser & Gary Moncrief

THE IDEA OF term limits has been around since the founding of our nation. The Articles of Confederation limited representation in the Congress to "three years in six." By 1777, seven states limited the number of terms that an executive officer could serve, and several states (Pennsylvania, Delaware, New York, and Virginia) passed some type of limit on legislators or requirement for their rotation in office. Moreover, six states—Delaware, Maryland, New Jersey, New York, Pennsylvania, and South Carolina—limited the terms of some local offices (Petracca 1992). The concept of term limits for members of Congress was proposed and debated during the Constitutional Convention but was not included in the proposed constitution. The process of ratification featured vigorous debate on the wisdom of term limits. Although left out of the Constitution, term limits and rotation in office remained popular principles throughout the nineteenth century, with most legislators voluntarily leaving office (Swain et al. 2000).

The modern push for limiting the terms of members of Congress and state legislatures took root in the late 1980s and early 1990s. The 1988 Republican Party platform called for limits on congressional terms. While early term limit initiatives in 1990 in California, Colorado, and Oklahoma appear to have been driven by local activists, most of the term limit initiatives in play by 1992 were organized and largely funded by a national organization, U.S. Term Limits (Rausch 2003, 230).

Almost all of the term limit proposals between 1990 and 1995 placed term limits on both congressional and state legislative office. By the close of 1994, twenty states had limited congressional terms, and twenty-one states had limited state legislative terms. For many people, the real motivation for term limits appeared to be to limit congressional tenure (Rausch 2003, 226), and many observers suspected that one of the primary goals of the term limit movement was to advantage the Republican Party in congressional elections, since the Democrats held a substantial majority of the congressional seats. This suspicion was reinforced by the GOP support of term limits in the 1994 Contract with America—the platform on which many Republicans ran for Congress.

But in 1995, congressional limits were ruled unconstitutional by the U.S. Supreme Court (*U.S. Term Limits, Inc. v. Thornton* 514 U.S. 779). The Court noted that states cannot place restrictions on qualifications for a federal office. State legislative limits, however, were allowed to stand. Ultimately, therefore, congressional term limits were abolished before ever being implemented. Twenty-one states were left with term limits on state legislative office. Eventually, term limits were repealed or invalidated by courts in six of those states, leaving fifteen states with legislative term limits currently in effect.

In four states—Massachusetts, Oregon, Washington, and Wyoming—the state supreme courts overturned term limits. In Massachusetts, Washington, and Wyoming, term limits were established via initiative change to the state statutes. All three states' supreme courts ruled that term limits constituted an additional qualification for office and that it was impermissible to establish constitutional qualifications for office in the statutes. None of these three states has a process for amending its constitution by initiative. In Oregon, the court case involved a different issue: whether an initiative may address more than one subject. The court ruled that since the 1992 initiative that imposed term limits in Oregon addressed more than one section of the state's constitution, it was in violation of the single-subject rule. In two other states, the legislatures repealed term limits. In both Idaho and Utah, term limits were statutory, rather than constitutional, meaning that the legislatures were free to repeal them without a popular vote. The Idaho legislature met resistance in the form of a gubernatorial veto, which was overridden, and then in the form of a popular referendum qualified by term limits proponents. The referendum sought to nullify the legislature's bill repealing term limits. But in 2002, Idaho voters rejected the referendum, leaving the repeal in place. The Utah legislature met little resistance when it repealed term limits in 2003. In all the states where term limits have been repealed, the term limits were established by statute (either through the statutory initiative or by direct legislative action) rather than by an amendment to the state constitution. None of the states in which term limits were established through initiatives to change the state constitution have seen term limits repealed.

The most recent elections involving term limits showed mixed results. In 1999, Mississippi voters defeated an initiative proposing term limits for legislators. In 2002, as previously mentioned, Idaho voters declined to reinstate term limits after the legislature repealed term limits earlier that year. Yet there were several elections in which term limit proponents were victorious. In 2000, voters in Nebraska approved term limits for the fourth time, after state courts had overturned the previous three attempts. Most recently, in 2004, the Arkansas and Montana legislatures presented voters with measures that would extend term limits to twelve years in either chamber (to replace the more restrictive six- and eight-year term limits passed in those states in 1992). Both measures were rejected.

Currently, then, fifteen states have term limits for legislators. Table 1.1 lists the states that have term limits for legislators. It gives the year they

TABLE 1.1.   States with Term Limits on State Legislators

State	Year Enacted	House Limit (in years)	House Year of Impact	Senate Limit (in years)	Senate Year of Impact
Arizona	1992	8	2000	8	2000
Arkansas	1992	6	1998	8	2000
California	1990	6	1996	8	1998
Colorado	1990	8	1998	8	1998
Florida	1992	8	2000	8	2000
Louisiana	1995	12	2007	12	2007
Maine	1993	8	1996	8	1996
Michigan	1992	6	1998	8	2002
Missouri	1992	8	2002	8	2002
Montana[a]	1992	8	2000	8	2000
Nebraska	2000	n.a.	n.a.	8	2006
Nevada	1996	12	2010	12	2010
Ohio	1992	8	2000	8	2000
Oklahoma[b]	1990	12	2004	12	2004
South Dakota	1992	8	2000	8	2000

[a]Montana limits state representatives and state senators to eight years of service in their respective chamber during any sixteen-year period.

[b]Oklahoma legislators are limited to a total of twelve years, which may be served in either chamber or split between the two chambers.

were enacted, the length of the limit by chamber, and the year that the first legislators in each chamber were (or will be) forced out of office.

States have adopted term limits with varying provisions. Some term limit laws are more restrictive than others. The most common limit is eight years in one chamber. But Arkansas, California, and Michigan impose a six-year limit in the House, and three states have a twelve-year limit. There is also the question of whether an individual can return to service after sitting out for a specified period. In some states (e.g., Arizona and Florida), state representatives can serve four consecutive terms (eight years), sit out a term, and then run again for the same chamber. In other states (e.g., Michigan and Missouri) term-limited legislators are barred from ever returning to that chamber; in other words, there is a lifetime limit. Table 1.2 shows the length of time an individual can serve in the fifteen term-limited states and whether the term limits in those states apply to consecutive terms or impose a lifetime ban. Thus, the severity of the term limit law varies by state. As discussion in later chapters will show, the restrictiveness of the term limit provision can significantly affect legislative career incentives and patterns, tenure, and power of legislative leaders, as well as interchamber relations and relative influence.

The 1996 election marked the first time that legislators were forced out of office by term limits, with a total of fifty-two members termed out in California and Maine. The impact in the 1998 election was much more dramatic. Half of the 100 House members in Arkansas and 63 of Michigan's 110 House members could not run for reelection. The Oregon

TABLE 1.2.   Term Limit Provisions

Limit (in years)	State Affected	
	Consecutive Terms	Lifetime Ban
6 House, 8 Senate		Arkansas, California, Michigan
8 total	Nebraska[a]	
8 House, 8 Senate	Arizona, Colorado, Florida, Maine, Montana,[b] Ohio, South Dakota	Missouri
12 total		Oklahoma
12 House, 12 Senate	Louisiana	Nevada

Source: National Conference of State Legislatures.

Note: A lifetime ban means that legislators cannot again serve in the same chamber after the specified number of terms is completed (except for in Oklahoma, where the ban refers to the total number of years served in either house of the legislature).

[a]Nebraska is a unicameral legislature, with only a Senate.

[b]The Montana law stipulates that a legislator may serve only eight years in any sixteen-year period in a specific chamber.

House lost 22 of its 60 members to term limits that year (before term limits were later struck down by the Oregon Supreme Court). In Colorado, the Speaker of the House, the president of the Senate, the majority leaders in both chambers, the House minority leader, four of the six members of the joint budget committee and more than half of the twenty-six committee chairs were forced out by term limits.

By 2004, term limits had forced members out in twenty-six chambers in thirteen states. A total of 257 legislators in twelve states were ineligible to have their names placed on the ballot in 2004. At the end of that year, a total of 1,214 legislators nationally had been removed by term limits. Table 1.3 shows the number of legislators prevented from running for reelection in various years as a result of term limits. In addition, many other legislators have left before their terms have been completed, to run for other office in anticipation of term limits. In several states (e.g., Arkansas, California, Maine, and Michigan), term limits are now in a "second-generation cycle," in which those legislators who replaced term-limited legislators have now exhausted their term limit and themselves been replaced. Meanwhile, term limits are not yet even in the "first-generation cycle" in Louisiana or Nevada; no one will be barred from office due to term limits until 2007 in Louisiana and 2010 in Nevada.

Between 1999 and 2004, 139 bills to modify or repeal term limits were introduced in seventeen states. Most bills to modify term limits would require voter approval, because they amend the state constitution. In other words, these bills are actually referenda, which must be passed by the state legislature first and then submitted to the public. To date, very few bills to modify term limits have passed in state legislatures and subsequently been submitted to the voters. Just one has met with voter approval. In 2002, the Missouri legislature referred to the ballot a question that would exclude service resulting from elections to finish partial terms from the calculation of term limits, and voters approved the measure. As previously mentioned, in November 2004, legislatures in two states—Arkansas and Montana—proposed constitutional amendments to increase the limit on terms to twelve years in each chamber. Both measures were rejected by voters. The only other term limits bills to pass state legislatures were repeals of statutorily imposed term limits. These bills passed in Idaho in 2002 and Utah in 2003. (See the NCSL table on term limits legislation for 1999–2003 at http://www.ncsl.org/programs/legman/about/BillsAmndRplTL.htm.)

Just one state—California—has tried to modify term limits with a citizen initiative. In the March 2002 primary there, voters declined to pass an initiative proposal to lengthen term limits for their legislators. Proposition 45 would have allowed a termed-out legislator to petition for the right to run for up to four more years after reaching the constitutional limit. The measure received just 42 percent of the vote. The distinction between statutory term limits and constitutional term limits is therefore an important one. No state with constitutionally imposed term limits has repealed them or even modified them in any significant way. By comparison, most states in which term limits were imposed through statute have now repealed the limits through either judicial or legislative action.

TABLE 1.3.   Numbers of Legislators Removed from Office by Term Limits, 1996–2004

Chamber (size)	1996	1998	2000	2002	2004	2006
Arizona House (60 members)			15	9	5	9
Arizona Senate (30 members)			7	6	2	6
Arkansas House (100 members)		49	25	14	36	14
Arkansas Senate (35 members)			13	11	0	11
California Assembly (80 members)	22	16	19	20	18	20
California Senate (40 members)		11	8	7	8	7
Colorado House (65 members)		18	10	7	7	7
Colorado Senate (35 members)		9	11	5	5	5
Florida House (120 members)			55	14	7	14
Florida Senate (40 members)			11	12	0	12
Maine House (151 members)	26	11	17	28	21	28
Maine Senate (35 members)	4	1	7	8	7	8
Michigan House (110 members)		63	21	23	37	23
Michigan Senate (38 members)				27		27
Missouri House (163 members)[a]			8	73	15	73
Missouri Senate (34 members)[a]		1		12	10	12
Montana House (100 member)			33	7	10	7
Montana Senate (50 members)			14	15	6	15
Ohio House (99 members)			45	9	7	9
Ohio Senate (33 members)			6	4	5	4
Oregon House (60 members)[b]		22	17			
Oregon Senate (30 members)[b]		2	5			
S. Dakota House (70 members)			20	7	3	7
S. Dakota Senate (35 members)			13	4	7	4
Total	52	203	380	322	257	322

Source: National Conference of State Legislatures, http://www.ncsl.org/programs/legman/about/termedout.htm.

Note: Entries are the number of legislators who had completed the maximum number of terms allowed under their state's term-limit law. Some of these legislators might have intended to retire from the legislature at that time, irrespective of term limits.

[a]Because of a Missouri court ruling, eight House members and one senator who had won special elections were term-limited out prior to the actual 2002 term-limit implementation.

[b]Oregon's term limits for legislators were held unconstitutional by the state supreme court in January 2002.

The Term Limits Debate

The term limits debate in the late 1980s and early 1990s revolved around a basic issue that also faced the framers of the Constitution: does the value of rotating people in office outweigh the value of the knowledge and experience incumbent lawmakers bring to the job? Summaries of the basic arguments presented by the proponents and opponents of term limits follow.

Arguments in Favor of Term Limits

1. Term limits would allow more people to have the chance to serve in the legislature, thus retaining the notion of citizen legislatures.

Historically, one of the main arguments for rotation of offices is the desirability of moving officeholders back into private life and spreading the opportunity to serve to more people. Term limits would limit the time commitment, allowing people to take time out to serve in the legislature and then to return to their regular jobs. People working in the private sector and professions are not likely to run for office if they must spend ten to fifteen years in office to gain significant influence. Civic-minded individuals would be willing to serve for two, four, or six years and then go back to their careers. Term limits are a mechanism to ensure that legislatures remain citizen bodies, not organizations dominated by career politicians.

2. Those who run for office knowing that their terms are limited are more likely to represent their constituents' interests and to seek policy changes that might be opposed by entrenched interest groups.

Because term limits make it impossible to make a career out of legislative service, legislators would have less incentive to court interest groups for campaign contributions and other help in retaining their office. Because they know they will leave office in a short time, legislators elected under term limits will be more likely to take the political risk of opposing the desires of interest groups and to more vigorously represent the desires of the people.

3. Term limits reduce the extraordinary power of incumbents during elections. As a result, a more diverse group of people will be elected to state legislatures.

During the time that term limits were being debated, the reelection rate for incumbent members of Congress was over 90 percent. Although there was more turnover at the state legislative level, most of that turnover occurred through resignations, not electoral defeat of incumbent members. With the increased number of open seats due to term limits, it is likely that more women and racial minorities will be elected to state legislatures.

4. *Interest groups would be weakened under a system with term limits, because such groups would not be able to develop long-term relationships with legislators.*

It takes time for lobbyists to get to know legislators and develop solid working relationships with them. Career legislators come to be heavily dependent on lobbyists and interest groups for campaign contributions and develop long-term relationships with them. As a result, long-tenured members become less responsive to the general public. Under term limits, lobbyists will have to work constantly to get to know the new legislators and develop relationships with them. Because they do not plan to make a career out of legislative service, the legislators elected under term limits have less need for the campaign contributions and other favors that interest groups can provide.

5. *Most states already limit the number of terms that governors can serve. Term limits on legislators are just an extension of this policy and level the playing field for all officeholders.*

Legislators should be treated the same as governors in terms of having a limited amount of time in office. The limits on governors have worked effectively and help to ensure that the executive branch is infused with new ideas and fresh approaches to policy questions.

Arguments against Term Limits

1. *Term limits interfere with the fundamental right of voters to elect their representatives. If voters do not want a person to represent them, they can vote him or her out of office.*

We already have term limits—they are called elections. The people are the best judge of whether a person represents them effectively. Although term limits may remove ineffective or corrupt legislators, they also force hardworking, effective legislators from office.

2. *By removing experienced and knowledgeable legislators, term limits weaken the legislative branch of government. A weak legislature upsets the balance of power that is the basis of the democratic form of government.*

Legislatures comprised of new and inexperienced members will be at a disadvantage in terms of knowledge and the power that it brings. The governor and staff within the executive branch will gain power at the legislature's expense. Because the legislature is the branch most open and accessible to the people, the people will have less ability to influence the outcome of decisions on policy questions. By removing experienced members from the legislature, the ability of the legislature to effectively oversee the operations of the executive branch is reduced.

3. *Term limits ignore the value of experience in crafting and managing public policy.*

Term limits would remove legislators just as they are developing a working knowledge of how the legislature and state government operates. The loss of this institutional knowledge about what actions were taken before and why severely limits legislators' ability to make good policy. It takes time to acquire certain skills needed to be an effective legislator, such as bargaining, being willing to compromise, appreciation of parliamentary procedure, and capacity to listen to people. Term limits do not provide sufficient time for legislators to become truly skilled at their jobs.

4. *Term limits encourage legislators to opt for short-term solutions or quick fixes, over more-difficult solutions that are best over the long term.*

Because they hold office for only a short time, legislators under term limits do not have as much incentive to think about long-term solutions to policy issues. They are more likely to vote for solutions that are popular at the time but that may have negative consequences over the long term. Legislators elected under term limits will be less interested in devoting the time necessary to mastering complicated policy issues and sponsoring legislation that may only be enacted over the course of several legislative sessions.

5. *The power of lobbyists, legislative staff, and bureaucrats increases under a system with term limits, because they possess institutional knowledge about policy issues and what went on in the past.*

Although it is harder for lobbyists to develop long-term working relationships with legislators elected under term limits, the lobbyists are a source of institutional knowledge and policy expertise. Inexperienced legislators elected under term limits may be forced to turn to lobbyists, legislative staff, and state bureaucrats for information about issues and how to handle them. While the lobbyists and others may be a good source of information, they are not elected and therefore are not answerable to the people.

Literature on Term Limits

The literature on term limits can be divided into three basic categories. The first category, the earliest work, was largely speculative or, in some cases, polemic. Most of the early writers on the subject took one or the other side of the argument for why imposing term limits was a good or bad idea (Mitchell 1991; Will 1992; Crane and Pilon 1994); or they produced propositions as to potential consequences—propositions that might be tested in the future (Malbin and Benjamin 1992; Cain 1996; Grofman 1996). The second category of literature was historical, documenting the term limit movement itself—the initiative campaigns, why limits passed, who supported and who opposed term limits and why (e.g., Olson 1992). The third category, comprised of research into the actual effects of term limits, has only recently emerged, since it was necessary for some time to pass before any observable effects might begin to occur. In the years since term limits first took hold in California and Maine, however, research into term limits and their consequences for legislatures has become possible. This third category—involving empirical research testing specific hypotheses about the effect of term limits—is of particular concern to us here.

The number of research studies is thus far quite small, although the body of work increases each year, as term limits go into effect in more states. Virtually all of the research focuses on the effects of term limits in one or more of the following ways: (1) electoral consequences, (2) the effect on individual legislators, (3) how the legislative institution and its operation have changed (including the consequences for the selection and power of legislative leaders), and (4) the relative strength of the legislative institution. Much of this research is reviewed in the topical chapters of this book, so here we simply offer some observations about the broad contours of the early empirical research.

Most of the first empirical studies were single-state studies, focusing on just one or a few of the broad topics mentioned in the previous paragraph. For example, Daniel and Lott (1997) produced an early study of the electoral consequences of term limits in California, Allebaugh and Pinney (2003) did the same for Michigan, and Caress (1999) examined the impact of term limits on women candidates in California. Other single-state studies include Clucas's (2003) analysis of California; Penning's (2003) study and the Wayne State collaborative effort (Sarbaugh-Thompson et al. 2004) on Michigan; and work by Moen, Palmer, and Powell (2004) on Maine and by Straayer (2003) on Colorado.

A few researchers undertook cross-state studies that were confined to an analysis of just one of the four topics mentioned previously. Examples include Carroll and Jenkins's (2001) study of the effect of term limits on women candidates, the analysis by Caress et al. (2003) of the electoral effect on minority candidates, Francis and Kenney's (2000) study of the influence of term limits on legislators' electoral ambitions, and Kousser's (2005) analysis of rates of bill passage.

Understandably, almost all of the studies just mentioned were limited in scope—either by focusing on a single state or by focusing on a single topic across states. Moreover, almost all these studies attempted to discern the effects of term limits after a very few years' worth of observations. After all, while most of the current state legislative term limits were enacted between 1990 and 1994, they did not begin to move people out of the legislature until 1996 or later. Thus, while all these studies inform us about some of the more immediate effects of term limits, they cannot tell us much about the long-term effects. Furthermore, it is possible that some of the early effects were short-lived, becoming less of a concern over time, with the maturation of the term limit cycle. Thus, today, we are in a better position to assess the effect of term limits than we were five or six years ago.

To date, very few studies have undertaken an examination of the effects of term limits that is both comprehensive (analyzing more than one or two of the topics discussed earlier) and comparative (analyzing data from numerous states). Moncrief and Thompson (2001b) made an effort to study multiple (electoral, behavioral, and structurally influential) effects in five states in which term limits had been implemented, but the lack of control states in their study means we must be cautious in drawing definitive conclusions. Of the early empirical research, only the Carey, Niemi, and Powell (2000) study can be said to be comprehensive (covering numerous hypothesized effects of term limits), comparative (using data from all states), and controlled (using data from both term-limited and non-term-limited states).

Additional empirical studies of the effect of term limits are appearing. These studies have the benefit of more years of data as we move further away from the implementation date of term limits in many states. Some of these studies are single-state analyses; some are comparative but not comprehensive (focusing on just one topic—often the electoral effects of term limits). The advantage of the Joint Project on Term Limits is that it allows a comprehensive, cross-state, controlled data set. The data and analysis in this volume is drawn from that project and thus represents the most thorough analysis yet of the true effect of term limits.

Composition of Legislatures

Gary Moncrief, Lynda W. Powell, & Tim Storey

IN 2003, a group called Oregon Term Limits began an effort to reinstate legislative term limits in their state. The preamble to their proposed initiative is a concise statement about some of the presumed benefits of a term limit law. It reads: "WHEREAS: Limiting the terms of legislators promotes varied public representation, broadens opportunities for public service, and makes the electoral process fairer by reducing the power of incumbency and the professional lobby . . ." (see http://www.ore gontermlimits.org/index04.html).

There are at least four separate assumptions in this statement. First, it is assumed that term limits will create a broader demographic mix within the legislature ("promotes . . . public representation"). Second, it suggests that more people—presumably average citizens—will be able to serve ("broadens opportunities for public service"). Third, it suggests that electoral competition will increase ("reducing the power of incumbency"). Finally, it presumes that lobbyists will lose influence ("reducing the power of . . . the professional lobby.")

In this chapter, we examine the evidence as it bears on the first three of these assumptions. The early proponents of term limits argued that term limits would eliminate "careerist" legislators and expand the opportunity for "average" citizens to participate (e.g., Fund 1992). Cain and Kousser (2004, 10) noted in their report on California, "Some supporters hoped that term limits would produce a mix of representatives that more closely resembled the general population's characteristics and attitudes: more women and minorities, fewer career politicians, fewer people obsessed with the electoral bottom line, and fewer representatives corrupted by lobbyists and party leaders."

Obviously, this argument has a lot to do with the electoral advantages of incumbency, as well as the notion that there is a class of people in American society (citizen politicians instead of professional politicians) who want to participate but who are currently shut out of the system. From these premises, other propositions can be drawn. One is that term limits will open the system to participation by a more diverse group of people— more women, more minorities, and a broader cross section of the population by age and occupation. Another, often implied assumption is that term limits will alter the partisan makeup of legislatures. Based on the Joint Project on Term Limits—its 2002 National Survey of State Legislators, 2003 Survey of Knowledgeable Observers, and case studies—this chapter explores the evidence gathered thus far in regard to these potential effects of term limits. We begin with the most obvious and likely potential effect—an increase in turnover in the legislature.

Turnover and Tenure

The basic premise that term limits will lead to higher turnover and lower average tenure is one of the first potential consequences of term limits identified by proponents and analyzed by researchers. Early research (Moncrief et al. 1992; Opheim 1994; Luttbeg 1992; Everson 1992) relied on data from previous retention rates to project how term limits would affect future retention rates. One of the important, if obvious, findings of this early research was that the nature of the term limit law and the nature of current retention rates were not the same everywhere and that, consequently, the effect of term limits on retention would be different under different conditions. Another early line of research was pursued by Francis and Kenney (2000), who argued that term limits would actually have a larger impact than assumed because of what they called "churning"—the likelihood that individuals would leave to pursue other opportunities prior to their term limit deadline.

Fortunately, this is one area in which we now have good objective data. It is a relatively easy (albeit tedious) process to determine turnover trends before and after the implementation of term limits and to compare those trends to turnover trends in states without term limits. We can also rely on the mean tenure figures that some of the case studies provide. Much of this work was done by Moncrief, Niemi, and Powell (2004) in conjunction with the JPTL.

Quite clearly, term limits impact the turnover rate. Generally, the imposition of term limits led to an average increase in turnover of about 14 percent (see figs. 2.1 and 2.2). There are variations, of course—based on type of legislature and chamber, type of term limit, historic turnover rates in a particular state, and so on. A legislative chamber with a six-year term limit (e.g., the California Assembly) should experience a more dramatic impact than, say, Nevada's House of Representatives, which has a twelve-year term limit. In other words, the shorter the potential term is, the greater is the potential impact. Moreover, full-time, professional legislatures are likely to experience greater immediate effects from the imposition of term limits than are part-time, citizen legislatures. Because the incentive structure to stay (including pay, perquisites, staff, and legislative career opportunities) is greater in full-time, professional legislatures, such legislatures usually have a lower turnover rate than part-time legislatures (Moncrief et al. 1992; Opheim 1994; Moncrief, Niemi, and Powell 2004).

In Ohio, where turnover previously averaged about 20 percent in the House over each two-year election cycle, turnover rocketed to over 50 percent in the year that term limits kicked in. But it then dropped to about 30 percent in the subsequent election. In Colorado, where turnover was relatively high to begin with (averaging about 30 percent), turnover after term limits has been only slightly higher (averaging about 35 percent). In states where twelve-year limits are in force (e.g., Oklahoma and Nevada), it is unlikely that turnover will change much except in the year of implementation, in which the initial "hit" will wipe out all the old-timers.

Overall, there is no doubt that term limits increased turnover. What is less clear at this point is the sustained effect. Turnover rose dramatically in many states in the years immediately surrounding the implementation of term limits. In most states, there was a decline in turnover after the initial implementation, but we simply do not have enough data yet to determine at what point turnover reaches equilibrium after term limits are implemented.

Demographics

Carey, Niemi, and Powell (2000, 18) noted, "There are widely shared expectations that term limits will generate greater turnover and that increased turnover will change the characteristics of legislative candidates

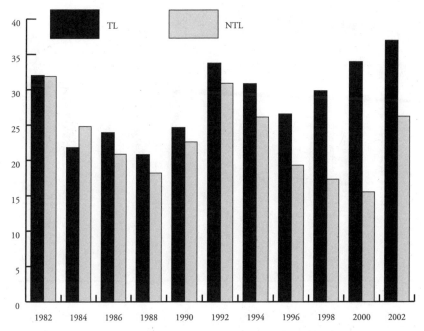

Fig. 2.1.   House turnover in term-limited and non-term-limited states. (Data from Moncrief, Niemi, and Powell 2004.)

and of legislators." The argument is simple enough: because so many incumbents are white, older males, any increase in turnover naturally ought to lead to an increase in the election of groups traditionally under-represented in state legislatures (Cain and Levin 1999, 175). The list of such groups can be long and diverse, but many analysts predicted that term limits would lead to an increase in at least the number of women and minorities. Others argued that term limits would also increase legislatures' economic and ideological diversity and age distribution.

Early assessments, extrapolating retention rates from the 1970s and 1980s into the future, contended that more women were likely to be elected under term limits (e.g., Thompson and Moncrief 1993). Most incumbents were men, and incumbents are difficult to defeat, but term limits would replace incumbent-held seats with open seats. The assumption was that women candidates would be more likely to win open-seat contests than elections in which they are challenging an incumbent. But the early work after term limits were implemented found little or no such

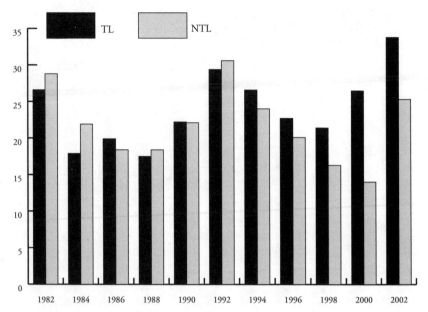

Fig. 2.2.   Senate turnover in term-limited and non-term-limited states. (Data from Moncrief, Niemi, and Powell 2004.)

evidence (e.g., Carey, Niemi, and Powell 2000, 24–27). In fact, some researchers concluded that there appeared to be an overall decline in the number of women representatives in term-limited states, especially in the lower chambers (Carroll and Jenkins 2001).

Based on analysis of the 2002 national survey, Carey et al. (2006, 115) found that the number of women elected had increased slightly in both term-limited and non-term-limited states during the time period under study. However, after controlling for systemic variables, they concluded, "[W]hile the overall prospects for women candidates have improved over time, we are unable to attribute any part of this change to the extraordinary opening up of legislative seats that occurred as term limits took effect." In other words, there is no evidence that term limits have actually led to an increase in the number of women serving. Table 2.1 demonstrates this fact in a simple manner. Comparing the number of women in term-limited state legislatures in the year just prior to implementation of term limits to the number of women in those same state legislatures today reveals virtually no change. Obviously, such a comparison does not account for other factors that may be at work. Nonetheless, the table makes it quite clear that term limits have not led to a discernible increase in the number of women serving.

The state-by-state pattern varies, of course. Cain and Kousser (2004) calculated that because of term limits, an average of about three additional women was elected in each election in California. But for most states, there is virtually no change overall. Interestingly, in several term-limited states, the overall number of women legislators actually declined after term limits took effect, while in others, such as Arizona and Maine, the number of women in the House dropped, but the number of women in the Senate increased substantially. The reason behind this phenomenon is that many of the women who were term-limited out of the lower chamber success-fully ran for the Senate. This is almost assuredly a short-term effect, how-ever. As these women are term-limited out of the upper chambers, there will be fewer women currently in the House to replace their senatorial sis-ters. Based on the JPTL case studies and 2002 survey and on the careful work of Carroll and Jenkins (2001), it is clear that term limits have thus far

TABLE 2.1.   Women in Term-Limited Legislatures

State	Year of Term Limits Implementation	Women in Legislature in Year before Term Limits	Women in Legislature in 2005	Change
Maine	1996	48	44	−4
California	1996/1998	25	37	12
Colorado	1998	35	33	−2
Arkansas	1998/2000	23	22	−1
Michigan	1998/2002	34	30	−4
Florida	2000	38	38	0
Ohio	2000	28	26	−2
South Dakota	2000	14	17	3
Montana	2000	37	37	0
Arizona	2000	32	30	−2
Missouri	2002	45	42	−3
Oklahoma	2004	18	22	4
Net change in number of women in states where term limits have been implemented				1

Source: Compiled by Tim Storey from information from the Center for American Women and Politics (Rutgers University).

Note: In states where term limits were implemented in different years for the House and Senate cham-bers (California, Arkansas, and Michigan), the year of the House implementation appears first.

simply not led to an increase in the number of women serving in state legislatures and, in some cases, may actually be detrimental.

Race, Ethnicity, and Gender

There were a few early analyses (e.g., Thompson and Moncrief 1993) predicting little change in racial/ethnic diversity due to the imposition of term limits. The premise was that since most minorities are elected in relatively safe majority-minority districts, term limits would not open up many new seats except those in which white incumbents had held the seat for a long time in districts that had changed demographically over time. Where this condition held, there were some significant gains in a few specific states. For example, the number of Latino legislators in California and African American legislators in Michigan increased after term limits went into effect (Caress et al. 2003). The same is true, to a lesser extent, in Arizona (Latinos) and Arkansas (African Americans). But on the whole, these are isolated events, and in some cases, they may be due more to redistricting than to term limits (Berman 2004, 2; Caress et al. 2003).

Cain and Kousser (2004, 10) noted in their analysis of California: "[M]inorities have been elected to office more frequently, resulting in an increasingly diverse Legislature. Some of this transformation can be attributed to term limits, yet we also find that much of the diversification resulted from other trends that term limits merely accelerated." The key word here is "accelerated." In a few states (e.g., California), term limits provided the accelerating impetus for trends that were already at work (e.g., the demographic shifts in the Golden State's population). As incumbents (often Anglo) in such states were no longer able to run for office, statewide demographic trends could be reflected through open-seat legislative elections.

But for most states, such demographic representation was not significantly lagging behind prior to the imposition of term limits, so term limits did not appreciably alter the demographic mix in the legislature. A typical case is Colorado. John Straayer and Jennie Bowser (2004, 11) noted: "Ethnic diversity in Colorado's General Assembly was minimal before term limits, and it is minimal today. So in this respect, term limits appear to be irrelevant." Overall, therefore, Carey et al. (2006, 115) found "no systematic differences between legislators from term-limited and non-term-limited states" in terms of the increase in racial or ethnic minorities.

This is a conclusion supported by almost all the cases studies conducted by the JPTL.

Economic Background

Another contention in support of term limits is that people of diverse backgrounds, including different economic backgrounds, will be more likely to run for office if they know that their tenure will be relatively short and that they do not have to run against an incumbent. If the aim of imposing term limits is to create a true "citizen legislature," citizens from all walks of life might be encouraged to run. Yet there is virtually no evidence that this has come to pass.

Based on their 1995 data, Carey, Niemi, and Powell (2000, 40) found no evidence that term limits have created a difference in income level, occupational background, or level of education of legislators. This null finding is corroborated by the 2002 data. Carey et al. (2006, 114) found no differences in these variables due to term limits and concluded that the new data "strongly reinforce the conclusions from the 1995 study."

Age

Early on, there was anecdotal evidence that some very young legislators were elected in term-limited states. This seemed to be particularly true in Maine, where several college-aged legislators were elected. In Arkansas, Shane Broadway became Speaker of the House at the age of twenty-eight.

Ambition theory suggests that term limits might have an effect on who runs for legislative office under a term-limited scenario. If lengthy legislative careers are precluded, one might hypothesize that there would be an increase in two types of candidates: very young candidates who see the legislative experience as a valuable résumé item for future employment and much older—likely retired—candidates who have the time to engage in public service because they have concluded their private careers. But analyses based on the 1995 and 2002 surveys find no such evidence.

The case studies yield inconsistent evidence in this regard. While the average age dropped in California from about forty-seven years to forty-two, it increased by four years in Maine, and it held essentially steady in Ohio. In at least two states (Colorado and Arizona), the mean age did not change discernibly for House members but increased in the Senate, as some term-limited old-timers in the House moved to the upper chamber. The non-term-limited control states mirrored this inconsistency; the average increased in Indiana but stayed unchanged in Illinois and Kansas.

Political Orientation

Partisan Effects

The previous chapter notes the speculation by some observers that the term limits movement was driven in part by partisan motivations. The assumption was that the Republican Party, which was the "out party" at the time the term limit movement emerged, would benefit. Carey, Niemi, and Powell (2000, 35) addressed precisely this issue: "The inevitable effect on turnover will, in time, spill over onto the partisan composition of the state legislatures. Initially, there will be a partisan imbalance that will be pro-Republican [because] Democrats dominated most state legislatures. Thus through the year 2000, most legislators legally prohibited from reelection are Democrats." Carey, Niemi, and Powell argued, however, that party reversal will be short-lived, as many Republicans who are elected because of term limits will eventually be term-limited out themselves. This portends an "ebb and flow" process in which the minority party (the "out party") may become the "in party" during the term limit duration but then will suffer losses as its own members are term-limited. Carey, Niemi, and Powell (2000, 36) concluded that "long periods of one-party domination of state legislatures may as a result be less frequent and may be replaced by shorter-term fluctuations as first one party then the other finds its incumbents forced from office."

Elsewhere, Meinke and Hasecke (2003) found a partisan effect of term limits, but only in "mid-range" professional legislatures (i.e., those legislatures not at the very top or bottom of the professionalization scale). In particular, their study concluded that term limits provide a hindrance to Democrats in these states because the short-term legislative compensation level is not great enough to overcome the disincentives created by term limits. There are, of course, many factors beyond term limits to contend with here, including national partisan tides, redistricting, and campaign finance trends that make analysis more difficult. For example, another study found that term limits actually strengthen the incumbent party in a legislature by giving the majority party more latitude in redistricting (Schaffner, Wagner, and Winburn 2004).

Ideological Effects

Since term limits are often viewed as part of an ideologically conservative, antigovernment movement, one might wonder whether the imposition of term limits encourages an ideological shift. There are two components to this argument. First, states that adopt term limits are exhibiting a stronger antigovernment (or at least limited-government) attitude, and this attitude might be more attractive to ideologically conservative potential candidates. Second, limited government and bounded service (service limited to a specific number of years) are compatible ideas. Ideological conservatives might be willing to engage in legislative service if they know it is only for a specified period.

From the 1995 and 2002 surveys, there is almost no evidence that these propositions are true. Carey, Niemi, and Powell (2000, 34) found that there was a shift toward a more conservative ideology in both term-limited and non-term-limited legislatures. They concluded, "[T]he initial effects of term limits on state legislator ideology appear to be marginal, if not negligible."

Ambition and Careers

The motto on the banner of the U.S. Term Limits Web site is "Citizen Legislators, *Not* Career Politicians" (http://www.termlimits.org). This statement captures much of the public sentiment in support of term limits. The American public has a long history of distaste for the idea of "career politicians," and this distaste is, we think, one of the reasons for the success of term limit initiatives.

There are two implicit assumptions embedded in the argument against political careerism. The first assumption is that there were many careerists in state legislatures prior to the imposition of term limits. The second assumption is that career politicians will be thwarted due to term limits. Both of these assumptions are testable.

The first assumption—that many state legislators were careerists who spent long periods in the legislature—is true for some states and not true for others. The critical variable was the type of state legislature. Moncrief et al. (1992) showed that the proportion of legislators who remained in the chamber for twelve years was clearly related to the professionalization of the legislature. In the eight state legislatures characterized as "full-time, professional," 40 percent of the House members and 60 percent of the senators remained in office for at least twelve years. But in the seventeen states characterized as "part-time, citizen legislatures," less than 20 percent of the House members and 26 percent of the senators stayed for as long as twelve years.

Clearly, the incentive structure worked to foster careerism in some legislatures but not in others. Of the states in which term limits were originally imposed, only three were in the "full-time, professional" category, while nine were in the "part-time, citizen" group. In other words, term limits were imposed disproportionately in states that did not have many "careerists" in the first place. The reason for this phenomenon largely has to do with the geographic distribution of the initiative process in the United States. More western states permit the initiative process; most western states are relatively rural, low-population states where legislatures are more prone to be part-time. The conclusion is that while term limits can indeed preclude the existence of careerist legislators, there were not many careerists to begin with in most term-limited states.

Concerning the second assumption in the argument against political careerism, one way in which term limits clearly affected such careerism is by eliminating the cadre (quite small in some states, much larger in others) of legislators who had served for long periods in one chamber. Long-term careers within a single chamber can no longer occur in term-limited states. In Colorado, for example, the average number of years served in the chamber dropped in the House and Senate, respectively, from 4.2 and 8.0 in 1993 to 2.5 and 6.3 by 2003. In Arkansas, the mean years served dropped from 6.5 to 3.5 in the House and from 9.4 to 7.0 in the Senate. The mean Senate figures are likely to drop a bit further yet, as term limits were imposed in most upper chambers one or two electoral cycles later than in the House.

The implications for this trend are particularly strong in states with shorter (six- or eight-year) limits and are likely to play out in especially dramatic ways in leadership positions (including committee chairmanships). For example, Cain and Kousser (2004, fig. 3.1) found that the average years of tenure for committee chairs in California was 5.6 in the period just prior to the passage of term limits but had been reduced to 2.5 by 1997–2000. Similar dramatic decreases in experience levels are documented in the case studies for party leadership position in Arkansas, Ohio, and other states.

However, to preclude "career legislators" is not the same thing as eliminating "career politicians." The assumption of many was that once elected officials were forced to leave the legislature, they would retire from politics and return to private endeavors. But is this in fact what occurs? Term-limited legislators can no longer make a career serving continuously in one legislative chamber. After a period of service variously determined by the different term limit laws, a legislator must decide among running for another office, finding a nonelective career in politics, returning to a nonpolitical career, or retiring (or, in some states, sitting out at least one election cycle and then running for reelection). Table 2.2 shows the future plans of members in both term-limited and non-term-limited states; the term-limited states are further divided into those where term limits have been adopted but have not yet gone into effect and those where term limits are already forcing members out of office.

The first row of the table shows that at the end of their service in the current chamber, fewer term-limited legislators plan to retire compared to legislators in states without term limits. Further analysis of these data show that most younger members—those under forty-five—simply do not

TABLE 2.2.   Future Career Plans of Legislators in Term-Limited and Non-Term-Limited States

| | Term Limit Status | | | | | |
| | Lower Chamber | | | Upper Chamber | | |
Future Plans	None	Adopted	In Effect	None	Adopted	In Effect
Retire	36%	26%*	18%*	36%	28%	28%
Return to previous nonpolitical career	29%	30%	23%*	29%	48%*	29%
Lobbying/consulting	16%	16%	11%*	15%	18%	16%
No further office	17%	16%	8%*	17%	16%	11%
Appointive office	14%	11%	11%	12%	15%	14%
Run for other chamber	23%	26%	52%*	1%	5%*	13%*
Run for local office	10%	11%	12%	4%	11%*	14%*
Run for statewide office	15%	17%	15%	24%	26%	21%
Run for U.S. House or Senate	13%	13%	14%	20%	14%	19%
Number of cases for each cell in column	1,246	235	406	384	134	15

Source: 2002 National Survey of State Legislators.

Note: Each entry shows the percentage of respondents who indicate that future plan. Since respondents could check more than one possibility, the entries sum to more than 100% for each column. The survey question was "After service in the present chamber, what are you likely to do?" Respondents were instructed to check all the options that applied. States in which term limits were adopted and then removed are excluded.

*$p < .05$ (two-tailed) compared to states without term limits for that chamber

express the intention to retire at the end of their period of service, except for a small percentage (4 percent in the upper chambers and 7 percent in the lower) who serve in states without term limits and envisage a complete career in their chamber. Older members—those sixty-five and over—largely plan to retire at the end of their service. Over 60 percent indicate they will retire, although these numbers are reduced by term limits and especially by limits in effect. The largest effect of term limits is among the middle-aged—those forty-five to sixty-four. In the lower chambers, for example, 31 percent without term limits plan to retire when they finish service, compared to 20 percent in states that have adopted term limits and 16 percent in states where limits have come into effect. Numbers are virtually identical in the upper chambers.

The percentage planning to retire is especially low where term limits are in effect in lower chambers. The sharp drop in numbers in the lower chambers where term limits have taken effect may be largely due to differences in the age distribution of members in these chambers. The percentage of younger legislators—those under forty-five—has increased significantly only in the lower chambers where term limits are in effect and therefore actually forcing members out of office. Here, 24 percent are under age forty-five, compared to 16 percent in lower chambers without term limits and in those that have adopted but not implemented term limits. Members of upper chambers are typically first elected to the chamber at an older age. Thus, only 12 percent of all legislators in the upper chambers are under age forty-five, and the percentage of those under forty-five in chambers where term limits have taken effect is only 2 percent greater than in states without term limits.

The percentage of legislators planning to return to a nonpolitical prior career shows no consistent relationship with term limits. Although advocates of term limits largely envisioned citizen legislators who would return to their nonpolitical careers after service in the legislature, this does not seem an accurate characterization. Nor are these individuals planning to use their expertise and contacts gained by their legislative service to move into careers in lobbying or consulting.

Members in term-limited states are more likely to plan to run for another office. Although there are only modest declines in states among the small percentages that plan no further official service, there are quite specific and substantial differences in which offices legislators intend to seek. Many legislators in the lower chambers see an opportunity to continue their political career by running for the upper chamber—indeed, an incredible 52 percent of legislators in states where term limits have taken effect indicate a likelihood of running for the Senate when their service ends in the House. At this point, House members are faced with the necessity of making a decision in the next or next few elections. These legislators also know when the seat in the upper chamber must be vacated by its incumbent.

Even some senators are considering the previously unusual choice of running for the House. Term limit laws in eight of the fifteen term-limited states allow legislators to move to the other chamber and thereby extend their service in the legislature beyond the length of time they could serve in a single chamber—and they can rotate indefinitely. These are the states listed in table 1.2 as having provisions for "consecutive terms" (with the exception of Nebraska). The remaining term-limited states limit the total length of service in the legislature, and this limit cannot be evaded by moving from one chamber to the other. Prior to the implementation of term limits, it was extremely rare for a state senator to move to the state House. But now, according to the 2002 national survey, 13 percent of upper chamber members in states where term limits are in effect believe it is likely they will run for the lower chamber, compared to 1 percent in states without term limits. Moncrief, Niemi, and Powell (2004, 379) identified fifteen cases in which state senators moved to the House in term-limited states in 2000; they found no such cases in non-term-limited states.

Table 2.2 does not show that the legislators surveyed had any increased intention to run for either the U.S. Congress or statewide office, although it does show an increased intention of running for local office, especially among members of upper chambers. Members of lower chambers have a more obvious next career goal—the upper chamber—than do members of the upper chambers. Although some members of upper chambers are willing to consider running for the lower chamber, the data show that others may find local office slightly more attractive. It is also possible that members of upper chambers in term-limited states look slightly more often to future appointive positions to continue their career than do members of upper chambers in states without term limits.

The lack of a relationship for statewide or congressional office may appear anomalous, especially since both are frequently career goals for state legislators. Just over one-half of the members of the U.S. Congress, for example, have previously served as state legislators. Yet from the perspective of the state legislators, relatively few can hope to serve in Congress. The median state has six U.S. House members, two U.S. senators, and about five statewide elective offices (besides U.S. senators). The typical state House of Representatives contains 110 members, the Senate about 40. Thus, there are potentially 150 state legislators interested in thirteen offices—offices frequently occupied by incumbents (with high likelihood of reelection), often of the same party as the legislator. Thus, when respondents say it is likely they will run for these offices, they may be expressing more a hope than a practical plan.

A prior study by Carey, Niemi, and Powell (2000) also showed no increased intention to run for the U. S. Congress among either House or Senate members in states that had adopted term limits. However, these authors examined whether state senators in office in 1992 actually ran for the U.S. House in 1994 or 1996. In particular, the authors wished to determine whether the adoption of term limits (few had taken effect by 1996) increased the number of state senators running for the U.S. House. The authors found that the effects of term limits varied considerably by circumstances. Almost no legislators were willing to challenge an incumbent in their own party, whether they faced term limits or not. In contrast, open seats in the U.S. House are usually attractive to state legislators, and in some circumstances, the presence of term limits increased the already high propensity of state senators to run for the small number of open races. The major effect of term limits occurred in challenges to incumbents from the other party. The likelihood that a state legislator challenged an incumbent in the other party was much greater in term-limited states, and the likelihood increased as legislators' end of service in the chamber approached. Thus, term limits may have a greater effect on the broader electoral arena than table 2.2 reflects.

Evidence from the case studies corroborates the finding that careerism does not end with term limits. David Berman (2004, 2) notes in his study on Arizona, "Contrary to the hopes of term limit supporters, the reform has not filled legislative chambers with citizen legislators with little or no political ambition who are willing to return to their private lives after a few years of service." In almost all the case study states, when legislators were forced out of the chamber due to term limits, most of them continued to run for (and usually win) other offices. The most immediate impact thus far has been to fill the Senates with termed-out House members. In California, for example, 90 percent of the senators now have previous experience in the Assembly. In Ohio, the figure is 75 percent. But the move to extend one's political career is not limited to switching chambers. Overall, as the national survey indicates, there has been an increase in termed-out legislators running, often successfully, for statewide, congressional, or even local offices.

Conclusion

In a few respects, term limits have fulfilled the promise of their supporters. Certainly, turnover has increased in most state legislatures where term limits have been imposed. Clearly, it is now impossible to have the extremely long careers within a chamber that some legislators previously enjoyed. But for the most part, the contention that term limits will lead to a "new breed" of diverse, citizen legislators remain, as Carey et al. (2006, 113) state, the "dog that won't bark."

We find almost no evidence to support the first of the arguments for term limits listed in chapter 1 of the present volume. The notion that term limits will sweep out the old politicians is true (almost by definition), but the idea that term limits will sweep in a new breed is not. The case studies and 2002 national survey conducted by the JPTL team and the bits and pieces of research conducted by others show that term limits have not increased the number of women or (with a few exceptions) the number of minorities being elected to legislatures. There is no substantial difference in the age or occupational backgrounds of legislators elected under term limits, and while term limits clearly put an end to chamber careerism, it has had very little effect on political careerism.

Perhaps it was naive to think otherwise. After all, there appear to be limited segments of American society who exhibit the characteristic known as political ambition—who are willing to undergo the rigors of a political campaign and to engage in public service. Once these individuals commit themselves to public life—once they have incurred the costs (personal, emotional, and sometimes economic)—it is unlikely they will simply walk away.

CHAPTER 3

Constituent Attention and
Interest Representation

Lynda W. Powell, Richard G. Niemi, & Michael Smith

REPRESENTATION IS what legislatures are all about. As soon as a society is large enough that direct democracy is impossible, we rely on other individuals to represent our interests. How well they do that depends on a host of factors—how they are chosen, how the representative body is organized, and how they relate to other governmental bodies. Many of these elements of representation are dealt with in other chapters of this book. In this chapter, we deal more directly with the way in which legislators act as representatives.

In focusing on individual legislators and their roles, we discuss classic questions of representation: Do legislators think of themselves as trustees or as delegates? How do legislators weigh state interests against the narrower interests of their own individual constituencies? How attentive are legislators to their constituents—how much time do they spend keeping in touch with constituents, doing casework, and securing government projects and money for their districts? How much of their time is spent raising money and campaigning for reelection? How do they divide their time between legislating and other aspects of their job? How knowledgeable are they about issues and about the legislative process?

Our particular interest here, of course, is whether legislators in term-limited states are different on any of these matters from legislators in states without term limits. These are relevant questions because both proponents and opponents of term limits argue that limiting the length of time in office results in legislators less focused on the goal of retaining their positions. However, proponents and opponents differ greatly with regard to the consequences of severing the electoral connection.

Proponents argue that term-limited legislators will engage in a more deliberative style of representation, spending more time legislating and less time on campaigning and other activities designed primarily to get them reelected (Will 1992; Petracca 1991). Their representative style tends toward the Burkean: they pay more attention to broad interests rather than to the wishes of a narrow slice of constituents. As a consequence, advocates of term limits argue, term-limited legislators would produce better legislative decisions.

Opponents argue that it is the electoral connection that ensures that legislators act in the interests of their constituents (Polsby 1997; Glazer and Wattenberg 1996). Legislators should, in general, be working for constituency interests, not implementing their own preferences or those of other groups, including state or national interests as well as special interests or constituencies that the legislator might wish to represent in the future. Further, unlimited length of service allows legislators to develop policy expertise, and expertise and accountability allow the people's branch to have both power and legitimacy in government (Rosenthal 1992).

As in the other chapters of this volume, the question here is whose expectations are met in practice. Term limits, by definition, sever the electoral connection after six to twelve years of service in one chamber. Some studies have focused on "shirking"—the tendency of legislators to pay less attention to legislative duties in their last terms (Sarbaugh-Thompson et al. 2004, 107; Rothenberg and Sanders 2000). However, term-limited legislators appear to be as interested in long-term political careers as those in non-term-limited states (Carey, Niemi, and Powell 2000; see chap. 2 in the present volume). That suggests that they will give undiminished attention to legislative tasks in the hope of building a record that will serve their career ambitions beyond their current office. This attention may, however, be selectively directed to some activities more than to others, and the constituency that is of interest to a member may shift as well. For example, members who are thinking of running for a state office may adapt their policy positions and attention to a statewide constituency. In this chapter, we will examine the evidence from the Joint Project on Term Limits—from the case studies, the 2003 Survey of Knowledgeable Observers, and the 2002 National Survey of State Legislators—and from the existing literature on these issues.

We have organized the chapter around three questions. First, what are legislators' conceptions of their roles? In particular, to what extent do they think of themselves as trustees rather than as delegates for their constituents' interests, or as representing the interests of the whole state rather than those of their own constituency? Second, how do legislators report spending their time in terms of more-concrete duties attending to their constituencies? Finally, what are some of the broader consequences of attitudinal and behavioral decisions by legislators—including how well legislators represent their constituents on issues, how much time they spend on legislation, and whether term limits have increased or decreased their power to represent their constituents?

Legislators' Attitudes toward the Role of a Representative: Shades of Edmund Burke

Edmund Burke (1774, 1854–56), in his "Speech to the Electors of Bristol," discussed the perspectives legislators may take when establishing priorities and making decisions. Drawing on Burke's observations, two perspectives are commonly juxtaposed: that of "delegates" (legislators who focus heavily on the interests and opinions of their constituents) and that of "trustees" (legislators who focus less on the interests of their constituents and more on the perceived interests of the entire state or on their own consciences). These contrasting perspectives are most commonly thought of in connection with legislators' votes, but they in fact apply to larger questions about how representatives view their jobs.

Advocates of term limits argue that such limits result in legislators engaged in a more deliberative style of representation. They maintain that such legislators serve the interests of citizens, are less beholden to the short-term opinions and passions of the voters, and are less attentive to the demands of clamoring interest groups (e.g., Will 1992). In short, term-limited legislators are considered more likely to think of themselves as trustees than as delegates. In research on term limits, investigators have studied this question in a variety of ways.

When asked directly about their legislative styles, legislators in a recent Michigan study frequently objected to simplifying their decision making to a trade-off between conscience and constituency (Sarbaugh-Thompson et al. 2004, 111). In part, this is because they often see their own and their constituents' views as being basically the same (Rosenthal 2004, 45). They are also aware that most constituents have well-conceived points of view on only a small number of the issues on which they are expected to vote (Rosenthal 2004, 38–41).

In interviews in which legislators were pressed about the matter of conscience versus constituency, they gave little indication that term limits made a difference. In interviews in the mid-1990s (Carey, Niemi, and Powell 2000), legislators only occasionally talked about such differences. For example, a Washington House committee chair noted that he might have soft-pedaled policy differences with constituents in the past, but he commented of his perspective under term limits, "I'm much more likely to tell them 'I think you're simply wrong'" (Carey, Niemi, and Powell 2000, 57). He viewed this relative independence from constituents favorably. Similarly, a former legislator from Maine noted:

> I experienced that myself. . . . When a member has decided not to seek reelection . . . they don't tend to be as concerned about the winds of what the public is screaming about. . . . They seem to be a bit freer. (Carey, Niemi, and Powell 2000, 59)

Not all legislators view this development favorably. One Colorado legislator stated: "No one has a stick on term-limited members. They vote as they please and are no longer concerned about their districts" (Straayer and Bowser 2004, 38).

In net, although this topic is certainly not spontaneously raised by legislators and although many would consider it an oversimplification, interviews suggest that term limits may indeed encourage a trustee orientation among legislators. The 1995 and 2002 surveys of legislators, which are based on large numbers of respondents, allowed us to examine the effects of term limits carefully, controlling for a range of other factors, such as demographic differences between constituencies and partisan differences between legislators. Both surveys included an item at the heart of Burkean concerns, by asking legislators about their priorities regarding district interests.

> When there is a conflict between what you feel is best and what you think the people in your district want, do you think you should follow your own conscience or follow what the people in your district want?

Answers were on a seven-point scale ranging from "Always District" (1) to "Always Conscience" (7).

In the 1995 survey, legislators mostly likely to take a "trustee" approach were the "newcomers" (those elected in the 1990s or afterward) in term-limited states. In the center of the spectrum were the "old-timers"—those that began legislative service before 1990, when no states had yet passed legislative term limits. Closer to the "delegate" end of the spectrum were the newcomers in non-term-limited states. (The difference between the newcomers in the two types of states was statistically discernable; the differences between old-timers and either group of newcomers were too small to be statistically significant.) Thus, it appears that some degree of Burkean detachment "can be encouraged through long tenure and incumbency, although not as much as through term limits" (Carey, Niemi, and Powell 2000, 61).

At the time of the 1995 survey, term limits had been adopted but not yet implemented in any of the states. In analyzing the new survey of legislators, Carey et al. (2006) found that compared to legislators in states without term limits, legislators in states where term limits had been implemented were more likely to follow their conscience than to follow what the people in their district wanted. Moreover, term-limited legislators for whom fewer years remained were more likely to follow their own conscience; this suggests that legislators in term-limited states with the shortest length of service allowed will be more likely to follow their conscience than those in states allowing more-generous limits.

In 2002, term limits had taken effect in many states. Consequently, the authors used a "chamber-specific" model, categorizing states by whether they had adopted but not implemented their term limits or whether they had both adopted term limits and put them into effect. (Of necessity, there was another small category, comprised of states that had adopted term limits but subsequently repealed them—a category mostly ignored in our analysis.) The results concerning "district versus conscience" are summarized under the first survey item in table 3.1, where the large, positive coefficient for the "adopted and implemented" category indicates the tendency of term-limited legislators to place themselves more toward the conscience end of the continuum.

Similar results were reported by Cooper and Richardson (2006). In a survey of legislators in eight states, they found a trustee orientation more predominant among term-limited legislators. However, the term-limited states they included had all implemented term limits, so they could not speak to differences between the subset of states that had implemented term limits and those that had only adopted them. They also did not consider the length of time that legislators had remaining in the chamber.

Closely tied to the Burkean advocacy of the legislator as a trustee rather than a delegate is the orientation toward broader, rather than narrower, interests. Reform advocates believe that by limiting the electoral incentive, legislators will be more likely to consider broader interests than those of their districts (Will 1992). Carey et al. (2006) found legislators in states that had implemented term limits to be more concerned with the needs of the state as a whole and less concerned with district needs than were legis-

TABLE 3.1.   Summary of Findings from 2002 National Survey regarding Representational Matters

Survey Item	b	Standard Error
Follow conscience or demands of district when there is conflict between the two:		
Always District = 1 to Always Conscience = 7		
Adopted but not yet implemented term limits	−.022	.101
Adopted and implemented term limits**	.204*	.091
Look after needs of district versus state as a whole:		
District = 1 to State as a Whole = 7		
Adopted but not yet implemented term limits	.099	.098
Adopted and implemented term limits	.191*	.088
Keeping in touch with constituents:		
Hardly Any = 1 to A Great Deal = 5		
Adopted but not yet implemented term limits	.096	.056
Adopted and implemented term limits**	.256*	.050
Helping constituents with problems with government:		
Hardly Any = 1 to A Great Deal = 5		
Adopted but not yet implemented term limits	.040	.059
Adopted and implemented term limits**	.180*	.053
Making sure your district gets a fair share of government money and projects:		
Hardly Any = 1 to A Great Deal = 5		
Adopted but not yet implemented term limits	.217*	.067
Adopted and implemented term limits	.189*	.060

Source: 2002 National Survey of State Legislators.

Note: The residual group in each equation is non-term-limited states. Each equation also contained a large number of control variables and a separate category for the small number of states that had adopted term limits and then struck them down. The N's for each equation are approximately 2,550. See Carey et al. 2006.

*$p < .05$

**$p < .05$ for difference between "adopted but not yet implemented" and "adopted and implemented" categories.

lators in states that had not adopted term limits. In states that had adopted but not implemented term limits, findings related to needs of the state and conscience were not statistically different from those in the non-term-limited states (table 3.1, second survey item). As we will continue to see, states that have implemented term limits are most likely to show the effects of term limits. Frequently, we also find that the fewer years the individual legislator has before being termed out, the stronger the effects are. Although it was not possible to look at variations in the maximum length of service allowed in term-limited states, the effects for "years remaining" suggests that states mandating the shortest service would similarly strengthen any effects of short time horizons.

The studies here cited suggest that the differences between term-limited and non-term-limited legislators—whether differences due to the direct effects of term limits (not being able to run for reelection) or due to indirect effects (e.g., the need to appeal to a broader constituency to promote a further electoral career)—mean that the former have a reduced focus on their constituencies, at least once term limits have taken effect. Moreover, the less time legislators have left in office, the more pronounced the effect is. Ironically, similar, though more modest, shifts in perspectives may come about through long service—an alternative precluded by term limits.

Spending Time: How Term Limits Affect Legislators' Priorities

In this section, we examine whether term limits, in shaping legislators' views of their roles, influence how they allocate their time in office. We expected that legislators in term-limited states, especially those approaching the end of their allowed service in the chamber, would spend less time being attentive to the constituency that elected them. Helping constituents with problems with the government, keeping in touch with constituents, and securing government monies for district projects are typically thought of as classic means of securing and maintaining electoral support, which is irrelevant under term limits. Thus, we expected time spent on these activities to diminish. In addition, we expected campaigning and fund-raising—activities even more closely tied to elections—to diminish as well. In this section, we also examine time allocated to studying and developing legislation. If less time is needed to attend to constituency and campaign matters, is more spent on legislating itself?

Evidence from the case studies seems to suggest more stasis than change with respect to matters of constituency attention. This stasis is shown by, as much as anything, the absence of legislators' and observers' commentary about the matter. Analysts in Maine noted, "These issues were rarely, if ever, mentioned in our interviews with legislators and legislative observers unless prompted by our questions" (Powell and Jones 2004, 12). The few remarks that do appear in case study reports are relatively uniform.

> Term limits do not appear to affect the extent to which legislators communicate with their constituents, respond to district concerns and do case work. . . . Most agree that term limits have had little effect on the amount [i.e., number] of "pork" projects in the budget. (Powell and Jones 2004, 12)

> Term limits have had little effect on constituent relations. (Berman 2004, 4)

> We found no change in the time spent on [helping constituents] before and after the implementation of term limits. (Sarbaugh-Thompson et al. 2004, 106)

> Members may be a little more active in helping with constituent questions and problems, but the slim data pointing in that direction may simply reflect the expanded availability of staff assistance. (Straayer and Bowser 2004, 36–37)

The last of the preceding comments may point to a difference across time—namely, that as legislatures become more professionalized, members increasingly rely on staff to perform constituency service. This tendency was observed in Colorado, where, to help deal with constituent service problems, members are making growing use of a support unit that was established two years before term limits were adopted. In Illinois, a non-term-limited state, the analysts observed simply that the "new breed of legislator tended to use staff for constituent service and working in the district rather than for policy research" (Mooney and Storey 2004, 29). In Michigan, a highly professionalized legislature, a research team reported that many legislators noted how much staff time was spent on constituency service (Sarbaugh-Thompson et al. 2004, 106).

The 2003 Survey of Knowledgeable Observers asked four questions about legislator-constituent relations, with mixed results (table 3.2). Observers thought that compared to sessions before term limits, legislators in most of the term-limited states spent slightly less time talking to constituents and solving constituent problems. Yet they thought that these same legislators spent more time sending newsletters to constituents and seeking state funds for district projects. Still, observers of non-term-limited legislatures noted larger and more consistent changes. These reporters felt that "their" legislators now spent more time on all constituency-related activities, and the increases with respect to newsletters and seeking state funds considerably outpaced the increased time reported in the term-limited states. Overall, the mixed results in the term-limited states, like the comments of legislators themselves, suggest that not much has changed due to the imposition of limits on tenure. Whatever the institutional constraints, contemporary legislators in all bodies pay a good deal of attention to district interests. Nonetheless, the larger, more consistent changes in the control states hint at the possibility that term-limited legislators are different.

Both the case studies and the survey of observers indicate the importance of distinguishing the effects of term limits from other changes that are occurring concurrently in both term-limited and non-term-limited states. The JPTL national surveys of legislators allow us to separate these two types of effects. In addition to data from a representative sample of legislators in all ninety-nine chambers, we have data from two constrastive years: 1995, when term limits had been enacted in most places but had not yet taken effect, and 2002, when term limits had taken effect in a number of chambers and states. In both surveys, there were three items intended to measure the classic types of constituency attentiveness. We asked the leg-

TABLE 3.2.   Legislators' Attention to Their Constituencies before and after Term Limits

Legislators in 2003 Compared to a Decade Before	Term-Limited States	Non-Term-Limited States
Spend time talking to constituents	2.94*	3.11
Spend time solving constituents' problems	2.86**	3.19
Seek state funds for projects in their districts	3.19**	3.50
Send newsletters or other mailings to constituents	3.16**	3.72

Source: 2003 Survey of Knowledgeable Observers.
Note: Ratings were on a five-point scale from "Quite a Bit More" (1) to "Quite a Bit Less" (5).
*$p < .10$
**$p < .05$ (based on t-tests for significance of differences in means between term-limited and non-term-limited states)

islators how much time they spent on the following activities, using a five-point scale ranging from "Hardly Any" (1) to "A Great Deal" (5):

- Keeping in touch with constituents
- Helping constituents with problems with government
- Making sure your district gets a fair share of government money and projects

In both time periods, evidence from multivariate analyses suggests that there was movement toward lower levels of responsiveness to constituents' needs and demands (Carey, Niemi, and Powell 2000, chap. 3). In the 1995 survey, the key comparison was between the newcomers in term-limited and non-term-limited states. In all three cases, this difference was significant; new legislators reported that they less often kept in touch with constituents, less frequently helped them with their problems, and were not as diligent about making sure that they received their share of pork projects (Carey, Niemi, and Powell 2000, 51–55). Most striking was the large difference with respect to pork, where newcomers in term-limited states reported spending substantially less time aiding their constituents—almost half a point less on the five-point scale. The authors wrote, "[T]his finding is particularly remarkable given that these two groups are equal in their intentions to run for reelection, suggesting that legislators in term-limit states are less intent on pork-barreling in their efforts to secure electoral support" (Carey, Niemi, and Powell 2000, 54). The findings were not without qualification. Interviews in Maine, in particular, suggested that the small districts there guarantee that legislators are held accountable to constituents regardless of whether they can be reelected. Nevertheless, the size and consistency of results across questions suggests that legislative behavior was rapidly altered upon adoption of limits on legislative terms.

In 2002, when longtime legislators had been prevented from running for office and newcomers knew that their time in office was short, we took another look at whether representation styles had changed (Carey et al. 2006). As noted previously, the analysis in 2002 used a "chamber-specific" model, categorizing states by whether they had adopted but not implemented their term limits or whether they had both adopted term limits and put them into effect. The differences we observed are consistent with those observed in the 1995 survey. Legislators in term-limited chambers, for example, reported spending less time keeping in touch with constituents than did those in non-term-limited states. Among states that had implemented term limits, the difference was large and significant relative both to the non-term-limited residual group and to those that had adopted limits but not yet put them into action (table 3.1, third survey item). A similar pattern applied with respect to legislative casework. Legislators in term-limited chambers engaged in less constituent service than did those who did not face limits, but the difference was greatest where limits had already been implemented (table 3.1, fourth survey item). The results suggest that legislators respond to environmental incentives (i.e., that they do not respond as keenly to constituents) as soon as term limits are passed, but the effect is most marked once limits actually kick in.

Other results reinforce this sense of differential attention to constituencies when term limits are in place. Term-limited legislators in 2002 reported spending far less time than those in non-term-limited states on securing government money and projects for their districts (table 3.1, fifth survey item). In addition, among term-limited legislators, efforts to secure pork varied with the number of years remaining in their possible tenure; those with less eligibility spent less time trying to secure rewards for their district. The effect is relatively large, translating into an expected shift of one-third of a point (on the five-point scale) between a legislator with six years more to go and one facing imminent removal.

Thus, the national survey evidence consistently supports the notion that term-limited representatives behave differently from those who served earlier in the same legislatures and from those now serving in non-term-limited institutions. Similarly, we expect that other activities related to the electoral connection will be diminished in term-limited states. Most notably, we expect the amount of time devoted to campaigning and fundraising to be affected—at least among those legislators with a short period of remaining service. Indeed, this is exactly what we found. Carey et al. (2006, 118) reported: "At the aggregate level (the level of the term-limited chamber), there is no appreciable decline in the priority and energy devoted to such activity. We see no suggestion, for example, that the overall demand for money in the system should decline. If we disaggregate, however, we find that the efforts devoted to campaigning and fundraising among term-limited legislators are imbalanced: those with substantial eligibility remain active, while those for whom the guillotine looms closer slow down." Similarly, then, we would anticipate that legislators in states with shorter term limits would put forth less effort compared to legislators in term-limited states with longer career horizons.

Both constituents and legislators might argue that spending less time on campaigning and fund-raising is beneficial to representation. As already noted, however, the overall effort devoted to these activities is not reduced in term-limited chambers, even though term-limited members do spend less time on campaigning and fund-raising as the end of their service approaches. In theory, spending less time on campaigning and fund-raising would allow representatives to focus on legislation and constituency attention. Yet it is not clear that reducing campaign-related activity—activity that is, after all, one way of relating to constituents—means that representatives will allocate more time to activities that constituents value more.

Indeed, if less time is spent on all constituency and electoral activities, do we see more time expended on other aspects of the job of a legislator? On the same five-point scale, we asked how much time legislators spent on the following activities:

- Studying proposed legislation
- Developing new legislation
- Building coalitions within own party to pass legislation
- Building coalitions across parties to pass legislation

By any of these measures, time spent on legislating itself did not seem to increase in term-limited states. Severing the electoral bond did not result in allocating more time to the business of legislating itself.

The Externalities of Term Limits on Representation

In addition to changing legislators' own roles and behavior, term limits have had broad-reaching, systemic consequences for the political system. These changes include less contact between citizens and their representatives, legislators who are less knowledgeable about both legislative processes and policy matters, and lessened power of the legislature relative to other actors in the policy process. In this section, we briefly review the evidence for these varied effects.

For there to be meaningful representation, citizens need to have some sense of who their representatives are. Minimally, democratic accountability rests on voters having sufficient knowledge of incumbents' legislative performance to decide whether to vote to reelect them or to oust them. Term limits, rather than resuscitating the connection between citizens and those who represent them, might make it less likely that ordinary people would know who their legislators are. More-frequent rotation in office—turnover—inevitably lessens the likelihood that citizens have had sufficient contact with their representatives to be knowledgeable about them. Moreover, lacking knowledge of who their representatives are, they might interact with them less.

Information on this aspect of representation comes from a study that two of the authors of this chapter conducted in 1999 (Niemi and Powell 2003). Even in the self-selected sample used in that study, only a minority of individuals were able to recall the names of their state legislators. The percentage able to do so was lower in term-limited states, even though, at the time, no legislators had yet been prevented from running in a number of the states classified as term-limited. Taking advantage of nested House and Senate districts, we were able to show that an important explanation for the inability to name their legislators was length of service. As term limits inevitably shorten average tenure of representatives, their abbreviated service reduces their contacts with constituents. This, in turn, makes constituents unable to recollect their names. Significantly, they were also less likely to have contacted their representatives.

Here, then, is another reason for a weaker connection between legislators and their constituents under term-limited regimes. Lack of personal ties—some as simple as knowing the representative's name—can reduce the likelihood of contacts and therefore the knowledge that representatives have of their constituents and the influence that constituents are likely to wield. Since this effect is not likely immediately upon adoption of term limits, it is likely to have grown recently, as numerous legislators have been prevented from running. The shorter the length of tenure allowed, the greater the effect will be.

Citizens themselves are especially concerned about these issues. Attentiveness of the legislator—keeping in touch, helping constituents who have problems with the government, and knowing constituents' interests—are aspects of legislative service typically rated as important by constituents themselves. The 1978 National Election Study found that citizens ranked "keeping in touch with the people about what the government is doing" more important as an activity for U.S. House members than any of the other activities they listed, slightly edging out "working in Congress on bills concerning national issues." For U.S. senators, keeping in touch ranked second to working on bills, but it was ranked more important than any other type of activity (Hinckley 1980, 450–51). Thus, for citizens, this aspect of the job of a representative is critically important.

Term limit advocates wish for citizen legislators more in touch with their constituents. Limited tenure often seems to have had contrary results. Where legislative terms are limited, citizens are less likely to have the familiarity with their legislators that fosters knowledge about their representatives and that facilitates contacts for help; consequently, rather than making legislators more in touch with constituents, term limits seem to lessen the ability of citizens to hold their representatives accountable in the election booth. As we have seen from the legislator survey, term-limited legislators spend less time trying to keep in touch with and help constituents in dealing with the government. Thus, under term limits, both citizens and legislators take less initiative in establishing a relationship, and the effect of both dynamics works to reduce the extent of constituency contact that underlies the relationship between the two.

For democratic theorists, the core of the relationship between representatives and their constituents involves working in the legislature on bills and establishing public policy. This activity of a legislator was also ranked highly by citizens. In the 1978 National Election Study, it was ranked as the second most important task of House members and the first task of senators; in a survey by Hibbing and Theiss-Morse (1995, 66), it was at the top of the list. At the heart of the relationship is the responsibility of legislators to create policy consistent with the wishes (a delegate view) or interests (a trustee view) of their constituents. Between term-limited legislators and those without term limits, are there any differences in whom they represent? With regard to legislators' perceptions of proximity to the average constituent on liberalism or conservatism, there is no difference between term-limited and non-term-limited chambers or between new and old members in those chambers. There does not appear to be any difference in the extent to which legislators specialize in one policy area versus being equally active in many areas. Here, we find no impact of term limits, although our data on this point is quite limited. Of course, regardless of legislators' intentions to represent their constituents, doing so also requires a good deal of knowledge of state problems and policies and of legislative processes. Anecdotal accounts differ in the degree to which lack of experience hampers the quality or quantity of legislation produced under term limits, but the lack of knowledge itself is a thread running throughout accounts in virtually every chapter of the present volume.

The 2003 Survey of Knowledgeable Observers likewise indicates that compared to members in states without term limits, members in term-limited states knew less about statewide issues and about how the legislature operates. This is not surprising, of course, in that members in states where term limits are in effect have much less experience in the legislature. As of 2002, for example, we calculated that in states where term limits were in effect, 46 percent of the members had served two years or less, compared to only 18 percent in states that had not adopted term limits. Of perhaps greater import, only 8 percent had served eight or more years, compared to a whopping 54 percent in states that had not adopted term limits. Legislators in term-limited states are thus likely to lack the attributes—especially knowledge—that are associated with length of tenure. Hence, although members may give more emphasis to the needs of the state as a whole in term-limited states, they are less knowledgeable about the substance of these issues.

Interviews and the survey of observers indicate that term-limited members know less about matters that come before their committees. Details of legislation are often drafted and negotiated in committees, and observers of the legislative process emphasize the special importance of knowledge in this context (see chap. 5). The lack of understanding in this domain demonstrated among many term-limited legislators also hampers quality representation.

Finally, the accumulated evidence indicates that term limits have had an impact on the power and influence of the legislature in state government relative to other parts of the government. Both interview and survey results indicate that administrative agencies, legislative staff, lobbyists, and party caucuses all gained influence relative to the legislature in term-limited states (see chap. 10). This means that the political actors who are charged most directly with representing the people—their elected legislators—have evidently lost power to unelected individuals and to the executive branch. Thus, one could reasonably argue that citizens' representation has been diminished in term-limited states.

Conclusion

Term limit advocates hoped for a return to the Burkean, or "trustee," model of representation, whereby legislators would pay less attention to particularistic interests of their districts and more to the broader needs of society. These hopes have been, at best, half-filled. According to the surveys of legislators and observers alike, term limits have indeed weakened the link between representatives and individual districts. Observers report that legislators in term-limited states spend less time talking to their constituents and solving their problems than legislators did a decade ago; this shift is especially noticeable when compared to what has happened in non-term-limited states. In the nationwide survey, new legislators in term-limited states report themselves more likely to follow their consciences—and less likely to follow the will of constituents—than do their counterparts in non-term-limited states. Furthermore, newly elected, term-limited legislators pay less attention to constituency issues than do their counterparts that lack term limits. Most notably, term-limited legislators claim to place less emphasis on securing pork for their home district (while knowledgeable observers see term-limited legislators as having grown in their use of pork, but less so than legislators in non-term-limited states). Overall, the presence of term limits seems to mean that legislators devote less time and effort to constituency issues. These changes would please advocates of a trustee model of representation and, presumably, those who support term limits because they feel that legislators are too wrapped up in campaign and reelection activities.

However, there is a downside to weakening links with constituents. Though they may have wished for legislators to be less absorbed in narrow interests (even those located in their constituency), term limit advocates also wished for citizen legislators to be more in touch with their constituents. Limited tenure seems to have the contrary result. Reducing the time legislators are in office means that citizens have less time to become familiar with them. This, in turn, makes constituents less likely to interact with their legislators.

Moreover, having reduced their focus on constituency interests, Burkean legislators are expected to give increased time and attention to statewide issues, and on this front, term limits are a disappointment. The nationwide survey shows term-limited legislators being less attentive to statewide needs than those in non-term-limited states and, according to a number of measures, spending no more time on the task of legislating. Perhaps owing to this lack of attention, as well as to their shorter time in office, members in term-limited states were judged—by both case analysts and knowledgeable observers—to know less about statewide issues.

Finally, regardless of the interests legislators represent and the knowledge they possess, a concern expressed in all parts of the research project is that term-limited lawmakers are less effective in mastering legislative procedures and in dealing with other parts of the government. Reforming the legislature is a goal of term limit advocates. Weakening the legislature and possibly diminishing the level of citizen representation appears to be an unintended by-product, at least in terms of the public rationale for the adoption of term limits. Some citizens may, however, find less government activity preferable to more. For them, at least, this may be an intended and desired outcome.

CHAPTER 4

Legislative Leadership

Thomas H. Little & Rick Farmer

ALAN ROSENTHAL (2004, 209) indicates they are "the fulcrum on which much of the legislative work hinges." Jewell and Whicker (1994, 1) describe what they do as an "elusive and powerful phenomenon." Tom Loftus (1994, 47), who was one of them for a time, compares them to both "a teacher in front of the classroom . . . , a font of real knowledge, and someone in front of a firing squad who is fumbling with his blindfold and last cigarette in order to buy time." Robert Hertzberg, also formerly one of them, notes that they are "everybody's rabbi, priest and counselor" (State Legislative Leaders Foundation 2005). They are the elected and appointed leaders of the state legislatures—the Speakers, presidents, pro tempores, floor leaders, and whips.

Regardless of how you say it, one thing is clear: legislative leaders are central to the legislative process. Legislatures that have weak leadership are likely to be weak institutions (Rosenthal 2004). Strong leadership is associated with a strong and effective legislature. However, in the eyes of many, that very same strong leadership was a central impetus for the term limits movement that swept across the nation in the 1990s. Strong leaders—exemplified by the likes of Speakers Willie Brown in the California Assembly, John Martin in the Maine House, and Vern Riffe in the Ohio House—were used by many to promote the cause of legislative term limits.

Term Limits and Leaders: What Did We Expect?

While legislative term limits restrict the terms of every legislator, their most dramatic impact, many felt, would be on legislative leaders. A six-year limit on members realistically translates into a two- (or at most four-) year limit on leaders (Malbin and Benjamin 1992, 213). Under term limits, apart from the rather unique situation of a legislator returning to the institution after leaving, legislators would choose a leader with very limited experience in the chamber, and that legislator would be leading an institution dominated numerically by legislators with even less experience.

Expectations regarding the effect of term limits on leadership tended to fall into one of three categories. First and most obvious was leadership selection and tenure. By definition, term limits will affect (although not necessarily increase) leadership turnover (Jewell and Whicker 1994, 36, 193). Beyond turnover, there was also an expectation that term limits might influence leadership contests and the types of people who would seek and win those seats. According to Malbin and Benjamin (1992, 213), "members would trade their votes for favorable committee positions, as potential leaders seek to put together majority coalitions for their leadership races." This expectation is supported by Rosenthal (1998, 157–58). It would be particularly true in states where legislative tenure was generally a requirement for leadership selection. Moreover, as term limits are implemented, the importance of legislative seniority in determining leaders is minimized, as no candidate for leadership will have extensive tenure. Early work on leadership selection by Bowser et al. (2003) finds this to be true.

Second, most expected that term limits would have an effect on leadership activity and responsibilities (e.g., Jewell and Whicker 1994, 36–37). Not only might the leaders chosen be different, but so would the jobs to which they were chosen, allowing them to focus on different types of activities and responsibilities than had predecessors who were not bound by term limits. Leaders under term limits would have to spend more time "courting" and educating the new members. While some suggested that the ability of leaders to raise campaign money would be less important (e.g., Price 1992, 150), most suggested that with the increased number of open seats, campaign activities—especially the ability to raise money—would become central to gaining and retaining leadership positions and keeping members happy. Moreover, one could reasonably speculate that the increased number of open seats would increase the emphasis of leaders or future leaders on candidate recruitment and management.

Finally, the third set of expectations related to leadership effectiveness—both within the institutions (relative to their members and their ability to manage the legislative process) and with external players, including lobbyists, party leaders, and the governor (Jewell and Whicker 1994, 36–37; Rosenthal 1992, 207). Regarding internal effectiveness, Rosenthal (1992, 207) argued that term limits would accelerate the already evident trend toward decentralized and weakened leadership. Leaders would have less control over committee appointments, bill scheduling, and floor management. Concerning external effectiveness, it was accepted that the term-limited leader would have a weaker hand vis-à-vis the executive. Rosenthal (1992, 208) wrote, "What you are going to see with term limits is a shift, generally speaking, back to executive dominance." According to Malbin and Benjamin (1992, 215–16), this shift would occur because term limits alter the incentive structure, increasing the incentive for members to support the governor and decreasing their ability to withstand gubernatorial pressure. Moreover, while most governors are term-limited as well (Beyle 2003), they have the potential to serve at least eight years in most states, so it is quite likely that the newly elected, term-limited legislative leader will be facing an experienced executive.

The Effect of Context

The degree to which one would expect term limits to impact these three dimensions of leadership are tempered by two sets of factors: the nature of the term limit requirements and the nature of legislative leadership in the state prior to term limits. As noted in chapter 1 of this volume, term limit regulations vary in length (between six, eight, or twelve years), application by chamber (i.e., a limit of years per chamber versus a limit of total legislative service), and permanence (i.e., a ban on consecutive terms versus a lifetime ban). The combination of each of these qualities affects the nature and extent of term limit effects on legislative leadership. In other words, one can expect effects to be greater in institutions where the limits are shorter (six or eight years), specific to each chamber, and lifetime in nature than in states where the limits are longer (twelve years), allow for service of all years in a single chamber, and allow legislators to run again after a period of absence. For example, one would expect the impact on leadership to be greater in the Arkansas House (which has a six-year lifetime limit) than in the Louisiana House or Senate (which allow twelve consecutive years in each chamber).

In addition to the specifications of the term limits, one must also consider the nature of legislative leadership in the given chamber. If leadership in the chamber has traditionally been characterized by limited leadership tenure or relatively weak leadership influence, one can expect the impact of term limits to be limited. If powerful leaders with long tenures have historically characterized an institution, one can expect the impact of term limits to be greater. For example, one would expect the impact to be greater in the Ohio House, which had two powerful Speakers in the twenty-six years before term limits, than in the Arkansas House, which was characterized by rotating Speakers and strong committee chairs prior to the implementation of term limits.

Term Limits and Leaders: What Did We Get?

Regarding anticipated impacts on legislative leaders, there was little disagreement between the opponents and proponents of term limits. Both agreed that term limits would alter the selection process, the responsibilities, and the influence of legislative leaders. Proponents believed that would be a good thing (e.g., Fund 1992, 234). Opponents did not (e.g., Rosenthal 1992, 208). Now that a significant amount of time has passed since the implementation of legislative term limits, let us see if the anticipated predictions came to pass.

Leadership Selection and Tenure

While there was significant disagreement among scholars, proponents, and opponents of term limits regarding whether their effects would be, on the whole, positive or negative, there was consensus regarding one thing: they would have a significant effect on the selection and length of tenure of state legislative leaders. Indeed, for many proponents (reflecting on the power of Brown, Martin, and Riffe, mentioned earlier), this effect was a significant reason to implement term limits. The nine-state study conducted by the Joint Project on Term Limits (JPTL) reveals that the implementation of legislative term limits did indeed alter the selection process in one very predictable way: increased leadership turnover and competition for leadership positions. Since the implementation of legislative term limits, all six of the term-limited states in the JPTL study have had at least two different leaders presiding in each chamber. From 1980 to 1994, the California Assembly had one Speaker. From 1996 (the year term limits were implemented) to 2005, five different people have held that post. Likewise, the Maine House of Representatives had one Speaker from 1975 to 1995, but five different people have held the post in the ten years since that time. However, the significance of the turnover change varies considerably according to the nature of the limits and the historical leadership patterns in each state.

As indicated in table 4.1, leadership tenure after term limits is less than half of that of the three Speakers serving before the implementation of term limits. Dramatic change took place in the lower chambers of Maine, Colorado, Ohio, and California, with average tenure dropping by as much as six years. Because of the rapid turnover of Speakers (three in two years) following the 1994 election, the five-year average in California masks the fourteen-year tenure of Willie Brown. Effects were not limited to the lower chamber. Historically, key Senate leaders in Ohio and California served six or eight years prior to term limits. After term limits, that number decreased to a single term in each position, with the exception of Senator John Burton, who served as president pro tempore of the California Senate for six years before he was termed out in 2002. House leadership in both states was characterized by a marked decrease in leadership stability following the implementation of term limits. Table 4.2 suggests that leadership tenure in the control states remains significantly higher than in the term-limited states.

In Colorado and Maine, leadership turnover following the implementation of term limits generally returned to the level of the 1970s, when leaders in these states tended to rotate every two or four years. As reflected in table 4.1, the 1980s and early 1990s had witnessed an increase in leadership stability in these two states. In the non-term-limited Indiana legisla-

TABLE 4.1.   Comparison of 2005–6 House Leadership Tenure before and after Term Limits

State	Three Pre-Term-Limits Speakers Average Years	Post-Term-Limits Speakers Average Years (N)
Arizona	4	3.3 (3)
Arkansas	3.3	2 (3)
California	5	2 (5)
Colorado	6.7	2 (4)
Maine	8	2 (5)
Ohio	9.3	3 (2)
Average	6.06	2.38 (22)

ture, leadership turnover in the House has been motivated by majority change, and the Senate president pro tempore has been in place for more than two decades. Finally, the effect on formal leadership positions is less in Arkansas and Arizona. Before term limits, leaders tended to hold their formal posts for two or four years. After term limits, those terms were decreased to two years in Arkansas. Interestingly, the nature of term limits in Arizona created a position in the Arizona House where leadership after term limits might be more, rather than less, stable. In 2002, term-limited Speaker Jim Weirs ran successfully for the Senate. In 2004, he ran successfully for his old House seat and was promptly reelected Speaker for the 2005 session. Because Arizona limits legislators to eight years of consecutive service, Weiers could serve six more years as Speaker. In the less professional, non-term-limited Kansas legislature, leadership turnover has always been and remains relatively high. These results generally mirror the findings of the JPTL 2003 Survey of Knowledgeable Observers and 2002 National Survey of State Legislators, both of which found greater leadership turnover and less stability in term-limited states.

Relative to the period before term limits, members' level of legislative experience prior to becoming an institutional leader has gone down dra-

TABLE 4.2.   Comparison of 2005–6 House Leadership Tenure and Legislative Experience of Term-Limited and Non-Term-Limited States

State	Speaker	Years as Speaker	Prior Legislative Experience
Term-Limited States			
Arizona	Jim Weiers[a]	4	6
Arkansas	Bill Stovall	2	4
California	Fabian Nuñez	2	3
Colorado	Andrew Romanoff	2	4
Maine	John Richardson	2	4
Ohio	Jon Husted	2	4
Average		2.3	4.2
Non-Term-Limited States			
Illinois	Michael Madigan	20	18
Indiana	Brian Bosma	2	12
Kansas	Doug Mays	4	10
Average		8.7	13.3

[a]Jim Weiers had six years of legislative experience when first elected Speaker in 2002. After completing his tenure in the House, he served two years in the Senate (2003–4), then returned to the House to be reelected Speaker.

matically. In Maine, for example, the average years of legislative experience for new leaders decreased from fourteen to four years. The numbers were similar in each of the term-limited states. According to one Arizona legislator, "High turnover has produced a House where there is a very small pool from which to draw experienced members for leadership positions" (Berman 2004, 7). In Arkansas, where the offices of Speaker and Senate president pro tempore were historically based solely on seniority, the results were most dramatic. In the House, this has produced two of the youngest Speakers in American history. Bob Johnson was thirty-three when he was tapped as Speaker in 1999, but he was ancient compared to his successor, twenty-eight-year-old Shane Broadway, who was elected to the House at twenty-four and had completed his House tenure at twenty-nine (English and Weberg 2004, 38). Table 4.2 indicates that preleadership experience for legislators in term-limited states is significantly lower (just over four years) than for their counterparts in states without term limits (over thirteen years).

Finally, table 4.3 suggests that while experience in the chamber has decreased for all leaders, the drop in legislative experience is not nearly so great in the Senates, as more and more Senate leaders come to their positions with experience in both chambers. On average, Senate leaders came to their position with two years more legislative experience than did their House colleagues. Three of the six Senate leaders served previously in the lower chamber, while only one House leader had served in his state's Senate. In Maine, legislative experience for the 2003–4 leadership team actually increased, from about ten years prior to term limits to thirteen years

TABLE 4.3.   Legislative Experience of 2005–6 House Speakers and Top Senate Leaders in Term-Limited States

| State | House | Experience (years) | | Senate | Experience (years) | |
		Same Chamber	Total		Same Chamber	Total
Arizona	Jim Weiers	8	10	Ken Bennet	6	6
Arkansas	Bill Stovall	4	4	Jim Argue	8	14
California	Fabian Nuñez	3	3	Don Perata	2	8
Colorado	Andrew Romanoff	4	4	Joan Fitz-Gerald	4	4
Maine	John Richardson	4	4	Beth G. Edmonds	4	4
Ohio	Jon Husted	4	4	Bill Harris	5	10
Average		4.5	4.8		4.8	7.7

after term limits, with Senate leaders serving their full eight years in the House before coming to the Senate (Powell and Jones 2004, 17). Likewise, most of the leaders in the Ohio Senate served first in the House (Farmer and Little 2004, 9).

In most states, leadership selection has historically been highly correlated with seniority. Legislators have been required to serve extensive tenures and hold several other apprentice positions before moving to the top of the leadership ladder. However, term limits restrict the potential and importance of legislative tenure as a prerequisite for leadership selection. In the absence of seniority and experience, the selection process in term-limited states differs significantly from other states in at least three ways: competition, predictability, and qualifying factors.

First, in terms of competition, leadership positions are much more contested in term-limited states than in states without term limits. Each chamber in the six term-limited states in the JPTL study has experienced significant leadership contests in the past four years, including some rather bruising battles. At one point in the battle to succeed a term-limited Speaker, it appeared that two Ohio representatives were going to share the two-year term, one taking each year (Farmer and Little 2004, 10). Competition for leadership begins very early, often in the freshman term. One Colorado legislator noted: "There is early jockeying for leadership positions. As soon as Dean was elected Speaker, rumors started about who was running next. Everyone is posturing to be a leader, not waiting to learn the process, the trade, first—just posturing on positions" (Straayer and Bowser 2004, 49).

Second, leadership selection in the term-limited states was historically quite predictable. In Arkansas and Florida, the importance of seniority and the practice of rotating leaders every two years allowed one to predict leaders years ahead. In the other term-limited states, leadership ladders, tradition, and the importance of incumbency made leadership selection quite stable and predictable. Even where there was turnover, leaders followed a predictable pattern to the top. Following term limits, this predictability was replaced by virtual chaos. Following the fourteen-year leadership of Willie Brown, the California Assembly has had seven leaders in ten years. Legislators in Maine and Colorado seem to have returned to a relatively predictable pattern of leadership selection reminiscent of the days before term limits, generally elevating the floor leader to the presiding officer at the beginning of each term. As noted earlier, the 2005 Speaker of the Arizona House was formally a freshman (with eight years of House experience), having returned to the House after two years in the Senate. Leadership selection in the three control states is markedly different from that in the term-limited states. Leaders in Illinois, Indiana, and Kansas have considerably more legislative experience than their counterparts in the term-limited states. Of the top leaders in these states who held their posts in 2005, none had less than twelve years of experience in his or her chamber. In the six term-limited states, only one of the leaders in 2005 had served more than eight years in his chamber (Speaker Weirs of Arizona), with most having only four or six years of service.

Finally, in the absence of experience as the primary predictor of leadership ascension, other qualifying factors have become more important. While personal relationships have always been important in determining leadership positions in the legislature, they have become even more important in term-limited states. Upon election to their first legislative term, especially in Houses of Representatives, legislators interested in leadership begin building coalitions and relationships with other legislators for a run at leadership. In states with six-year limits, ambitious legislators can get most of the votes they need for Speaker by courting those legislators who were elected in their class, with a few additional supporters from the class before or after them. A second, related qualifying factor associated with successful leadership efforts revolves around campaign assistance. Many prospective leaders gain a foothold in the leadership race by assisting legislators with their campaigns, building a relationship that is both political and personal at the same time. One Maine legislator noted: "[T]he [House] majority leader made contact with new members by driving to their district to help with elections. He took the time, putting 40,000 miles on his car, and defeated two other candidates who did not spend the time working with and for new legislators. The majority leader got the votes from these new members. That is how leadership races will likely be run in the future" (Powell and Jones 2004, 22).

In the California Assembly, it has become the norm that new Speakers are selected and take office early in the second year of the biennial session, so that they can more effectively raise money and recruit candidates without the lame-duck status associated with leaders who are in the final months at their posts. Senate leaders also expend significant effort on candidate recruitment. However, their job is considerably easier than that of Assembly leaders, because of the number of term-limited Assembly members interested in seeking a position in the Senate.

In conclusion, leaders in term-limited states have, by definition, a limited number of years in both the legislature and their leadership position. The limits on legislative experience represent a significant decline in all of the term-limited states, relative to experience prior to term limits and relative to the states without limits. However, the degree to which the increase in leadership turnover (or decline of leadership experience) is a significant change from past leadership in the state depends on the patterns of selection present before term limits.

Leadership Activities

The general job description for most state legislative leaders (either individually or as a leadership team) varies little from one state to the next. According to Alan Rosenthal (1998, 245–92), all legislative leaders make appointments, preside, assign bills, administer the institution, serve the needs of members, work with the other chamber and the executive, build legislative coalitions, take the heat for wayward members, and help get members elected. Leaders who neglect these responsibilities are likely to find themselves back with the rank and file or among the general public. However, the emphasis that legislative leaders place on these functions varies from state to state, time to time, and even position to position.

A shift in emphasis was quite clear following the implementation of term limits. For the most part, leaders in term-limited states continued to be responsible for the institutional management and operation of the legislatures, just as they had been before the implementation of term limits. Leaders in both term-limited and non-term-limited states continue to preside over floor sessions, assign bills to committee, make appointments, negotiate with the governor and the other chamber, and represent their institution to the public. While the ability of some leaders to effectively perform these duties may have declined, their obligation to perform them did not. However, the balance of responsibilities often shifted quite dramatically in two areas: serving and educating the membership and campaign activities.

With as many as 40 percent of the legislators new in some chambers at the beginning of each session, member education and training have become high priorities in states where legislative terms are limited. Scholars in all six of the term-limited states found an increased emphasis on membership training and education that was not evident in Indiana, Illinois, and Kansas. Legislative leaders employed a broad spectrum of tools to try and bring the large classes of legislative neophytes "up to speed" as quickly as possible. In Ohio, Speaker Larry Householder paired senior legislators with new members from safe Republican districts even before the general election was held. In Arkansas, Speakers Shane Broadway and Bill Stovall would open up their apartments for dinners for small groups of freshmen prior to the beginning of a session. In the California Assembly, leaders established the California Assembly Program for Innovative Training and Orientation for the Legislature (CAPITOL) Institute, designed specifically to quickly educate new legislators, staffers, and spouses. A more thorough discussion of these and other steps taken by leaders to better equip their new members can be found in chapter 11 of this volume.

Leaders in most of the term-limited states also find increased pressure to be involved in campaign activities, especially candidate recruitment and fund-raising. The JPTL case studies found such shifts in Arkansas, Colorado, Maine, Ohio, and California. It is difficult to determine the impact of term limits on campaign activities in Arizona, because the implementation of limits there coincided with implementation of legislation for campaign finance reform.

Because term limits create so many open seats with each election cycle, legislative leaders are under constant pressure to recruit effective and qualified candidates. In the Ohio and Maine Houses, recent leaders won their posts by recruiting and working closely with successful candidates across the state. There are a growing number of midterm vacancies, as term-limited legislators leave to take advantage of opportunities that present themselves. According to Richard Powell and Rich Jones (2004, 19), leaders in Maine "are expected to recruit candidates, help raise campaign funds and get their party's candidates elected." Powell and Jones explain, "Although leaders were expected to play an electoral role prior to term limits, this role has become more important because of the increased turnover caused by term limits."

In Arkansas and California, term limits necessitated a temporal shift in the cycle of leadership selection, so that a lame-duck leader would not hamstring the caucus campaign efforts. The new Speaker of the California Assembly takes his position in the spring of each even-numbered year, months before the fall elections. In the Arkansas House, the Speaker designate is in place and active a full year before being formally sworn in as Speaker in January following the elections. These changes seem to be working, as scholars found a significant increase in fund-raising and electoral activities in the California Assembly and the Arkansas House. In 2004, Arkansas Speaker-elect Bill Stovall III established the first leadership political action committee (Leadership Arkansas '05), which raised and distributed more than thirty-five thousand dollars to new and incumbent candidates. Almost 90 percent of the money was distributed to candidates who proved to be successful.

While campaign activities are important for leaders in most states, leadership studies revealed no increase in the importance of such activities in recent years in Illinois and Kansas compared to California, Ohio, Arkansas, Colorado, and Maine. As noted earlier, election-related shifts in Arizona are difficult to attribute to term limits, because they coincide with significant changes in campaign finance regulations and rules. While leaders are considered very powerful in Illinois, the case study of that state made no mention of campaign-related activities as a source of that power. In recent years, the Indiana House has seen an increase in leadership campaign activity and targeting, which is attributed to the increasingly competitive nature of that chamber, where the majority has consistently been up for grabs for almost two decades.

Interestingly, the JPTL surveys of legislators and observers offer mixed results regarding leadership priorities. The only significant differences between term-limited and non-term-limited states found in the survey of legislators suggests that leaders in term-limited states are less—not more—interested in recruitment, fund-raising, and general campaign activities. However, this may reflect the fact that states with term limits tend to be less professional and less competitive than those without them. While knowledgeable observers find an increased focus on fund-raising in the last decade, there was no significant difference between term-limited and non-term-limited states regarding changes in efforts in candidate recruitment.

In conclusion, the case studies suggest that term limits have caused legislative leaders to shift their priorities and focus a bit. They tend to be more likely than their counterparts in non-term-limited states to focus attention on meeting the immediate needs of the new legislators (especially information and education) and on maintaining or gaining the party majority in the increasingly competitive electoral environment created by constant legislative turnover and open seats. These trends were more evident in Houses than in Senates. Because senators increasingly come from the House, most are well versed in the nuances of the legislative process (if not the nuances of the Senate), so education efforts are not as critical. Moreover, because most candidates for the Senate are moving over from the other chamber, candidate recruitment and fund-raising are not as critical.

The results from the surveys reveal less impact than the results from the case studies.

Leadership Effectiveness

At the end of the day, the only thing that really matters for legislative leaders and the legislature is results. If leaders have less experience and less stability but still get the job done, term limits really do not matter. If leaders have to spend more time educating and courting members but still hold their own with the governor, the legislative institution and the balance of power will be all right. Therefore, our final question in this chapter is perhaps the most important. Are leaders in term-limited states effective leaders?

The case studies of the six term-limited states suggest that while legislative leaders in most of these institutions are working hard, are doing a remarkable job in light of their situation, and are usually the most influential players in their chambers, they are not as powerful as their predecessors or as their counterparts in states not constrained by term limits. They seem to have maintained their internal positions of influence, but as the influence of their institutions has decreased, they are much like big fish in a shrinking pond. Further, other fish seem to be almost as big and are perhaps getting bigger. In terms of external leadership effectiveness, the discussion in this chapter and the findings in chapter 9 in this volume clearly indicate that the institutional influence of the legislative leadership and the legislature relative to the executive is generally decreased in recent decades but that legislatures with strong and effective leaders can hold their own.

The JPTL studies of individual states and surveys of legislators and observers suggest that the effects of term limits on internal influence have been mixed. Similar to the findings of Sarbaugh-Thompson et al. (2004) in Michigan, the JPTL studies suggest that legislative leaders remain influential in their respective chambers. However, these statements of strength are almost always prefaced or followed by the caveat that today's leaders (with the possible exception of those in Arkansas) are not as influential as their predecessors. For example, while Berman (2004, 5) notes that "power in the Arizona Legislature continues to be concentrated in its leaders," he adds that "leaders under term limits are less likely to do an effective job," and he cites three rebellions against leadership from 1999 to 2003.

The decline in leadership influence is generally attributed to three sources: the limited knowledge and experience of the leaders, the limited tenure potential of the leaders, and the career motivations of the members. First, as shown in table 4.2, legislative term limits have created a situation in which legislators are moving into institutional leadership with limited legislative experience, sometimes as little as two years of experience in the institution. Historically, a key source of leadership influence has been leaders' understanding of the legislative process—their grasp of the nuances of particular policies, their knowledge of the history of legislative issues, and their personal relationships with other legislators (Rosenthal 1998). In term-limited bodies however, legislative leaders, especially in lower chambers (table 4.3), seldom have the time and experience to build up such knowledge and skills. One Arizona legislator put the problem succinctly: "Term limits has meant that people received committee and other leadership positions before they were ready for them" (Berman 2004, 16). Members in each of the term-limited states noted that current leaders were less knowledgeable of policy and process than their predecessors of the non-term-limited era.

Second, legislative leaders in term-limited legislatures tended to find their influence lessened because of their lame-duck status. From the time a term-limited legislative leader takes up his or her position, everyone knows when that leader's term will end. Legislators, especially those in their first or second term, realize that there are limited long-term consequences in disobeying or offending legislative leaders in term-limited states, because they will be gone in two or, at most, four years. Legislators in each of the term-limited states cited this fact as an explanation for decreased influence. According to one Colorado leader, "Just days after I was elected, I heard members of my own party asking, 'who's going to take over in two years.' And the campaign began" (Straayer and Bowser 2004, 48–49). Another Colorado legislator added, "[Leadership] is weaker, they have no stick, a two-year cycle, a lack of continuity and discipline" (Straayer 2004, 50).

Finally, the nature of the membership and the fact that they, too, face limited tenure has weakened legislative leadership. Term-limited legislators are generally more concerned with achieving their own short-term goals than they are in working with the leadership or "taking one for the party." Various Maine legislators noted: "Leaders cannot control the members"; "Members have no allegiance to the leaders. They openly defy and ridicule them"; "Committee chairs disregard the deadline" (Powell and Jones 2004, 21, 29, 41). Rebels in the Arizona House defeated the leadership budget twice in three years, despite embarrassment to the Republican leadership and despite public relations victories for the Democratic governor (Berman 2004, 6). In Ohio, Speaker Larry Householder was able to overcome a similar challenge by recruiting and assisting candidates and building an esprit de corps among his caucus members prior to and during his first term as Speaker (State Legislative Leaders Foundation 2004). However, the unique and precarious nature of this success is evidenced by the fact that a scandal within his staff had rendered him completely impotent by the end of his second term (Smyth 2004). Personal power, which may be exercised under term limits, is much more tenuous than institutional power, which the limits most assuredly weaken. While the case studies reported a loss of leadership influence, the survey of observers did not reveal comparable findings. However, it did reveal that relative to the non-term-limited states, term-limited states suffered a significant loss in the influence of the party caucus, a central tool of party leadership.

In contrast to the case studies of leaders who tend to see their power decreasing, case studies in the control states of Indiana and Illinois recorded no such loss, while studies in Kansas showed that Republican leadership there has suffered from some internal party splits. Leaders in the Illinois legislature are considered among the most influential in the country because of their knowledge, their experience, their control of the budget process, and their control of the floor. Legislative leaders in Indiana are considered powerful, "more respected than feared" (Wright and Ogle 2004, 5). Leadership in the Kansas legislature in recent years has been hampered by a split within the majority party—a split that has rendered the state, at least in the eyes of many, a three-party state.

The story of leadership power in the Arkansas legislature is so unique that it must be explained. Most believe that term limits have actually increased the power of the Speaker of the House and the president pro tempore of the Senate, relative to their influence before term limits. This result is quite rare in term-limited states, but it stems from the fact that these positions were so weak before term limits. Prior to the implementation of term limits, power in the Arkansas legislature lay in seniority and key committee chairs, not in the elected leaders. In fact, some went so far as to describe these positions as ceremonial. However, as term limits leveled the playing field in regard to seniority, legislative leaders took a much more active and visible role in agenda setting, bill assignment, committee assignment, and public relations (English and Weberg 2004).

Legislative leaders wear two distinct hats when it comes to influence. They need to influence other legislators within their institution, and they also need to influence actors outside the legislative institution, on behalf of the legislature. We now turn to the effects of term limits on that second, external role.

One of the most consistent and persistent arguments made by opponents of the term limits movement was that they would upset the constitutional balance of power between the legislative and executive branches of government that have served the states and the nation so well for two centuries. It was believed that the legislature, hamstrung with inexperienced leadership, revolving-door staff, and high membership turnover, would be at the mercy of stable, well-staffed, and ambitious governors. Extensive analysis of changes in Michigan politics following term limits supports this proposition, revealing that term limits have increased the influence of the office of the governor relative to its power before term limits (Sarbaugh-Thompson et al. 2004, 192).

The JPTL studies of leadership in nine states suggest that the legislative leadership is indeed losing power relative to the executive, but it is unclear how much of that loss is due to term limits and how much is due to other factors, including increased institutional, personal, and political powers for the executive. In four of the six term-limited states, respondents indicated quite clearly that the legislature and its leadership had lost power relative to the executive branch (both the governor and the bureaucracy). A respondent in Maine summed up the line of thought: "Term Limits have shifted power to the executive. The rotation of presiding officers weakens leadership because of the steep learning curve. There are a number of members who are posturing for leadership positions in the next legislature. It is hard for the leader to sanction members. Legislative leaders are unable to hold their own with increasingly effective executives" (Powell and Jones 2004, 21). In the other two states (Arkansas and Ohio), the picture is a bit different. In Arkansas, presiding officers have gained power at the expense of key committee leaders, and increased influence in Ohio appears to be a function more of personalities than of institutional change. In Illinois, Kansas, and Indiana, only respondents in Illinois suggested that the role of the executive had changed significantly in recent years, with the executive having increasing influence relative to the legislature and its leaders.

In conclusion, our findings generally agree with those in chapter 9 of this volume: there has been a decrease in the influence of leadership relative to the executive and the bureaucracy in term-limited states. However, it is not clear that this shift is completely and solely related to legislative term limits. Instead, it appears that term limits may have accelerated a shift that was already occurring in many states. One Maine legislator noted: "Executive power has been increasing at the expense of the legislature for 30–40 years. It is not related to term limits. The best way to serve as a counterweight to the executive is by being decentralized and inclusive" (Powell and Jones 2004, 63).

Leaders under Term Limits: The Impact
Depends on the Context

In some ways, the impact of legislative term limits on legislative leaders is clear and as anticipated. Term-limited legislative leaders serve shorter tenures and arrive to their posts with less legislative experience than their predecessors who served before term limits. Term-limited leaders have less experience and time to develop the skills usually associated with successful leadership. Legislative leaders in term-limited states spend more time educating and leading legislators and expend more effort on candidate recruitment, training, and fund-raising than did their predecessors or than do most of their counterparts in other legislatures. With some exceptions, term-limited legislative leaders have less long-term impact on public policy and the nature of legislation that is passed by their chambers than did their predecessors. In short, term-limited legislative leaders have less control over legislative members, the rules, and the agenda.

However, in line with previous studies of leadership in term-limited states (e.g., Peery and Little 2003), we find that the consequences may not have been as universal or as dramatic as many anticipated, for several reasons. First, hardworking leaders have done everything within their power to maintain the influence of their legislative institutions despite term limits. Having less experience does not mean that leaders are less intelligent, less diligent, or less inclined to maintain the integrity of their institutions. Term-limited legislative leaders have virtually invented tools and ways to maintain their influence and that of their chambers relative to the executive. Second, politics and personalities can limit or exacerbate the effects of legislative term limits. Leaders with outstanding political skills will lead despite term limits, and leaders who find themselves facing executives or other legislators with strong skills may find term limits a convenient excuse for their relative failures. Institutional differences play a key role. Finally, even within similar chambers, the effect of term limits is a function of unique institutional qualities, including the level of influence and stability of leaders prior to term limits and the nature of the term limit requirements in that institution. Leaders who were very strong before term limits, for example, have much farther to fall than those who exercised limited power.

CHAPTER 5

Committees

Bruce Cain & Gerald Wright

THE ROLE OF committees in a legislature reveals a lot about the stature and power of that legislature. Nelson Polsby (1975) observed that in terms of initiating and amending legislation or investigating the executive, legislative committees tend to be weaker when the legislature as a whole is more subordinated to the executive branch, stronger when the legislature is "transformative." Congressional committees, for example, are stronger under the U.S. separation of powers than in the British parliamentary system.

While all states except for Nebraska have now adopted the bicameral federal model, the role of committees in the states tends to be different from that found in Congress, where some committees are as easily at the service of the party leadership as is the case in Britain. The difference is that the seniority rule, which was close to absolute in the modern Congress until the reforms of the 1970s, never fully took root in the states; rather, majority leaders in the lower houses of most state legislatures retain appointment of committee chairs (Clucas 2001; Erickson 1996). Nevertheless, all of the state legislatures use standing committees to deal with the workload of considering at least hundreds and often thousands of bills each session. Most state legislatures do not meet all year, but even those that do could not survive trying to consider, evaluate, and act on all proposed legislation from the floor (Francis 1989; Krehbiel 1991).

Apart from Alan Rosenthal's (1974) analysis of state committee systems and their effectiveness in the policy process, much of what we have learned about committees comes from two large data collections, both made before the advent of term limits. In 1981, Wayne Francis administered a fifty-state survey of some two thousand state legislators. He used the resulting data to explore the factors that affect the balance of power between committees and party leadership, optimal committee size, and members' satisfaction with different institutional arrangements (Francis 1989). Ronald Hedlund, Keith Hamm, and their collaborators have several collections of information on committees in the state legislatures, including measures of the evolution of state committee systems over most of the twentieth century. In addition to providing an overview of committee systems from colonial times to the present (Squire and Hamm 2005), they analyze changes in rules and procedures of committee decision making (Hamm, Hedlund, and Martorano 2001), the evolution of committee property rights (Squire et al. 2005), and the degree to which majority parties dominate committees (Hedlund and Hamm 1996), and they provide an accounting of the numbers of committee positions in the legislatures (Hamm and Hedlund 1990). Also available are descriptions of aspects of the committee systems, including the increasing staff in recent decades (Neal 1996), while recent work has examined the representativeness of committees relative to their full chambers (Battista 2006; Overby and Kazee 2000). This body of research provides a foundation for our effort here, but virtually all of it predates term limits. Almost by definition, term limits influence committee membership stability, which is a key factor in how committees function (Basehart 1980).

In this chapter, our approach to assessing the effects of term limits on the performance of committee systems in the states is to begin by identifying the key functions of the committees and then to assess how term limits affect these functions in our six term-limited states. The first function we will examine is the informational role of committees (Krehbiel 1991). As part of the division of labor, committees also develop expertise among their members through strategic committee placement of legislators with appropriate backgrounds and stability of service. The accumulated experience of committee members then provides a source of evaluation independent from the data, reports, and testimony supplied by outside sources, such as the governor, agencies, and lobbyists.

One question here is whether the committees serve the interests of the full chamber or the majority party. Given the substantial powers that the majority leadership in most chambers exercises over the structure, membership, leadership, and often the jurisdictions of committees, the arguments of Gary Cox and Matthew McCubbins (1993) concerning the operation of majority parties as "cartels" may well prove to be even more applicable in the states than it has been in Congress (see also Cox and McCubbins 2005). In either case, the committees' capacities to provide sound policy information on legislative proposals are vital for the effectiveness of the leadership or the chambers.

The key aspects of the informational role of committees are the division of labor, which yields efficiencies over full floor consideration of bills and resolutions, and the development of expertise that comes from specialization and immersion in the subject matter of the committee. The yield for the legislatures is quality analysis and information that is not dependent on outside agencies. If committees are effective here, they develop solid reputations for knowing what they are doing and thereby achieve a level of deference from the larger chamber. The division of labor is a given, since all the chambers use standing committees, so we will focus on specialization, expertise, and gains expected from committees.

The second function we will examine is deliberation. The process of getting the views and ideas of a variety of sources, selecting among the best, and discussing the best alternatives underlies the deliberation function of committees. While the idea of floor debate as a forum for exchanging ideas may hold sway in the popular imagination, the actual work of fashioning legislation happens in smaller groups, largely the standing committees and subcommittees of the legislatures. An important element here is the willingness and ability of the chair to draw on the potential contributions of members of the committee. This includes considering the views of the minority party, fairness in hearing a range of proponents and opponents in testimony, incorporating perfecting amendments to make better public policy, and general management of the committee so that it can function effectively in its informational role. Ruling committees with an iron fist, shutting out the minority party, and passing on bills without adequate access for those with an interest are examples of undermining the deliberative function. Good deliberation would include political as well as purely policy considerations, because it is in the interest of the committee to put forward only legislation that will succeed. By overturning or substantially amending proposals on the floor, the full house sends the message that the committee did not do its job well.

Finally, the last function we will consider in this analysis is gatekeeping. While the rules of the state chambers differ, a primary expectation in most is that committees will regulate the flow of legislation passed on to the full chamber. This includes keeping "bad" bills off the floor. Of course, what is "bad" is in the eye of the beholder: it includes bills that would not achieve their policy ends, those that have no chance of passing but would consume limited floor time, and bills that majority leadership does not want on the floor (Cox and McCubbins 2005).

Information, Experience, and Expertise

A strong committee system relies heavily on stability and experience for creating and retaining expertise. Indications of this include the amount of experience chairs have with a committee before they assume their leadership roles and the duration of committee tenure. The more experienced the committees and chairs are, the more time they have to become expert on the subject matter before the committee, through attending hearings, hearing witnesses, reviewing bills and reports, talking to lobbyists, and so on. Since term limits put a ceiling on the continuous service of legislators on committees, an anticipated impact is a substantial decrease in levels of experience following term limits.

This effect is nicely illustrated by California statistics. The highly specialized and professional committee system pioneered by Jesse Unruh before term limits resembled that of the U.S. Congress. California's limits are particularly strict, allowing Assembly representatives only six years and state senators eight years before they must permanently rotate out. With such a short time horizon, the experience and tenure levels of chairs and committee members have decreased substantially, especially in the Assembly. For example, prior to 1990, when limits came into effect, Assembly committee chairs had an average of 3 years of committee experience before they assumed their leadership position, but after term limits, that number dropped to essentially one term, or 2.2 years. Moreover, whereas Assembly chairs stayed in their role for 5.6 years during 1979–90, that number dropped to 2.5 years during 1997–2000.

To add to the problem, the average tenure of chief consultants in the Assembly's standing committees fell from 8.7 to 4 years between 1989 and 2000. However, the same pattern was not found in the Senate, where the average tenure of consultants rose from 5.3 to 7.8 years (Cain and Kousser 2004, 37). Partly, this reflects the higher turnover rate of members in the Assembly, but it also reflects the greater freedom Assembly chairs have to replace consultants when they take over a committee. The Senate adopted a policy that new chairs could not change consultants for six months and could change no more than one consultant at a time. This illustrates an important point: staff can be used to offset—as opposed to amplify—the effects of inexperience that come with short term limits.

Term limits have also affected levels of committee experience in Colorado, Arkansas, and Maine. Statistics in all three states clearly illustrate the impact. Chair turnover has always been high in the Colorado legislature and remained so after term limits. John Straayer and Jennie Bowser (2004, 56) note, "[T]he data show a considerable drop in aggregate chair experience, both as members and committee chairs." In Arkansas, the most powerful committees had been controlled for decades by a few party leaders. They had a strong seniority system, so that younger members, as well as those who offended the leadership, were shut out of any formal positions. That changed dramatically with term limits, as the senior members were termed out and the leadership positions were more widely distributed among the membership (English and Weberg 2004, 34–35). In Maine, by 2001, the years of legislative experience among committee chairs had declined from 8.8 to 4.7 in the House and from 8.3 to 7.4 in the Senate. We see the same pattern (perhaps in even starker form) in Michigan, where twenty-seven of thirty-four committee chairs were termed out in 1998 (Sarbaugh-Thompson et al. 2004, 135). Prior to term limits, the committee chairs averaged 8.9 years of service on the committee under Democratic control and 7.5 years of experience under Republican control. In contrast, after term limits took effect in 1999, committee chairs had an average of 1.7 years of prior service. Under the best of circumstances under term limits, Michigan chairs will probably have 4 years of experience on their committees (Sarbaugh-Thompson et al. 2004, 137–38).

The impact of term limits on experience is conditioned by the backgrounds members bring with them to a committee. Here, the Senates provide an interesting caveat to the generalization of declining experience among legislative committee members and chairs. Because the trend in many term-limited states is for representatives who are term-limited out of the House to move to the Senate, the experience levels of the Senate remain higher after term limits because they are infused with new members with House experience. This is one of the natural, unintended compensations of bicameralism. Before term limits, the primary argument for bicameralism was that the Senate provided for representation of larger geographical units for (in most states) longer periods of time. But with term limits encouraging more interhouse movement, the Senates serve to offset the complete inexperience of the Houses. This has not gone unnoticed by legislators. One Maine House member stated, "The Senate is stronger because of the experience of the members who are moving over from the House" (Powell and Jones 2004, 21). There was a huge difference between the experience of committee chairs in the House and Senate in Ohio. In the House, zero of twenty-one committees in 2001–2 and three of twenty-one in 2003–4 had experienced chairs. By comparison, thirteen out of fourteen Senate chairs in 2001–2 and thirteen out of fifteen in 2003–4 had experience. Term limits in many states have created a new bicameral tension between the more experienced Senate and less experienced House. At one level, the career path from House to Senate is a successful adaptation to the lack of experience engendered by term limits. But it also can erode norms of deference and mutual cooperation between the chambers.

The effect of term limits on experience may differ in the states with reentry provisions. In Arizona, members can and do return, and legislative leaders have sometimes tapped returning veterans for chair assignments in order to give some experience to a committee. The number of chairs with previous experience in the committee they come to head varies greatly from year to year (Berman 2004, 8). Arizona has also used vice-chair positions as a means of training future chairs, a method that has helped alleviate the inexperience problem somewhat.

The trend toward less experienced chairs and leadership in the term-limited states was not apparent in our control states, where there has been little change in recent years in experience and tenures of committee chairs. Committees remain powerful in Kansas, where the short duration of the legislative sessions means that the legislature relies heavily on interim session committees (especially the appropriations committees) to prepare legislation for the next year (Smith and Erickson 2004, 9). The Kansas report found that committee chairs were chosen for their loyalty to the leadership and that it was unheard-of for freshman members to get committee chairmanships as they do in term-limited states. In Indiana, also, there "have not been any large-scale changes in how the committees operate" (Wright and Ogle 2004, 12). Committee chairs are typically experienced: fifteen of seventeen House chairs in the 2001–2 session continued as chairs in 2003–4, as did fifteen of the twenty chairs in the 2001–2 Senate.

In Illinois, weak committees and high levels of membership instability have been the norm for some time and remain so. The party leadership has complete control over the number, names, and jurisdiction of the committees as well as their membership. General Assembly committees have no "permanent or clearly defined jurisdictions" and deal with "whichever bills the rules committee assigned to them." Since rules committees are small and controlled by the legislative leaders, the "majority leader could easily assign a bill to whichever committee he wished" (Mooney and Story 2004, 24–25). This kind of leadership would not be possible under term limits, since rapid turnover of leadership undercuts the power of leadership substantially.

In sum, the term-limited states show a trend toward less stability and experience in committee chairs and membership, although the degree varies somewhat between California and Arizona. The non-term-limited states have not shifted from their normal patterns. In some states, that means strong committees, but in others, it means committees subordinated to strong leadership (which is itself missing in the term-limited states).

The important question is whether these decreases in experience translate into notable declines in expertise. The answer drawn from the evidence of our case studies is a resounding yes. The Colorado study reports that "interview respondents have noted a propensity of newly appointed and inexperienced chairs to 'make mistakes' and 'get rolled' by minority party committee members" (Straayer and Bowser 2004, 55). A Colorado interviewee noted that "members lack experience and also knowledge of existing law" and "don't know why a law may need to be changed" (Straayer and Bowser 2004, 64). An Arizona informant reported that "term limits have meant that people received committee and other leadership positions before they were ready for them" (Berman 2004, 8). The authors of the Ohio study note: "[T]he constant flow of new members, inexperienced committee chairs, and revolving door leaders has created a much more chaotic and unpredictable process. Further, the relative inexperience of many of the members has significantly increased the workload for everyone associated with the legislature" (Farmer and Little 2004, 17–18).

Respondents in the 2003 Survey of Knowledgeable Observers conducted by the Joint Project on Term Limits reported a similar pattern. In comparing the term-limited states with the control group of three states without term limits, we find some of the greatest differences in whether members are knowledgeable about issues, how the legislature operates, the concern for clarity and precision in legislation, and specialization of issues. These differences are found in responses to questions about all the legislators, not committees, but the impact of such ignorance and attitudes would affect members on committees. Specifically, the knowledgeable observers agreed that the committee members in the term-limited states are significantly less likely to be knowledgeable about issues before the committee.

The impact of lack of experience on expertise was also noted in the Michigan study. The authors assessed expertise by asking members who they consulted with on difficult legislation. They found that members were slightly more likely to consult their chairs before term limits than after. More telling for the impact of term limits is that committee members were significantly more likely to consult their chairs when the chairs had a clear experience edge (Sarbaugh-Thompson et al. 2004, 146).

The evidence is quite consistent. Term limits have cut the number of years of committee experience for both members and chairs, and that decrease is accompanied by a widespread perception that the now less experienced members, who face foreshortened careers in their chambers, are less knowledgeable about issues and about both general legislative and committee procedures. Committee members and chairs are also believed to be less concerned about fine-tuning legislation, exactly the informational role generally expected of committees.

Deliberation and Partisanship

Our hypothesis is that shorter terms on committees, coupled with a knowledge that one is not going to be interacting with one's fellow legislators for the long haul, produces a short-run orientation. One effect of this, we expect, is impatience with the traditional apprenticeship norms of career legislatures. Inexperienced members have had less time to get to know one another and develop trusting relationships, especially those that would cross party lines and foster bipartisan approaches to committee work. In addition, inexperience is likely to affect the leadership's ability to select committee chairs who can and are willing to do the hard work of producing sound bills and who will effectively draw on the full talents of the committee membership.

Viewed in these terms, the impact of term limits on deliberation has not been positive. For example, in Michigan, members report that chairs are more likely to silence the opposition and to ram bills through than was the case before term limits. Knowledgeable observers report that committees in the non-term-limited states are slightly more likely to be collegial and courteous in committee. These sources comport perfectly with reports from the case studies. In Ohio, "committee meetings are more rancorous than before term limits" (Farmer and Little 2004, 10). One Colorado interviewee noted, "[T]he civility is gone, chairs are gaveling down colleagues, there is disrespect for the system" (Straayer and Bowser 2004, 58). In Arizona, committee members reportedly seem "less collegial and willing to compromise" (Berman 2004, 8).

As in Congress and non-term-limited state legislatures, committee partisanship has been on the rise in term-limited legislatures. In Michigan, one-fifth of the respondents serving before term limits said there was little or no partisan conflict on their committees; only 11 percent agreed to that after term limits were in place (Sarbaugh-Thompson et al. 2004, 140–42). The Colorado study reports, "[O]ver eighty-four percent of the mail survey respondents saw the legislature as a whole as more partisan, and data on the kill rate of minority party bills seems to reflect heightened partisanship in committees as well" (Straayer and Bowser 2004, 58). The higher partisanship in the term-limited committees may be an indication of less deliberation and an unwillingness of the chairs to draw members of the minority party in, at least where possible without changing the fundamental purposes of the legislation. By comparison, interviews with the minority Democratic leadership in the Indiana Senate revealed a conscious effort to go along with the majority where possible so that they were not shut completely out of the process. The working relationship there between the leadership of the two parties grows out of long years of interaction. Interviewees there agreed that term limits would make the understandings they have achieved difficult, if not impossible.

Our conclusion, then, is that the accelerated clock of the term-limited states appears to result in some tendency for chairs to push legislation through with power rather than seeking consensus—that is, differences are less likely to be expressed in a collegial fashion that would enhance working relationships. It may also be that the lower loyalty to the chambers that the knowledgeable observers perceive in the term-limited states (in response to survey question 12; see the appendix in the present volume) means that members generally find less incentive to develop long-term working relationships. Such relationships have their basis in reciprocity that develops when interactions are expected to extend well into the future (Axelrod 1981).

Gatekeeping and Committee Deference

Another effect that term limits have had is on committee gatekeeping functions. When committees have experience and knowledge and the legislative rules delegate to them the right to screen and amend bills, the exercise of that responsibility is called gatekeeping. In essence, the committees hear the bills and then screen some out, preventing infeasible bills from reaching the floor. Sometimes, a powerful chairman may bottle up a good bill for reasons of personal prejudice or self-interest. But if the system is working well, the committees should be screening weak bills and those that stand little chance of getting support. In so doing, they keep the legislature focused on a feasible agenda.

In most states, committees have the power to choose whether or not to consider a bill and then whether or not to report it out. Some states have the requirement that every bill submitted be considered by the committees and reported out. An example are the "G.A.V.E.L." rules imposed on the Colorado legislature through the direct initiative that prevents committees from burying bills and prevents party caucuses from implementing a binding vote (Straayer and Bowser 2004; Kousser, Cox, and McCubbins 2005). For such legislatures, one means of gatekeeping is to report bills with a recommendation not to pass. The recommendation is a committee's signal to the full chamber that it has looked at the bills and found them wanting. In most cases, that recommendation is tantamount to killing the bill.

We can illustrate the impact of term limits on committee gatekeeping by looking at California (where we expect the results to be strongest). One indicator that legislative committees have lost their screening power is the rate at which bills are killed in committee and not allowed onto the floor for a vote. A comparison of the fate of a selection of bills from a sample of sessions before and after term limits shows that this indicator of gatekeeping has declined, especially in the less experienced house. Before term limits, the Assembly stopped 36 percent of Assembly-originated bills in committee; after term limits, the number dropped to 23 percent. In the Senate, there was a smaller drop—from 17 to 12 percent—in the kill rate of bills that originated on its side (Cain and Kousser 2004). These data are consistent with the testimony in interviews of numerous members and staff. One former senator who had chaired various committees and served in the executive branch stated that "there has been an essential evisceration of the hearing process" and that, as a consequence, "nothing dies anymore." A Senate committee consultant noted that there was "less scrutiny of legislation and less quality in both houses, but a much steeper decline in the Assembly." An Assembly committee consultant put it bluntly: "[N]o one wants to kill each other's bills anymore" (Cain and Kousser 2004, 37, 41).

Another aspect of gatekeeping is the ability and willingness of committees to alter and amend bills they hear. Again relying on a sample of bills in a sample of sessions before and after term limits, the California study found no change in the overall rate of bill amendment but some significant differences in where the amendments occur. Specifically, fewer amendments happen in the originating policy committee, and more occur on the floor and in other committees—or, to put it another way, later in the process.

Consistent with other findings, Assembly bills were more likely to be rewritten by other committees, especially after being heard in the Senate policy committee. In general, the Senate was amending a larger percentage of Assembly bills, while the Assembly was less frequently amending Senate bills. The California study concluded: "[T]he fact that amendments are now made more frequently at nearly every stage of the legislative process indicates that bills passed out of committee need more 'fixing' or that less deference is given to committees. Either way, the patterns support the contention that term limits have eroded the committee process" (Cain and Kousser 2004, 43).

Finally, the back-loading of the legislative process—with less work done in the originating policy committees and more in the other house or conference committees—has policy consequences. The multilayered process of bill review ensures that bills are fully aired and considered. The danger of back-loading is that it opens the door to secretive last-minute deals and to less scrutiny by the press and interest groups, scrutiny that might expose what is happening before the final vote. One manifestation of this danger is the rise in "gut and amend" actions, defined as instances when the entire contents of a bill are stripped and replaced. A comparison of the frequency of "gut and amend" actions in a session before and after term limits reveals that the rate has almost doubled. Many of these bills, as longtime *Sacramento Bee* columnist Dan Walters puts it, have "multibillion-dollar consequences" (quoted in Cain and Kousser 2004, 48). The "gut and amend" stratagem received national attention when it was used to resurrect a bill permitting same-sex marriage. The bill, which had failed in the Assembly earlier in the session, was substituted as completely new content into an Assembly environmental bill (Benson 2005). The altered bill then passed the Assembly but was vetoed by the governor.

The changes in other states echo some of the findings in California, sometimes with a different emphasis. A Maine interviewee observed: "[C]ommittees are deferential to the executive branch. More new people are accepting of the bureaucracy. There is not enough healthy skepticism.

In the past, committee chairs were more aggressive with the executive"
(Powell and Jones 2004, 64). A report from Colorado laments: "[C]ommit-
tees used to be a filter that ensured that good work products came to the
floor. Not any more" (Straayer and Bowser 2004, 63).

We might expect that the lack of expertise and gatekeeping that we
have attributed to the term-limited legislatures would also result in the
committees being reversed on the floor more often and in more floor
amendments being offered. This does not square with the perceptions
recorded from the survey of observers. There is no difference in their
reports of changes in the willingness to offer amendments to bills or the
success of committee recommendations on the floor (survey questions 5
and 35; see the appendix in this volume). Offsetting that perception are
perceptions like those reported from Maine: "According to a number of
observers, committee reports are more likely to be challenged on the floor
now than in the past. . . . One legislator told us about a unanimous committee report that was overturned on the floor because a group of legislators knew more about the particular issue than the committee members"
(Powell and Jones 2004, 25).

The evidence is not consistent across all the term-limited states. For
example, the breakdown in the committee system's ability and willingness
to screen bills is more mixed in Colorado. On the one hand, the overall kill
rate for bills originating in policy committees has not changed. Moreover,
there is no evidence that there is more screening on the floor as opposed to
in committee, as in California. On the other hand, interviewees from Colorado repeatedly told the researchers that committees were "doing their
work less well" and "passing inferior products onto the floors" (Straayer
and Bowser 2004, 60). Colorado has also seen a slight decline in the number of interim committees, which were used in the past to study broad topics (e.g., transportation) in preparation for introducing bills into the next
session.

The effects of term limits on the gatekeeping functions of Maine legislative committees are similarly mixed. On the one hand, there has been a
rapid increase in the sheer volume of bills introduced, for all of the reasons
discussed elsewhere in this volume: the shortened time horizons of members, the need to accomplish as much as one can in a limited term, and the
inexperience of knowing a good bill from a bad one. But the kill rate in
committees, which was practically zero before, has risen in some years to
between 10 and 15 percent. Still, the general impression is that members
are less likely to defer to committee reports and recommendations.

"[T]here is much less deference given to committees," said one interviewee, "because others don't think they are any better specialists than they are." The interviewee asked, "Why should I trust some other member with no more experience in an area than me?" (Powell and Jones 2004, 31). In addition, committee chairs, being less experienced, are "less skilled at building consensus," which "leads to divided reports" (33). As a consequence, minority reports are more commonly reported on the floor, and there are even more challenges to reports voted out of committee unanimously.

The general pattern is that committee recommendations seem to carry less weight in sessions on the floor after term limits. However, perhaps because they, too, are less experienced, members not serving on the committees do not consistently make more attempts to overturn or amend committee bills. In some cases (as appears to be the case in Michigan), the committees still perform a gatekeeping function but appear to do so more at the beck and call of the party leadership and less based on the committee's consensus on the soundness of the proposed legislation (Sarbaugh-Thompson et al. 2004, chap. 8.)

We can compare the impact of term limits on committee functions by looking at what has happened in the control states without term limits. The sample clearly shows that non-term-limited states have not experienced the same general decline in their committee systems. The committee systems in Illinois, Indiana, and Kansas have either remained the same or evolved in ways that were influenced by other factors. For instance, in Indiana, interviews revealed that "there have not been any large-scale changes in how the committees operate" (Wright and Ogle 2004, 13). Moreover, Indiana has had "few amendments to bills reported out of committee on the floor." Indeed, the leadership is very respectful of bills that come out of committee, "honoring the author's preference for referral and not altering the substance of what the bill intends to accomplish." There are some small differences between the House and Senate in this regard, and there is also a perception in the Senate that "an important part of the committee work is 'cleaning up' after the sloppy bills passed by the House, thereby making better legislation and protecting the legislatures from likely challenges in the courts" (12). This reminds us that interhouse rivalries are common in bicameral systems. It is more correct to say that term limits exacerbated a preexisting problem than to suggest that they created one.

Kansas is another state where the committee system is alive and well: "Several legislators and staffers proudly told interviewers that in Kansas the attitude of 'fix it on the floor' does not hold sway." Interviewees reported that "the committee gate keeping system works relatively well in screening bills" (Smith and Erikson 2004, 8). Partly, this is a function of time; since the legislative sessions are only ninety days, it is not realistic to fix bills on the floor. Also, the shortness of the sessions puts the burden of legislative preparation on the interim committees, especially the appropriations committees. This has not changed in recent years. There are some changes to note, such as an uptick in the number of committee-sponsored bills, which is indicative of party leaders' firm control over the committees. Committee chairs continue to be chosen based on how they vote in the election for the speaker, and freshman committee chairs "are unheard of in Kansas, though occasionally a promising new legislator will rise immediately to the position of vice-chair" (Smith and Erikson 2004, 10).

In states where the committee systems were already weak and dominated by party leaders, they have remained so. This is the case, for instance, in Illinois. The "names, jurisdictions and even existence of committees" in the Illinois legislature are "far more fluid than they typically are in Congress." Also, leadership on the committees is not stable, "with between 50 and 100 percent of committees in each General Assembly being chaired by a legislator who had not chaired the committee in the previous General Assembly." The legislative leaders keep a firm hand on committee appointments, and seniority matters little. As a consequence, the committees "typically did very little screening of bills during the study period, with few bills dying in committee . . . and most committee votes being unanimous." Committee recommendations were usually followed, but this was because the committees typically had leadership behind them. The so-called control committees, such as the rules committee, were "dominated by legislative leadership" and controlled the flow of legislation very tightly in terms of schedule and content (Mooney and Storey 2004, 25).

The patterns of change that term limits have brought to the states' committee systems were not witnessed in the non-term-limited states. The decreased experience of chairs and members on the committee has yielded committees with lower levels of experience in the term-limited states. Thus, they are less adept at performing the fundamental informational function that is one of the benefits legislatures gain from having committees. We also find evidence for weakened deliberation in the committees of the term-limited states. We saw this in the form of higher levels of partisanship, disorderly proceedings, and more conflict within committees.

Finally, the gatekeeping functions of committees appear to be less efficient under term limits. The lower levels of expertise in committees undermine the deference accorded to committees on the bases of careful and thorough work. The shortened time horizons of the term-limited legislators might similarly undermine the development of norms of reciprocity based on distributive considerations of implicit logrolls—that is, understandings in which legislators allow each other their way in their own bailiwicks. The case studies also provide some evidence of a reverse deference. Newer members expressed reluctance to amend or kill bills in committee when such action could provoke the same treatment for their own bills.

Conclusion

We find no evidence that term limits have helped the committee process. The one possible exception is that in some states where senior party members have controlled the key committees, term limits removed them from power and resulted in a significant decentralization of power (Smith and Erickson 2004). However, even here, it is not clear that this change enhanced the fundamental functions of committees. The benefits of the committee division of labor are realized with some longevity of service on the committees, by which members develop expertise in the policies, actors, and possibilities for policy change in their areas. Members with appropriate backgrounds are often effective sooner than neophytes, but committee service enhances the informational, deliberative, and gatekeeping effectiveness of the committee systems. When viewed from the perspective of the traditional functions of the committee system, the goal of term limits, which is to bring in new faces and new ideas, translates simply to inviting innocence and ignorance.

The changes wrought by term limits have important implications for the distribution of power within the legislatures and between the legislature and other actors, specifically the executive and organized interests. The effectiveness of the committee system rests on the ability of the committees to benefit the full legislatures. As an incentive to develop the expertise and do the hard work of fashioning good legislation and weeding out the bad, committee members are given property rights—that is, some level of power—in their areas (Krehbiel 1991). These trades of power for specialized work in committees net the legislature independent evaluations and bases for making policy. Without those, the legislature necessarily must rely on other sources of information. The evidence from our cases studies suggests that term limits have led to a loss of committee influence and effectiveness, particularly to the executive branch.

Cain and Kousser's (2004) study of California showed that term limits limited the ability of the legislature to rewrite executive proposals. There was also a decline in oversight and a drop in the number and score of audits of the executive agencies. The effect was similar in the less professionalized legislatures as well. The summary judgment for Maine is that "committees are deferential to the executive branch." The Maine report explains: "More new people are accepting of the bureaucracy. There is not enough healthy skepticism. In the past, committee chairs were more aggressive with the executive" (Powell and Jones 2004, 64). Similarly, in Arkansas, one interviewee admitted that "by making us change members so often we create a constant effect of less experience, and the executive branches become more powerful this way." This and similar evidence led to Smith and Erickson's (2004, 45) conclusion that "the largest impact of term limits on executive/legislative relations" is that they appear to have "institutionalized an inequality of power in the legislature's ability to oversee the executive branch bureaucracy."

The shift of power to the executive was also found in the Michigan study. There, the relative inexperience of committee chairs led to a marked increase in the impact of gubernatorial influence on committee chairs especially: "No respondent mentioned the governor's control over committee chairs prior to term limits. After term limits 22 percent of our respondents said that the governor exerted control over the chair" (Sarbaugh-Thompson et al. 2004, 139–40). The clear pattern is of enhanced dependence on and impact of the governor and agencies on committee proceedings. Similarly, the scattered evidence we have suggests that the already meager levels of agency oversight are diminished as well. This finding is consistent with one from the fifty-state survey of legislators by Carey et al. (2006, 124–25). They found that legislators perceived both the governor and the bureaucracy to have more influence in term-limited states.

The evidence also points, though less consistently, to enhanced leadership influence over committees. This is difficult to tease out, because the committees in the states with few exceptions are dominated by the party leadership or, in some cases, the party caucus. The less experienced members are more dependent on the leadership, but since the leadership is also less seasoned under term limits, it is less capable of appointing committees that can work effectively to produce the legislative package the leadership desires: "What has changed is the experience levels of members and chairs, and the continuity of leadership-chairmanship connections and the relationships and understandings" (Straayer and Bowser 2004, 55). This situation was noted in Michigan, where party leaders were named significantly more often as sources of control over committee work after term limits (Sarbaugh-Thompson et al. 2004, 140)

The effects of term limits on committees, then, can be summarized by noting, first, that senior powerholders were removed from office, which reshuffled and, in some cases, decentralized power in the legislatures. But one must note, second, that the informational, deliberative, and gatekeeping roles of the committees are undermined by term limits. All of these roles depend on time in office, which allows committee members to learn both substance and procedures, to develop positive working relationships, and to perform most effectively at fashioning legislation that the full chambers and their constituents will approve. The chief beneficiaries of this weakness in the term-limited committee systems seem to be the governor and agencies. If what Woodrow Wilson said about congressional committees—that Congress in committee is Congress at work—holds for the state legislatures, the quality of work of the state legislatures under term limits has suffered.

CHAPTER 6

Legislative Staff

Brian Weberg & Karl T. Kurtz

THE STATE LEGISLATIVE modernization movement was conceived in the 1960s and implemented with vigor throughout the remaining decades of the twentieth century. It aimed at making legislatures stronger, more competitive, and more capable public institutions. One pillar of institutional strength on which reformers placed their faith and their investment was the creation of expanded staff services for legislators.

In 1971, the Citizens Conference on State Legislatures got the staffing ball rolling with its landmark book of reform recommendations for state legislatures, *The Sometime Governments* (Burns 1971). Legions of reformers elected to state legislatures in the early and middle years of the 1970s—many of them made viable as candidates by the previous decade's landmark "one person, one vote" decision and motivated by President Kennedy's "Ask Not" inaugural call to public service—arrived energized at state capitals armed with the book and its recipe for institution strengthening. When they looked into the conference's cookbook for stronger legislatures, it told them:

> Adequate staffing must mean enough able people to supply leaders, committees, members, and party caucuses, on a regular basis, with the entire array of services . . . essential to an informed legislature. (Burns 1971, 125)

These reformers could not imagine an era of term limits. Quite the contrary, they came to build, lengthen, expand, and add muscle to the legislature. They wanted longer sessions, modern facilities, stronger leaders, more oversight, and better information.

The reformers took the conference's advice to heart, and legislative staffing levels in the states expanded at a rapid pace. However, states made different interpretations about what "enough able people" meant. Today, the number of full-time staff serving state legislatures differs tremendously from state to state. At the extremes, New York employs about thirty-five hundred people, while Wyoming manages its legislative business with the support of just over thirty full-time staff. No matter the approach, the addition of legislative staff is seen as the most important ingredient in the transformation of state legislatures of the 1960s and 1970s (Rosenthal 1981, 206).

Data on the growth in the number of staff is limited, with comprehensive fifty-state data existing only for the years 1979, 1988, 1996, and 2003 (National Conference of State Legislatures 2003). Still, these limited data provide a set of staff numbers that nicely span the years before and after term limits. At a minimum, they allow us to see the extraordinary growth of staff fostered by the 1970s-era reformers and their acolytes.

The first available estimate of the growth rate of legislative staff is for the period between 1968 and 1974—the initial burst resulting from legislative reform—and puts it at an astonishing rate of 130 percent (Rosenthal 1981, 206). Counts of total legislative staff between 1979 and 1988 by the National Conference of State Legislatures (NCSL) show continued rapid growth at a more measured pace of 45 percent. Growth tapered off considerably after this period, but legislatures continued to add permanent staff in the early 1990s, with a growth rate of 14 percent between 1988 and 1996. In the following era of tight budgets, public distrust of government, and declining government employment in general in the late 1990s and early 2000s, the growth in legislative staff numbers virtually ceased (National Conference of State Legislatures 2003).

With this influx of numbers came new roles and functions for legislative staff. Before the modernization movement, virtually all legislatures had clerks and secretaries offices to process legislation and at least one nonpartisan staff agency that did research and drafted legislation. Functions and offices that were added or expanded in the modernization period included fiscal offices and agencies that conducted legislative audits or program evaluations; public information offices to assist with media relations; and, perhaps most important, partisan staff for legislative leaders, party caucuses, and, in a few states, individual members (Kurtz 1974, 60–64).

It also is important to note that staff numbers expanded unevenly among the states. The size of state legislative staff is closely associated with levels of legislative professionalization. Indeed, since legislative staff size is one element of most indexes of professionalization, this is true by definition. Dividing legislatures into three categories of professionalized, hybrid, and citizen, the most professional ones on average employ over three times as many staff as the hybrid ones and nearly nine times as many as the citizen legislatures (National Conference of State Legislatures 2004, 2003). The professionalized legislatures have consistently employed over 50 percent of all legislative staff in the country in all periods for which data are available, and they accounted for over 65 percent of the staff growth reported for all of the states between 1979 and 1988. Clearly, during these years, the big got bigger, while many state legislatures fostered relatively minimal staff expansion (Weberg 1988, 190).

Of course, staff numbers are only part of the story of reform and the role of legislative staff. Perhaps as important are other trends, such as staff professionalization, specialization, decentralization, shifts toward partisan versus nonpartisan staff, and the role of staff as change agents within the legislative institution. Indeed, during the latter part of the 1990s, traditional, nonpartisan staff agencies began to sense and respond to a new slate of operational issues brought on by rapidly advancing technology, changing public attitudes toward the legislature, new and possibly more conservative views and expectations of legislators, and perhaps the advent of term limits. This "new age" for legislative staff—especially the permanent, nonpartisan variety—presents challenges of change and adaptation to which legislative staff continue to respond today (Weberg 1997, 26). Based on these trends in legislative staffing, this chapter explores whether term limits have altered the number, influence, roles, and responsibilities of legislative staff. In our discussion, we will draw distinctions between the influence and the importance of legislative staff.

Staff Numbers

There are three alternative hypotheses about the relationship between staff size and term limits. One is that term-limited states might have increased staff in order to provide more support and expertise to inexperienced legislators. A second is that term limits are a reflection of public distrust of legislative institutions and therefore that term-limited states would be unlikely to increase staff and might even decrease them. The third—in effect, the null hypothesis—is that term limits have little or nothing to do with changes in staff size over time. In fact, with the notable exception of California, our case studies of six term-limited states do not suggest any causal connection between term limits and staff size. Since this conforms to our personal observation of staff changes over time, we believe the overall evidence supports the hypothesis that there is no causal connection.

The NCSL staff counts for 1988 and 2003 coincide roughly with the periods before and after term limits and allow at least a partial test of the hypotheses. Table 6.1 shows the breakdown of numbers of permanent legislative staff by three levels of professionalization and term limit status for these two periods of time. The data for each period show that between term-limited and non-term-limited states, there is little difference in the staffing levels within each category. The rates of change between 1988 and 2003 bounce around a lot in ways that, with one exception, cannot be explained by term limits alone.

The exception is the nearly 10 percent decline in permanent staff in term-limited states before and after term limits. In California, Proposition 140 not only invoked strict term limits on legislators but also required the legislature to cut its annual budget by about 22 percent. These concurrent changes—term limits and budget cuts—resulted in major reductions in the staff of the California legislature. In 1988, three years before the passage of Proposition 140, California employed 2,865 year-round legislative staff. By 2003, that number had been reduced to 2,334, a cut of 531, or 19 percent (National Conference of State Legislatures 2003). Thus, California accounts entirely for the decline in the average number of staff in the category of professional, term-limited legislatures. Without California's reduction, the other three professional, term-limited legislatures—Florida, Michigan, and Ohio—would show an increase in average staff size compa-

TABLE 6.1.   Mean Total Number of Permanent Staff by Category of Professionalization before and after Term Limits

Category[a]	Term-Limited States				Non-Term-Limited States			
	States	1988	2003	% Change	States	1988	2003	% Change
Professional	4	1,564	1,411	−9.8	7	1,287	1,448	12.5
Hybrid	7	266	387	45.5	15	362	451	24.6
Citizen	4	112	141	25.9	13	119	173	45.8

Source: National Conference of State Legislatures 2003.

[a]Categories are as defined in National Conference of State Legislatures 2004, with "Red" and "Red Lite" combined as "Professional" and "Blue" and "Blue Lite" combined as "Citizen."

rable to that in the non-term-limited states. Thus, table 6.1 shows no evidence of a causal connection between staff size and term limits, except for the special case of California.

There is one more way in which the counts of legislative staff can illuminate our discussion of changing staff influence. NCSL's 2003 census of staff includes a breakdown between partisan and nonpartisan staff (not available in previous surveys) and reveals that there is a significant difference in the types of staff among professional, hybrid, and citizen legislatures (table 6.2). Partisan staff predominate in the professional legislatures. The mean proportion of partisan staff in term-limited states is somewhat lower than that in non-term-limited states, because three of the four professional legislatures that have term limits are at the low end of the range of percentages of partisan staff—Florida at 41 percent, Michigan at 53 percent, and Ohio at 52 percent. The California legislature, where 70 percent of the staff are partisan, is more typical of most professional legislatures. Citizen legislatures strongly favor a nonpartisan staffing approach and have very few partisan staff on which to draw. Hybrid legislatures have more substantial partisan staff resources than their citizen legislature counterparts but not nearly as much as the professional ones. The differences in staffing structure revealed by the staff counts are important for our discussion of the influence of staff under term limits.

Staff Influence

Many opponents of term limits argue that this reform only serves to empower the nonelected players and stakeholders who work within and near the legislative process. Lobbyists, experts from state agencies, executive bureaucrats, and, of course, legislative staff—each group with its potentially lengthy tenure, extensive institutional memory, and compara-

TABLE 6.2.   Mean Number and Type of Permanent Staff by Category of Professionalization, 2003

	Term-Limited States					Non-Term-Limited States				
Category[a]	States	Nonpart.	Part.	Total	% Part.	States	Nonpart.	Part.	Total	% Part.
Professional	4	612	799	1,411	56.6	7	300	1,148	1,448	79.3
Hybrid	7	298	88	387	22.9	15	316	135	451	29.9
Citizen	4	130	11	141	8.0	13	143	25	168	14.9

Source: National Conference of State Legislatures 2003.

[a]Categories are as defined in National Conference of State Legislatures 2004 with "Red" and "Red Lite" combined as Professional and "Blue" and "Blue Lite" combined as Citizen.

tively deep knowledge of the legislative processes and state programs—are seen to gain more influential policy and institutional roles compared to term-limited legislators. The elected members lose power in this equation, and opponents caution that America's state legislatures become less representative as a result.

The 2002 National Survey of State Legislators conducted as part of the Joint Project on Term Limits offers surprising results on the question of term limits and their effect on staff influence. In the survey, state legislators in term-limited and non-term-limited states rated the influence of legislative staff compared to other actors in the legislative process. Carey et al. (2006, 20) conclude that "there were no differences in responses attributable to term limit status in perceptions of . . . legislative staff," indicating "no shift toward greater staff influence in term-limited chambers."

The national survey results seem almost counterintuitive and refute a commonly held expectation about term limit dynamics within the legislative institution. Legislative staff are recognized as the most influential innovation of the legislative reform movement. By virtue of their specialized expertise, dedication to legislative goals and prerogatives, and establishment as a career service within the institution, legislative staff are key players in the everyday life of the legislature. One would expect term limits to enhance their role—if not by design, then simply by default, as term-limited members become less capable of (or less interested in) understanding the process, knowing the stakeholders, and comprehending the complexities of policy options and their ramifications.

Though perhaps surprising, the national survey's findings about staff influence are supported by results of a 2005 NCSL fifty-state survey of state legislative staff directors, conducted for the present analysis. NCSL asked this group of experienced staff several questions about staff influence and legislative trends during the previous ten years—approximately the time period during which term limits have been implemented in the states. As table 6.3 shows, staff directors who work for both term-limited and non-term-limited legislatures have similar outlooks on staff influence over the first decade of term limit implementation. They share almost exactly the same opinion about the growing influence of partisan staff, and they agree on whether nonpartisan staff have lost influence. For the most part, staff directors say that the influence of nonpartisan staff has remained the same or declined over the past ten years in both term-limited and non-term-limited legislatures.

The perceived increase in influence of partisan staff is closely related to the trends toward increasing partisanship in state legislatures (and Congress) as outlined in chapter 7 in this volume. Partisan staff are both a consequence and a cause of increased partisanship in the institution. They are a consequence in that their numbers and influence increase as the members become more partisan. They are a cause in that their advice and counsel may further polarize the legislature.

NCSL's 2005 survey of staff directors also asked respondents their opinion on future staff trends. These questions repeat ones first posed to this group in 1988. The results regarding staff influence are interesting because they illustrate how intuition and expectations about the impact of term limits on staff influence remain unchanged even in the face of experience that points elsewhere (table 6.4). Although current research indicates that staff appear not to have gained influence where term limits have been implemented, it is clear that those who are closest to this issue see something different in the future. Expectations remain for an influence effect in term-limited legislatures. Most senior staff in term-limited states do not anticipate a future of "business as usual," while three-quarters of staff directors surveyed in non-term-limited states expect little change to their balance of power within the legislative institution, just as they did in 1988. What explains this mismatch of expectations and outcomes? Perhaps those staff who were positioned to gain power and influence were not, for various reasons, inclined or prepared to accept it. Or perhaps we are looking

TABLE 6.3.   State Legislative Staff Directors' Perceptions of Changes in Influence of Legislative Staff, 2005

Survey Item[a]	Term-Limited States	Non-Term-Limited States	All States
Influence of Partisan Staff			
Increased	54%	55%	54%
Decreased	0%	4%	3%
Stayed the same	46%	42%	43%
Influence of Nonpartisan Staff			
Increased	13%	24%	21%
Decreased	25%	22%	23%
Stayed the same	63%	54%	56%

Source: National Conference of State Legislatures.

Note: Totals may not add to 100 percent due to rounding.

[a]The survey question began: "Looking back on the last ten years and with an overall view of legislative staff in your state, have the following increased, decreased, or stayed the same?"

too generically at legislative staff, "masking" as Carey et al. (2006) suggest, differences in staff roles, organizational position, and partisan and nonpartisan status.

In *Legislative Life,* Alan Rosenthal describes the influence exercised by legislative staff as "subtle and restrained." The restrained conduct of professional legislative staff may explain, in some way, why staff power has not expanded under term limits. This may be especially true for nonpartisan staff, who, as Rosenthal puts it, are "very conscious of the limits of their role" (Rosenthal 1981, 230). John Hird makes a similar observation in his study of state legislative nonpartisan policy research offices (NPROs).

> Their relationship to power and expertise has allowed NPROs to become influential in some sense but only influential in ways congenial to legislative demands for neutrality. Their power, mostly as information providers, has come at the expense of independence— they provide useful knowledge and remain trusted advisers—but at the heavy cost of losing the ability to challenge prevailing norms and bring new ideas, perspectives, and analysis to the legislative milieu. (Hird 2005, xv)

Before the era of term limits, nonpartisan staff—who predominate in all but the four professional legislatures among the fifteen term-limited states—probably had attained the maximum levels of power and influence possible for them under the strictures of confidentiality, neutrality, and legislator deference set out in their written and unwritten codes of conduct. With the advent of term limits, there may not be much room for

TABLE 6.4.   State Legislative Staff Directors' Expectations about Future Changes in Staff Influence, 2005

Future Staff Influence on Policy[a]	1988 All States	2005 All States	2005 Term-Limited States	2005 Non-Term Limited States
More influential	21%	24%	42%	16%
Less influential	3%	11%	13%	7%
About the same	76%	65%	46%	76%

Source: National Conference of State Legislatures.

Note: All states were non-term-limited in 1988. Totals may not add to 100 percent due to rounding.

[a]The survey question began: "Over the next five years, do you expect your staff to become: More influential in policymaking? Less influential in policymaking? Remain about the same?"

most of these staff to expand their influence without modification of these important, tradition-laden codes—an undertaking that most certainly would meet institutional resistance and take years to implement.

Partisan staff—legislative employees identified with a political party and working for individual members, leaders, party caucuses, and, in some states, committee chairs—would seem well positioned to gain influence under term limits. Partisan staff typically are closest to the members and often are recruited from campaign staffs. Leadership staff become gate-keepers for their bosses, providing them a unique point of leverage in the political process. Also, as partisanship and ideology come more to define the characteristics of today's state legislators, one would expect them—especially in their inaugural term—to look first to partisan staff for help and guidance.

For the states that have substantial partisan staff—mostly the ones in the professional and hybrid categories—we can try to reconcile, on the one hand, our expectation that partisan staff would make significant gains in influence under term limits and, on the other hand, the contradictory evidence that suggests that these influence gains may be marginal at best. One key to this contradiction is turnover. Partisan staff are well positioned to take advantage of influence opportunities presented by term limits, and they typically are less constrained than their nonpartisan colleagues to offer the kinds of support that term-limited legislators seem to need and want most—advice, ideas, and counsel about policy options and the political process. However, what partisan staff have going for them in terms of institutional position might be almost wholly negated by their relatively high turnover and subsequently limited experience with the legislative process (Kurtz 2006), public policy, and state programs. This turnover is especially evident among personal staff to individual legislators, as these staff come and go at least as quickly as their term-limited bosses. This relative lack of experience especially frustrates longer-tenured, more institutionally focused nonpartisan staff. A nonpartisan staffer in Ohio (in the same survey as Kurtz 2006 but not published there) summed it up saying, "With term limits, there are more inexperienced staff who are not effective and who are not aware of how the process actually works" (National Conference of State Legislatures 2006).

Leadership staff in term-limited states may turn over even more quickly than personal staff, but they also enjoy a privileged position of power. Anecdotal evidence from Oklahoma and Maine suggests that under term limits, "chiefs of staff" (the top aides to presiding officers) may be inclined to exploit a more influential institutional role, exerting the power of their office on decisions about legislative operations, procedures, and employment. Term limits bring into this role new people who may be more willing to exercise this power, along with new leaders who, due to their shorter overall legislative tenure and experience, are more willing to delegate institutional responsibilities to their chief of staff, circumventing the nonpartisan staff directors who traditionally have held responsibility for institutional management.

We do not yet know much about the impact of term limits on partisan caucus staff and their organizations. These staff groups tend to have longer-tenured employees. The only term-limited states with these more stable partisan staff groups are California, Maine (a staffing aberration among citizen legislatures), Michigan, and Ohio. In Michigan, for example, each caucus has a partisan policy office. These employees conduct policy analysis, track legislation, and assist with committee work. They turn over less than other partisan staff and tend not to be restricted in their approach to legislative work in the ways that nonpartisan staff can be, so their prospects for becoming more influential within the term-limited legislature are good. The Ohio term limits study reported: "[M]embers [under term limits] tend to depend on caucus staff for policy and political advice. As a result, according to knowledgeable observers, the power of the caucus staff has increased significantly" (Farmer and Little 2004, 11).

The California legislature relies primarily on partisan staff for committee staff support. As detailed in chapter 5 of this volume, there has been a precipitous decline in the experience and tenure of committee consultants in the Assembly since the imposition of term limits. The Senate has also experienced increased turnover in committee consultants, but not to the same extreme as the Assembly. The variance reflects both the greater experience levels of senators and the fact that the Senate has taken steps to stabilize the staff, even as the members change. Rapid turnover of partisan staff and their resulting inexperience may be as much of a hurdle for a term-limited legislature as are inexperienced members.

California's experience with legislative staff more generally (beyond committee staff) may be instructive about the prospects for partisan and nonpartisan staff under term limits. We previously noted that Proposition 140's combination of term limits and budget cuts was a toxic mix for California legislative staff, especially nonpartisan staff. Before Proposition 140, the California legislature had a mix of partisan and nonpartisan professionals, reflecting the legacy of former Speaker Jesse Unruh, whose vision was to create a fully independent and professional state legislature. California's nonpartisan Legislative Counsel, Legislative Analyst's Office, Assembly Office of Research, and Senate Office of Research earned national reputations as centers of policy and legislative expertise. These offices were complemented by large and sophisticated partisan staff operations that served the leaders and members of each caucus.

Proposition 140's one-two punch of term limits and budget cuts forced legislators to make quick and difficult decisions about the allocation of resources at the legislature. As Cain and Kousser report, these decisions made it clear where term-limited members, at least in the highly professionalized atmosphere of the California legislature, placed their immediate priorities. The ranks of veteran, nonpartisan staff declined rapidly as members protected, as best they could, the partisan staff resources available to them: "Veteran staffers with much expertise but high salaries have been phased out in favor of younger, cheaper staff who have often proven themselves to new members through their service in campaigns" (Cain and Kousser 2004, 44). Cain and Kousser (2004, 47) document a steep decline in staff employment at the Assembly Office of Research, the Legislative Analyst's Office, and the Senate Office of Research after Proposition 140. The Assembly Office of Research closed its doors only six years after the initiative was passed.

The lesson from California seems to be that partisan staff trump nonpartisan staff when budgets are tight and legislators are forced to decide between them. In these conditions, term limits enhance the influence and relevance of partisan staff. Where reelection stakes are high, as they are in California, these effects are probably amplified. Nonpartisan staff expertise, even at the sophisticated levels developed in California, can become vulnerable and marginalized under term limits. It remains to be seen how legislators in California react in the longer term to the decline of their nonpartisan agencies.

The addition of partisan staff to state legislatures has been an important organizational trend over the past few decades, as has been a slow but noticeable shift of power and influence away from nonpartisan staff to their new partisan colleagues. Term limits may accelerate this shift in situations where both types of staff are in place when term limits take effect. As an interviewee said in the Arizona term limits study, "Nonpartisan staffers provide information—partisan ones have more direct influence on policy" (Berman 2004, 9). The Maine term limits study reported that "many observers [of the Legislature] say that legislators now turn more frequently to the partisan staff for assistance because they are more likely to know them through their election campaigns and are initially less aware of the services available from the nonpartisan offices" (Powell and Jones 2004, 33–34).

Professional legislatures employ a much higher percentage of partisan staff than do hybrid or citizen legislatures, as shown in table 6.2. If these staff are relatively decentralized and experience high turnover, their ability to adapt to changing legislator needs and to serve roles in institutional management can be diminished. Cain and Kousser (2004) found this result in their study of the California Assembly. Indeed, it may be that lower houses are more vulnerable to this staff-related impact of term limits, because the members and their staff have less overall experience within the legislature. The Michigan House of Representatives, recognizing this problem at the institutional level, depoliticized its House Business Office early in its term limits experience in an attempt to lower staff turnover within the office and promote development of institutional memory and knowledge in the House's critical operational areas.

In the short run at least, the effect of term limits on staff influence appears to be situational. Legislative employees who have some degree of tenure, who work closely with key decision makers and related processes, who have special knowledge about complex topics and procedures, and who are relatively unbridled by institutional traditions and norms of conduct can and do expand their influence, if not by design, then simply by default. Staff who work on budgets, formulas for state aid, and taxes or who counsel leaders and committee chairs on parliamentary rules and procedures have an advantage (Rosenthal 2004, 113). These positions are influential without term limits. Term limits may enhance their power. In this framework, it is not surprising that Straayer's study of term limits in Colorado finds that although nonpartisan staff influence has, in general, grown only marginally, the nonpartisan budget staff have become "incredibly influential." As one observer commented, "the Joint Budget Committee members are losing their power to the staff with respect to ideas and options" (Straayer and Bowser 2004, 71).

All of this evidence and speculation about the power and influence of legislative staff requires some context, which is effectively provided by Sarbaugh-Thompson et al.'s (2004) study of the effects of term limits on the Michigan legislature. In their surveys of Michigan legislators before and after term limits, they asked where the legislators went first for information and guidance on policy issues. The legislators' responses suggest that staff do not play as big a role in legislator decision making as we sometimes presume. Perhaps legislative staff just are not really that influential to begin with. The fear, expressed by some, that they will come to dominate policy-making under term limits may be far-fetched. This is not to say that staff are not important and even critical to the effective operation of the institution, but concerns about their relative influence on policy-making decisions may be exaggerated.

Sarbaugh-Thompson et al. (2004, 154–57) present data that offer interesting insights into the decision-making processes of Michigan legislators. They show that legislators are more likely to seek expert opinion and guidance on technical issues (e.g., health care regulation) than on visible, big-ticket issues (e.g., school choice). But even on technical issues, legislative staff rank below House colleagues, constituents, and lobbyists on legislators' hierarchy of resources on which they depend for policy-making advice.

Surveys of legislators in Virginia and Michigan in 1974 showed similar results. When legislators were asked who they relied on for decision-making guidance in areas outside their specialization, legislative staff came in fifth behind the following: (1) other legislators; (2) debate in committee, on the floor, or in caucus; (3) lobbyists; and (4) executive agencies or the governor (Heaphey and Balutis 1975, 46). The 1970s survey responses are similar to those found by Sarbaugh-Thompson et al. nearly thirty years later.

In forming final decisions, legislators frequently depend more on political information than on facts. They want to know how a bill will affect their constituents and what its political implications might be. Traditional legislative staffing is set up to provide facts or services that often are crucial, but these staff rarely delve into the role of political counsel. Legislatures cannot operate without staff, but in most cases, staff remain deep in the background when legislators decide how to vote. Hird's study of nonpartisan research offices arrives at a similar conclusion: "Legislators see [NPROs] as one of the most important sources of information in helping them to understand and reach public policy decisions; and legislators view them as distinctly not influential over policy-making itself" (Hird 2005, 152).

New Staff Roles

The concept of staff influence can be ambiguous unless the aspects of legislative work and operations under consideration are clear. It appears that term limits have not unleashed legislative staff to dominate or even to more strongly influence legislator decision making, except in certain situations. However, term limits almost certainly have changed the way legislative staff work and have altered the roles that partisan and nonpartisan staff play in legislative life. Under term limits, legislative staff may not become more influential, but they clearly become more important to the effective work of legislators and the institution.

Term limits push nonpartisan staff to emphasize their role in educating members on the legislative process and how the legislature works. Where partisan staff exist in term-limited states, they tend to expand their roles as policy and political advisers. Each role is critical to the operation of the institution and the ability of legislators to get things done. A comment from the Arizona term limits study summarizes these trends.

> [L]egislative staff as a whole [have] become more important as a result of term limits: the nonpartisan staff in providing basic information and showing newcomers how to do things and partisan staff attached to leadership in providing policy direction. (Berman 2004, 8)

This conclusion from Arizona probably looks familiar to any observer of state legislatures, term-limited or not. There are more partisan staff in most state legislatures today, and they tend to take larger roles in policy matters and, to some extent, in institutional management. For a variety of reasons, nonpartisan staff spend more and more time teaching legislators about issues and the institution and marketing themselves to members who may have limited knowledge about their services. Term limits seem to accelerate these trends, just as they accelerate a shift of influence from nonpartisan to partisan staffers.

Term-limited members, knowing that they have only a few years to make their mark, want to hit the pavement running. Both partisan and nonpartisan staff help make this happen, but the burden of legislator education seems to fall mostly to nonpartisan staff, who have longer legislative experience and typically are more involved in the procedural aspects of legislative activity. A survey conducted in the term limits study in Arizona, where there is a mix of nonpartisan and partisan staff, illustrates that staff in term-limited legislatures play an increasingly important role as educators on operational matters (Berman 2004, 26). The Arizona researchers asked term-limited legislators, "When you were first elected to the legislature, how important were each of the following in terms of learning how to do your job?" Here are the results in order of importance:

1. Legislative staff

2. Working on a committee

3. Senior colleagues

4. Listening to debate on the floor

5. Trial and error

6. Formal training

7. Party leaders

These survey results provide an interesting contrast to the data that Sarbaugh-Thompson et al. (2004) provide on Michigan legislators' information sources. Legislators appear much more inclined to seek institutional guidance from staff than they are to entrust them as counsel on policy decisions. Again, we are confronted with the concepts of influence versus importance. For several reasons, influence is a difficult commodity for most legislative staff to accumulate. However, there seem to be ample opportunity and need for legislative staff to expand their roles as educators about legislative processes, public programs, and the skills it takes to be an effective legislator.

It comes as little surprise, then, that legislative staff in term-limited states—especially nonpartisan staff offices—are rapidly ramping up their orientation programs for new members and other strategies designed to help legislators step into their jobs quickly (see chap. 11 in this volume). These staff are also developing new strategies to promote their services to legislators. In Colorado, the nonpartisan Legislative Council and Office of Legislative Legal Services coordinate their efforts in an expanded "buddy program" that matches staff with legislators and is designed to personalize agency services and provide a trusted link for information and education (Straayer and Bowser 2004, 68). Staff at the Legislative Service Bureau in Michigan, who work in a bank building across the street from the Capitol, now participate in an extensive outreach program that requires staff to make routine visits to members' offices. In Wyoming, the small, nonpartisan Legislative Service Office redesigned the existing legislator orientation program into a new, comprehensive, multiday training event for term-limited legislators. The enhanced program was so successful that it was retained after the Supreme Court struck down the state's term limit law. The office also introduced into the curriculum a training program for committee chairs.

Staff in term-limited legislatures also need additional training, especially as partisan staff rotate more quickly through the institution. In Michigan, the House Business Office created "House University" to orient new staff to the legislature and train personal staff on such topics as constituent services, the legislative budget process, and how to work with lobbyists. California's C.A.P.I.T.O.L. Institute, which also serves legislators, has a similar mission as a House university for staff training, offering a range of subjects that include office management, scheduling tips, constituent casework, and training to be a chief of staff.

Conclusion

Although we found no link between term limits and staff numbers, term limits do make a difference for legislative staff. To many staffers, term limits are a plague on their institutions. Most who feel this way are nonpartisan, but this is not exclusively the case. Term limits put pressure on nonpartisan staff to change what they do and how they do it. Term limits also tend to elevate the institutional role of partisan staff, who, through their term-limited leaders, see the legislature from a different perspective than their longer-tenured, nonpartisan counterparts.

For nonpartisan staff, term limits can be threatening. Under term limits, they gain no new policy influence, and their work becomes more complex, as they adjust to the expanding need to become teachers and institutional counselors to legislators—roles that seem simply to add more work to their plate. Yet these new roles suggest a new level of importance for staff in term-limited legislatures. No legislature can operate without staff, and term limits make their work even more crucial—and not necessarily in ways that circumvent the prerogatives of the elected membership. Nonpartisan staff keep the legislative trains running, so to speak. Without them, term-limited legislatures might squeal to a halt or at least run off the tracks more often than a critical public would like to see.

Most legislatures have added partisan staff in recent years, and we speculate that term-limited states will feel particular pressure to do so. As discussed earlier, legislators want and need the kinds of political advice that only partisan staff are able to provide. They should get it from employees who are dedicated to their broader legislative goals, rather than from outside groups that typically are fixated on narrow policy interests. Partisan staff are close to the members and provide the stuff that members really want at decision time. Because of the partisan staff's relative proximity to the membership, legislators also come to trust these staff more.

CHAPTER 7

Legislative Climate

David R. Berman

HOW HAVE TERM limits affected how state legislators orient themselves toward their work and how they interact with each other? The answer, in part, depends on changes in legislative norms, which, simply stated, are "rules which establish the boundaries of acceptable legislative behavior" (Moncrief, Thompson, and Cassie 1996, 314). Scholars are not sure how to identify norms, though the idea that there are such objects is widely accepted.

One source notes: "[W] e may not know precisely how to detect a legislative norm, but if it walks like a norm and quacks like a norm, then we assume it must be a norm" (Moncrief, Thompson, and Cassie 1996, 315). Legislative norms vary from state to state. Some of the more common have to do with the following: (1) apprenticeship, the notion that new members should not immediately become full-fledged participants in the legislative process but should wait their turn; (2) specialization, the notion that members should focus on specific policy areas and become experts in these areas; (3) courtesy, the notion that members should do what they can to mitigate conflict with other members; and (4) institutional loyalty, the notion that members should put high value on their service and not discredit the institution (Thompson, Kurtz, and Moncrief 1996).

This chapter looks for term-limit-induced changes in legislative norms. Its inquiry takes in a variety of factors related to conflict and civility, including partisanship. Finally, the chapter examines how changes in interpersonal relations have affected the general legislative system.

Turnover, Knowledge, and Expertise

Term limits have fundamentally altered legislative behavior by increasing turnover (see chap. 2 in this volume). To varying degrees in all the term-limited states, term limits have encouraged or forced the departure of veteran lawmakers. With this departure has come a loss of institutional memory regarding programs, policies, and legislative norms; a loss of expertise or specialization in various policy areas; and a loss of senior members who might serve as mentors to new members. Conversely, the increase in the number of inexperienced legislators has produced legislative bodies in which members are less certain about how to do their jobs and relatively uninformed about the issues and the legislative process. Critics of term limits often cast doubts about whether term-limited legislators have either the time or the incentive to develop the expertise the job requires.

In some states, the decline in the level of experience has been sharp. For example, in Arizona in 1990, two years before the voters adopted term limits, the average House member had seven years of legislative service, the average Senator eleven years. By contrast, in 2003, the average number of years of service had declined to two for House members and six for Senate members (Berman 2004, 23). Similarly, though less spectacularly, in Colorado between 1997 (just prior to the enactment of term limits) and 2003 (when they had taken full effect), the average years of legislative experience dropped from 4.2 to 2.5 in the House and from 8.5 to 6.9 in the Senate (Straayer and Bowser 2004, 14).

Case studies in Colorado and Arizona highlight the significance of the loss of veteran members. Colorado had long experienced considerable legislative turnover. In the past, though, this did not matter so much because there were plenty of veterans around who were sources of both behavioral and policy cues: "The old-timers served as coaches on the culture and behavioral norms of the institution, and could relate policy history information and help the new ones figure out the interest group and lobbyist landscape" (Straayer and Bowser 2004, 18). All this changed as veterans were forced out of office. Speaking of the changes, one interviewee in Colorado concluded: "There is no institutional memory now. Some of the members now just do what they want, then say 'it's tradition' when it isn't and they have no way to know." Another interviewee added: "The new ones have no policy history, just quick, uninformed, knee-jerk reactions" (Straayer 2004, 23–24). In a similar manner, interviewees in the Arizona case study ventured the view that term limits have led to the departure of several old-timers and, with this, the loss of institutional memory regarding legislative norms, procedures, and protocol (Berman 2004, 11).

The 2003 Survey of Knowledgeable Observers conducted as part of the Joint Project on Term Limits (JPTL) suggested that legislators in both term-limited and non-term-limited states were less well informed on statewide issues than those of a decade before but that this problem was significantly greater in the term-limited states. In addition, as table 7.1 illustrates, legislators in term-limited states were viewed as significantly less knowledgeable both on specific issues before committees on which they served and on how the legislature operates. Not surprisingly, they were also perceived to be significantly more reliant on staff to draft legislation and less likely to specialize on issues. The latter finding is somewhat belied by the JPTL 2002 National Survey of State Legislators, which

TABLE 7.1. Legislators' Likelihood to Do Certain Things in 2003 Compared to a Decade Before

Survey Item	Mean Non-Term-Limited States	Mean Term-Limited States	Significance
Introduce bills	3.51	3.45	
Rely on staff to draft legislation	3.50	3.81	**
Sponsor interest group legislation	3.74	3.80	
Be knowledgeable about statewide issues	2.82	1.94	***
Be knowledgeable about how the legislature operates	2.70	1.80	***
Be concerned about clarity and precision in legislation	2.46	2.02	***
Specialize on issues	3.48	2.65	***
Deliberation (debate, negotiation, and compromise) takes place in the legislative process	2.56	2.41	
Leaders sanction rebellious legislators	2.85	2.99	
Floor leaders more or less collegial and courteous to other members	2.46	2.36	
Be willing to compromise in committees	2.46	2.44	
Be collegial and courteous in committee	2.52	2.29	*
Partisanship in the legislature as a whole	3.88	4.04	
Be knowledgeable about issues before the committee	2.71	1.96	***
Likely to follow parliamentary procedure on the floor	2.82	2.53	***
Support the institution of the legislature	2.45	2.04	***

Source: 2003 Survey of Knowledgeable Observers.

Note: Ratings were on a five-point scale from "Quite a Bit Less" (1) to "About the Same" (3) to "Quite a Bit More" (5).

$*p < .10$ $**p < .05$ $***p < .01$

found that term limits did not significantly affect whether legislators specialized in a single policy area or were equally active across many policy areas. That survey, however, did not deal with change over time and had more to do with how members allocated their time or attention than with how much they think they know about particular issues or whether they consider themselves experts in any particular area of policy.

Incentives and Attitudes toward the Job and Institution

Term limits have also fundamentally changed legislative incentives. With short time horizons, legislators have tended to be more anxious to make their mark earlier in their terms, by, for example, speaking out and vying for committee chairmanships and leadership posts. In term-limited legislatures, the norm of serving an apprenticeship period as a silent observer within the legislature has clearly gone by the board. Compared to the past, new members are more likely to expect and demand that they be treated as full-fledged participants in the legislative process.

Indications of these changes are found throughout the JPTL case studies. In Maine, for example, Richard Powell and Rich Jones (2004, 37) report that "the new members approach their legislative careers with a sense of urgency and impatience to get things done." They quote one observer as saying, "[T]he new members act as though they are always on the clock." Another interviewee added, "Because members feel as though they have to make their mark quickly and they have a predetermined limit to their legislative career, few are willing to serve apprenticeships within the legislature." Similarly, an interviewee from Colorado said: "Legislators come in wanting to make their 'mark' sooner. They don't spend a year watching and learning and listening. . . . The new ones come in to push an agenda right away, not to wait to fit in, learn the process, make connections. They just push" (Straayer and Bowser 2004, 78). As a way of justifying this aggressive behavior, a legislator in Arizona said, "When you realize you only have eight years at the most, everything has to happen much quicker" (Berman 2004, 11). The bottom line for many, as Art English and Brian Weberg (2004, 29) noted about Arkansas, is that "legislators now simply don't have time for an apprenticeship."

English and Weberg's study in Arkansas also links what we might call "the new aggressiveness" to a tendency to introduce more legislation: "Our interviews indicate that new members are coming to the legislative system with a greater desire to make an impact in their first term. The higher number of bill introductions in the Assembly seems to support that proposition" (English and Weberg 2004). Case studies in Arizona and Ohio, however, found that newcomers initially held back from introducing bills, waiting to become more familiar with the job and the process. In Ohio, observers suggested that it takes at least one full legislative session for new members to get acclimated to the legislative process and to have a good grasp on how to pass legislation (Farmer and Little 2004, 3). The California case study showed that bill introductions increased under term limits only in the period immediately before limits went into effect, because legislators wanted to take care of unfinished business before they were forced from office (Cain and Kousser 2004). The survey of observers also casts doubts on the effect of term limits on bill introductions, by indicating that respondents perceived that bill introductions had increased slightly in recent years in both term-limited and non-term-limited states.

Some of the case studies of term-limited states (e.g., Arizona and Ohio) suggest that proposed legislation is now likely to be of relatively "poor" quality—that is, ill informed, extreme, or poorly drafted. Observers believe that this is a result of legislators' lack of experience and their eagerness to make a record. The respondents to the survey of observers perceived a decline in the clarity and precision of legislation in both term-limited and non-term-limited states, but the problem was significantly greater in the term-limited states. Despite these perceptions in the case studies and among the knowledgeable observers, Kousser and Straayer were unable to find any evidence of systematic differences in legislation introduced in term-limited states (see chap. 10 in this volume).

The survey of observers (the source of table 7.1) also reports a decline in legislators' willingness to follow parliamentary procedure on the floor. Consistent with the short-term theme, the survey further suggests there has been a significantly greater loss in term-limited over non-term-limited states in the amount of support legislators feel for the legislative institution. In Ohio, a survey of lobbyists and other legislative observers found that 62 percent of the 291 survey respondents felt that the legislators were less likely than their counterparts a decade or more ago to defend the institution of the legislature (32 percent chose the response "Quite a Bit Less"), while only 5 percent said they were more likely to defend the institution (Farmer and Little 2004).

The case studies report that the aggressiveness and short-term orientation of term-limited legislators has led to a decline in respect not only for the institution as a whole but also for legislative leaders. From Maine, we hear that "the members are more aggressive with the leaders than they used to be" (Powell and Jones 2004, 42). The Colorado report noted, "[L]eaders are weaker, have no stick . . . [and] members chart their own course" (Straayer and Bowser 2004). Summarizing the situation, one observer in Arizona reported: "I have seen a decline in discipline, decline in the ability of leaders to rally troops even in their own party on procedural matters, leaders don't have that iron fist" (Berman 2004, 7). Knowing that leaders are not going to be around for long has made members less deferential to them and has in turn complicated the job of the leaders (see chaps. 4 and 9 in this volume). These developments have also helped elevate the level of conflict and, along with other factors related to term limits, have made the lawmaking process more chaotic.

Civility and Conflict

The JPTL case studies generally indicate that civility has declined in term-limited states over the past several years. Examples include the display of bad manners, the exchange of angry accusations and charges, or the unwillingness to give colleagues advance notice of coming amendments. In Colorado, one interviewee noted: "Respect for the institution, process, each other, is down. It is not as collegial as before" (Straayer and Bowser 2004, 23). In Arizona, meanwhile, observers complained about the decline in bonding and in the willingness to compromise and engage in consensus building. There was a feeling that "the legislature was friendlier in the past" (Berman 2004, 12). From Arkansas, English and Weberg (2004, 29) reported, "Several of our legislative and lobbyist respondents mentioned that legislators don't seem to care as much about their colleagues' feelings or keep their word with lobbyists about supporting legislation." Observers in Maine and Ohio also remarked on the decline in civility.

The case studies frequently mention increased aggressiveness, short-sightedness, partisanship, and extremism as reasons for the decline in courtesy and civility. In Arkansas, English and Weberg (2004, 29) credited much of the decline in institutional civility to the increased assertiveness setting in after term limits went into effect. In Arizona, short-timer status was equated by observers with chilling the legislative climate—making members less likely to take the time to get to know each other or to try to get along with each other, less willing to compromise, less inclined to listen to leadership, less respectful of the process, and less likely to care about the welfare of the institution as a whole (Berman 2004, 11). In Maine and Colorado, problems in civility were linked to increases in partisanship and extremism (matters I deal with more fully later in this chapter). One interviewee in Maine commented: "There has been an increase in the number of extremists. More extreme right and left. More 'all or nothing' attitude. It is a real challenge to bring people to the middle" (Powell and Jones 2004, 45).

One of the themes in the case studies is that term limits have contributed to the level of conflict by destroying former social networks and reducing both the opportunity and the incentive for legislators to get to know each other on a personal basis and to form friendships that cut across partisan or ideological lines and facilitate civility and cooperative action. Powell and Jones (2004, 37, 40) noted in Maine: "The members elected under term limits do not know each other very well and have not had the time to develop personal relationships with their colleagues. . . . This is particularly true for members from opposite parties. Legislators also have limited time to develop relationships with members of the executive branch, lobbyists, and others that come before the legislature. The lack of relationships makes the work of the legislature more confrontational and partisan before term limits." One interviewee in Maine added, "The legislature felt more family-like in the past than it does now" (Powell and Jones 2004, 41). Along similar lines, an observer in Arizona noted, "The legislature is, in a sense a family, but the solidarity has deteriorated over the years in part because members were not able to develop long-term relationships with each other" (Berman 2004, 12). Another added, "The legislature has new blood but has also lost congeniality because people don't know each other very well and have or will have less of an opportunity because of term limits to do so."

The findings about the effect of term limits on civility and interpersonal relations are not monolithic, however. The results of the survey of observers are more mixed on issues of courtesy and civility in term-limited compared to non-term-limited states. The survey found, for example, a significantly greater decline in the term-limited legislatures in the willingness of members to be collegial and courteous in committees. However, the willingness of members to compromise in committees declined in both types of legislatures, with no significant differences between them. Moreover, the survey of observers showed that floor leaders have become less collegial and courteous to other members in both term-limited and non-term-limited legislatures. Finally, there is little evidence—in either type of legislature—of any recent change in the frequency with which leaders move to sanction rebellious legislators.

The introduction of evidence from the control states suggests that factors other than term limits have affected the degree of socializing and, as a result, reduced camaraderie among legislators. In Indiana, the case study investigators reported that lobbyists are allowed to host receptions and dinners for the legislators and do it often. This appears to have facilitated interactions that cut across party lines and to explain the high level of interparty respect and cordial relations found in the Indiana legislature (Wright and Ogle 2004, 21). Conversely, Mooney and Storey (2004, 30) found that a decline in the number of receptions and parties sponsored by interest groups in Illinois during legislative sessions had resulted in less socializing among legislators in recent years. The Ohio case study noted that the state's gift law, which made it difficult for lobbyists to entertain groups of legislators, had a similar negative effect on socializing among members (Farmer and Little 2004, 14).

Some observers in the case study states suggested that term limits cut short a natural mellowing process that had in the past caused legislators who had served over long periods of time to become more cooperative. An interviewee in Colorado, for example, noted, "Longevity produces moderation, and longevity is gone and so is moderation." Another volunteered, "Members become more centrist with time and experience" (Straayer and Bowser 2004, 24, 83). From California came several expressions of the importance of time: "There is less time now to 'get over things,' such as being on the wrong side of a leadership fight. Time equals closer personal relations, equals working together better in and across parties. . . . The sharp edges are muted with time; the rigid ideological predispositions are softened. With term limits, of course, there is less time" (Cain and Kousser 2004). But while the moderating effects of time appear to be commonly assumed, there is some contrary evidence from California that, if anything, legislators become more extreme the longer they serve in office and that term limits may have made the legislature as a whole more moderate by halting the extremist drift that most members seem to experience over their careers (Cain and Kousser 2004, 77).

Generally, term limits have encouraged the elevation of conflict by encouraging members to strike out on their own. The new aggressiveness means they compete more intensely with other members for positions (which now open up more frequently). They also demand from their leaders more of an input in lawmaking and the budgeting process and, at the same time, feel less constrained by norms and party leaders.

Partisanship

Various indicators reveal a rise in partisanship in state legislatures. How term limits are related to this rise is difficult to determine. If important at all in this context, term limits may have only contributed to an ongoing national trend. Evidence from the general literature suggests that partisanship was increasing in state legislatures even before term limits took effect (Thompson, Kurtz, and Moncrief 1996). From the survey of observers, we find that partisanship has become more intense in both term-limited and non-term-limited states. Similarly, while there has been an upsurge of partisanship in term-limited state legislatures, the same thing has been true in non-term-limited Congress, which suggests that broader, national influences have been at work.

In Ohio and California, the case studies found an increase in partisanship but questioned how much it was due to term limits (Farmer and Little 2004, 13; Cain and Kousser 2004, 6). In Arkansas, partisanship became more of a factor because term limits facilitated changes in the party balance. English and Weberg (2004, 3) explain: "Term limits have had an important effect in the increase in Republican membership in the Arkansas General Assembly. This has especially been true in Democratic-termed seats moving Republican. Term limits have given Republicans a toehold in one of the nation's most dominant Democratic Assemblies." But as noted in chapter 2 in this volume, the open-seat opportunities brought about by term limits ebb and flow between the parties over time.

Some case studies linked upsurges in partisanship to the negative effect of term limits on social networking. The Ohio study reported: "Before term limits members got to know one another in committee, on the floor and at social events. These relationships grew over time. When those relationships were severed by term limits, civility was affected. A large number of freshmen enter the legislature each year. Many of these freshmen do not know anyone in Columbus except the caucus leaders and staff, who helped them get elected. They spend much of their time with caucus colleagues plotting how to defeat the other party. The relationships that would lead to civility are never developed" (Farmer and Little 2004, 12). Authors of a case study in Michigan also found a decline in cross-party friendships in sessions after term limits (Sarbaugh-Thompson et al. 2004, chap. 7). The story was much the same in Maine, though that state's case study also suggested that partisanship increased because party leaders had to hustle to find replacements for term-limited legislators and found it expedient to recruit true believers from the most extreme wings of the parties (Powell and Jones 2004, 39).

In addition to increased conflict between parties, it is conceivable that term limits might lead to greater intraparty conflict between different factions within the same party. The connection between term limits and intraparty conflict would most likely be indirect—tied either to the increase in open seats created by term limits and the ability of various ideological groups to take advantage of them or to the effects of a weakened leadership that is unable to effectively control intraparty conflict. The Colorado and Arizona case studies indicate the rise of intense and sometimes bitter intraparty conflicts driven by ideological divisions, most noticeably between moderates and conservatives in the Republican Party. In Arizona, moderate Republicans have challenged the control of conservative party leaders, who appear to be weaker as a result of term limits (Berman 2004, 3).

However, increased intraparty conflict can also be found in states without term limits. In Kansas, for example, the ideological divisions among Republican legislators have increased significantly (Smith and Erickson 2004, 1). In general, the evidence about the relationship between interparty and intraparty conflict is mixed. We do not have enough information to enable us to disentangle the effects of term limits from other influences, such as national party fortunes, redistricting, and changes in campaign finance.

Interchamber Relations

Finally, the material gathered for this and other studies suggests that term limits have impacted relations between members of the two legislative houses in a largely negative way. Limits have altered these relations in part by creating turnover and bringing about the addition of many new faces. These changes have broken old ties that stretched across the legislative bodies and have caused increased problems in communication. Term limits have also disrupted relations by encouraging legislators to switch from one legislative chamber to another. The importance of term limits as a factor promoting switching was commented on in several of the case studies and finds support in the general literature (Moncrief, Niemi, and Powell

2004). Since most of the switching has involved movement from the House to the Senate, the Senate has generally come out better than the House when it comes to legislative experience, especially at the leadership level. The increased gap in experience has, in some places at least, contributed to increased strain.

On the whole, the movement from one body to another has somewhat offset the general loss of expertise that legislatures have suffered due to term limits (see chap. 5). Theoretically, this cross-fertilization could also produce greater awareness and understanding of the other house and, perhaps, greater cooperation. Some case studies suggest, however, that, on balance, term limits have increased the strain in interchamber relations. In Ohio, for example, while the Senate has picked up many House members, the House has added so many new members that very few of them have relationships with members of the Senate, and House members often have trouble finding Senate sponsors for their bills. The lack of relationships has also meant increased difficulty in trying to resolve differences between the two bodies. Overall, the effects of term limits appear to have accentuated the differences between the House and Senate, with the Senate strengthening its status as the more experienced body. Because of this, Farmer and Little (2004, 14) predict that "the Senate may become the stronger of the two partners in the bicameral legislative process."

In Maine, where similar developments have taken place, House members complain that Senate members do not respect them and that the more experienced Senate leaders have attempted to take advantage of House leaders in explaining how things have traditionally been done. Partly because of term limits, there seems to be a general lack of trust among Senators and House representatives in Maine (Powell and Jones 2004). One finds a similar story in Michigan: term limits have increased the power of the Senate over the less experienced House, made it more difficult for House members to work with their Senate colleagues, and exacerbated House members' resentment of Senate members (Sarbaugh-Thompson et al. 2004, 179–80).

Underlying interchamber tensions since term limits—in Michigan and presumably elsewhere—is the increased possibility of electoral competition as members attempt to switch from one house to another. In particular, Senators have reason to worry about being challenged by termed-out House members. The possibility of challenges from legislators coming over from the other house for leadership positions also may chill relationships.

Conclusion

Term limits have fundamentally altered legislative culture because they have increased turnover—thus reducing the level of experience and knowledge in legislative bodies and destroying social networks—and because they have changed legislative incentives, making legislators more hurried, more aggressive, and less respectful of the process. Term limits appear to have helped loosen attachments to legislative norms, such as apprenticeship, specialization, institutional support, and civility. By encouraging turnover and changing incentives, term limits have also altered the environment in which legislators function—in particular, by weakening the control of legislative leaders. Particularly in the lower houses of states with the most restrictive term limits, legislative procedures seem more chaotic, less civil, and less predictable. Limits also seem involved in numerous ways in encouraging strained relations between legislative chambers.

We must view these results with some caution, however, because the evidence is limited and because there is evidence that some of these changes in legislative culture are present in states without term limits and were occurring before their onset. The effects of term limits on civility and partisanship are particularly complex and difficult to ferret out. Perhaps the most that we can safely say is that the shortened time horizons of term limits have fertilized seeds of change that are also growing, though not as vigorously, under other conditions in the legislative climate.

CHAPTER 8

Lobbyists and Interest Groups

Christopher Z. Mooney

LOBBYISTS AND INTEREST groups have always been an integral part of the state legislative process. Since the 1960s and 1970s, there has been an "advocacy explosion" (Nownes 2001, 25) in state capitals, just as there has been in Washington, D.C. The advocacy community in every state capital now consists of thousands of people working with and around the legislature to pursue their policy goals (Thomas and Hrebenar 2004; Nownes and Freeman 1998). Because these groups are so intimately connected to and concerned with the legislature, the major institutional change of limiting legislators' terms can be expected to affect their behavior and influence greatly. Indeed, much of the early debate over the adoption of term limits focused on the effects the reform would have on interest groups and lobbying (Payne 1991; Price 1992; Fund 1992; Struble and Jahre 1991; Will 1992). However, many of the early predictions about these effects were contradictory (Carey, Niemi, and Powell 2000, 83; Capell 1996; Sarbaugh-Thompson et al. 2004), and since then, only minimal systematic evaluation of these claims has been done.

Limiting the number of terms a legislator can serve may directly affect several of the American legislatures' fundamental characteristics that have a direct impact on the behavior and influence of interest groups and lobbyists. If legislators can only serve for twelve or eight or even six years, their turnover rate will increase in most states. Therefore, the membership of term-limited legislatures will likely be less experienced and knowledgeable in politics, the policymaking process, and policy. Moreover, under term limits, even "citizen legislatures" (e.g., those in Maine, Nevada, and South Dakota)—which frequently had 25 to 40 percent membership turnover each election even before term limits (Moncrief, Niemi, and Powell 2004)—will be purged of their long-serving members, those who often have substantial power and carry institutional memory. The forces of incumbent security, seniority influence, the norm of apprenticeship, and the reelection motivation—forces on which most theories of the legislative process are based—are likely to be substantially altered by term limits. What effects do these fundamental changes in the legislative institution have on interest group influence and lobbying, and how might the investigation of these impacts improve our theoretical understanding of the American legislative process?

In this chapter, I begin to address these questions by developing and testing several hypotheses about these effects, using a variety of qualitative and quantitative data from the Joint Project on Term Limits (JPTL) and other sources. On one hand, my analysis suggests that under term limits, there are more lobbyists, they are working harder, and their ethical behavior is sometimes worse. These lobbyists wield more influence in the legislative process, but this power is more evenly distributed among them. Paradoxically, less-experienced, term-limited legislators may need the resources and information of lobbyists more than do their non-term-limited peers, but new legislators tend to be especially distrustful of lobbyists. On the other hand, there is little evidence that term limits have any impact one way or the other on the broader, macrolevel influence of interest groups in state policymaking in general.

The Impact of Term Limits on
Interest Group Influence in Policymaking

Much of the debate over the adoption of term limits in the 1990s focused on their potential impact on interest groups' influence on policymaking. On one hand, term limits were supposed to decrease legislators' interest in reelection, thereby reducing the leverage that groups had over them through campaign contributions (Will 1992; Mitchell 1991; Struble and Jahre 1991). Term limits were also expected to reduce legislators' value to interest groups, by decreasing legislators' longevity, specialization, and security in office (Gordon and Unmack 2003; Daniel and Lott 1997; Tabarrok 1994; Kroszner and Stratmann 1998). It was thought that since legislators were less valuable to them, groups would not bother to build the long-term relationships with lawmakers that arguably result in groups' undue influence. On the other hand, opponents of term limits argued that the reform would actually enhance interest groups' influence, through their monopoly on the policy, political, and procedural information legislators need (Cain and Levin 1999; Corwin 1991; Polsby 1990) and through lame-duck legislators currying favor with groups and businesses for postlegislative employment or runs for other office (Cohen and Spitzer 1996; Carey 1998; Sarbaugh-Thompson et al. 2004; chap. 1 in the present volume).

The evidence of term limits' impacts on the macrolevel influence of interest groups in state policymaking has been no less mixed than the theoretical expectations. On one hand, in the JPTL 2002 National Survey of State Legislators, lawmakers saw no change in state interest group power with the implementation of term limits, nor did term-limited legislators assess interest group influence differently than their non-term-limited peers (Carey et al. 2006). These results match those of a similar survey undertaken in 1995 (Carey, Niemi, and Powell 2000). In addition, consider data gathered from academic and political observers since the 1980s by Thomas and Hrebenar (2004), assessing the "overall impact of interest groups" on each state's policymaking process. Table 8.1 displays the changes in these ratings in the term-limited and non-term-limited states from 1994 to 2002, showing clearly that the patterns are almost identical for these two types of states. Whether legislators were term-limited or not,

TABLE 8.1.   Change in the Overall Impact of Interest Groups in State Policy-making, 1994–2002

	Change in "Overall Interest Group Impact" Category, 1994–2002[a]		
	Less Influence	No Change	More Influence
Term-limited states[b]	1	8	1
	(10.0%)	(80.0%)	(10.0%)
Non-term-limited states	4	29	7
	(10.0%)	(72.5%)	(17.5%)

Source: Thomas and Hrebenar 1996, table 4.5; 2004, table 4.2.

[a]Each state was assessed as to whether and in which direction it changed in Thomas and Hrebenar's categorization of interest group impact between these years (no state changed more than one category between these surveys). The categories were "Dominant," "Dominant/Complementary," "Complementary," "Complementary/Subordinate," and "Subordinate." Values are the number of states with each type of change (with row percentages in parentheses).

[b]Includes only states in which legislators actually had been termed out by the 2000 general election.

overall interest group influence did not change in most states, and the states where it did change were fairly evenly divided between increasing and decreasing influence.

Of course, term limits' apparent lack of effect on group influence (as seen in table 8.1) may have come about through different processes. For example, Carey and his colleagues (Carey, Niemi, and Powell 2000; Carey et al. 2006) have suggested that this overall lack of effect may actually be the result of the two competing effects hypothesized by opponents and proponents of term limits; that is, the loss of established relationships caused by term limits may have weakened groups, while their greater relative information advantage over term-limited legislators may have strengthened them, resulting in no net change in influence. However, testing this hypothesis to sort out the causal processes would require different data than I have at my disposal here.

On the other hand, the qualitative evidence from the JPTL case studies suggests that close observers of policymaking in term-limited states believe that at least some lobbyists gained power with the reform, while those in the non-term-limited states saw steady or even decreasing lobbyist influence over the study period. Even though new legislators appeared to be more suspicious of lobbyists than were their more experienced colleagues, these observers felt that their lack of policy information and legislative experience forced term-limited legislators, especially freshmen, to rely heavily on lobbyists for information. One Arizona legislator stated flatly that new legislators "increasingly relied on lobbyists for information" (Berman 2004, 11–12). In California, some term-limited legislators reported that "over 90 percent of their bills were drafted or given to them by lobbyists" (Cain and Kousser 2004, 22). In Arizona, informants reported that "the big winners from term limits were lobbyists—before term limits, they had to deal with experienced people" and that "lobbyists never had more power" (Berman 2004, 13), while in Colorado, there was "broad agreement" that "the lobby corps has more influence now than in the pre-term limits era" (Straayer and Bowser 2004, 85). Even in Maine, which had the least professional term-limited legislature in the JPTL study, observers believed that lobbyists were stronger than before term limits, even if "the lobby has gained less power than was thought originally" (Powell and Jones 2004, 45). Indeed, in their study of term limits in Michigan, Sarbaugh-Thompson et al. (2004, 191) went so far as to give the reform an "F" for failing to achieve the reformers' goal of reducing lobbyists' influence in the process. Finally, respondents to the JPTL 2003 Survey of Knowledgeable Observers also believed that lobbyists recently gained more influence in term-limited than in non-term-limited states, but they believed this about legislative staff and administrative agencies as well (table 8.2).

What are we to make of the discrepancy between these various sources of evidence on the effect of term limits on overall lobbyist and interest group influence in state policymaking? Initially, there appears to be no evidence that term limits cause interest groups to lose influence, as reformers had hoped and some scholars had predicted (Will 1992; Mitchell 1991; Daniel and Lott 1997; Tabarrok 1994; Kroszner and Stratmann 1998). Neither is there strong evidence that opponents' worst fears of interest groups dominating the legislative process have come to pass (Cain and Levin 1999; Corwin 1991; Polsby 1990). But if we look at the evidence more closely, we see that while the influence of interest groups (according to the JPTL survey of legislators and the Thomas and Hrebenar data) does not appear to have been affected by term limits, there is the perception (according to the JPTL case studies and survey of observers) that the influence of lobbyists increased after the reform.

While these data are dissimilar in a number of other ways, it is worth considering the difference between the impact of term limits on the

TABLE 8.2.   Changes in the Influence of Lobbyists, Legislative Staff, and Administrative Agencies in Term-Limited and Non-Term-Limited Legislatures, 1993–2003

	Term-Limited States[a]	Non-Term-Limited States	p-Value of the Difference
Lobbyists	3.98	3.64	<.001
	(.88)	(.73)	
Partisan legislative staff	3.8	3.51	.001
	(.83)	(.69)	
Personal legislative staff	3.56	3.23	.004
	(.82)	(.58)	
Administrative agencies	3.22	2.83	.001
	(1.12)	(.84)	
Nonpartisan legislative staff	3.07	2.97	.276
	(.94)	(.57)	
N	437	114	

Source: 2003 Survey of Knowledgeable Observers.

[a]Values are the average responses rating the influence of these actors "relative to the legislature compared to a decade ago." Answers ranged on a five-percent scale, from "A Great Deal Less" (1) to "About the Same" (3) to "Quite a Bit More" (5). The standard error of each average is in parentheses.

influence of groups, on one hand, and their lobbyists, on the other. It may be the case that the dynamics of overall group influence are at such an aggregated, systemic level that institutional reforms have less effect, a slower effect, or a less perceptible effect on them, whereas the operational, day-to-day activities and influence of lobbyists might be affected more quickly and more noticeably by term limits. Further research is needed to sort this out, and further thought needs to be given to the theoretical and political implications of such a difference.

Of course, power is a relative concept. Aside from any absolute changes in interest group influence, did term limits affect groups' relative influence in the state political system? Term limits exacerbate the natural information asymmetries between legislators, on one hand, and interest groups, legislative staff, and executive agency officials, on the other (Carey, Niemi, and Powell 2000, 93; Moncrief and Thompson 2001b). Term-limited legislators have a great need for information, but they are more likely to trust those informed actors who have interests most in line with their own: their staff (especially partisan staff—see chap. 5 in this volume) and executive agency officials (Mooney 1991). Like interest groups, these actors have much of the information that legislators need to make decisions, but they are not suspicious "special interests" whose angle legislators must figure out before interpreting that information. Moreover, competing groups often present conflicting information, thereby confusing neophyte legislators and reducing each group's credibility. Less-experienced, term-limited legislators will have an especially difficult time judging the veracity of a group's information because of both a lack of experience and the public's (and, by extension, junior legislators') aversion to lobbyists and interest groups (Hibbing and Theiss-Morse 1995, 105–7). Thus, we might hypothesize that in term-limited states, interest groups will likely be less influential relative to legislative staff and executive agency officials than they are in non-term-limited states.

Again, the evidence on the hypothesis is mixed. In the JPTL survey of legislators, while term-limited legislators were more likely than non-term-limited legislators to report that executive agency officials were more influential, there was no such difference in the perceived influence of interest groups or legislative staff. In comparison, in the parallel 1995 survey (Carey, Niemi, and Powell 2000), staff were seen as being more influential by term-limited legislators. The qualitative evidence from the JPTL case studies provides some support for the hypothesis. For example, in California, newly elected, term-limited legislators were found to hire experienced personal staff so that they did not have to "depend on lobbyists and out-siders to provide expertise and knowledge" (Cain and Kousser 2004, 96). In Colorado, even though nonpartisan legislative staff were reluctant to assume a larger role in the policymaking process after term limits, the informants still felt that staff influence was increasing. In Arizona, the influence of leadership staff, in particular, was thought to be enhanced by term limits, so much so that lobbyists began lobbying them directly. Finally, the JPTL survey of observers found that the perceived influence of executive agency officials, partisan and personal (but not nonpartisan) leg-islative staff, and lobbyists increased more from 1993 to 2003 in term-lim-ited states than in non-term-limited states, with all of them increasing in influence by very similar amounts (table 8.2).

None of the evidence provides a direct comparison of interest group, staff, and agency influence. Yet it is suggestive of such a comparison. What emerges, then, is a picture of lobbyists being increasingly influential after term limits, but perhaps in tandem with a rise in the influence of legislative staff and administrative agencies.

The Impact of Term Limits on Lobbying Strategy and Tactics

If the impacts that opponents and proponents predicted term limits would have on the aggregate power of interest groups have not materialized clearly in the states, perhaps enough time has not yet passed to allow the processes involved to work through the system at that level. But lobbyists working in state capitols where term limits are a fact of life must grapple with their implications daily as they develop strategies and tactics to pursue their interests in the legislative process. Because of the demands of worka-day business in the statehouse and the pragmatic needs of these advocates, the first impacts of term limits may be seen not on interest groups' macrolevel power in the state but, rather, in the microlevel behavior of groups and lobbyists. In this section, I examine the processes behind these behaviors, to develop and test hypotheses of what might be term limits' most immediate impacts.

At root, interest groups attempt to influence policymaking by marshal-ing information about why the policies they espouse should be adopted and then communicating this information to policymakers (Nownes 2001). Groups communicate directly with policymakers about the potential sub-stantive and political impacts of policy choices. Groups also communicate policy information to citizens, with the hope that political information (the public's views on a policy) will be relayed indirectly to policymakers (Gold-stein 1999). Lobbying strategies and tactics, then, are decisions about how and when to communicate which information to whom. How would these decisions be different in states with and without term-limited legislatures?

A group planning its advocacy strategy must consider the receptivity of policymakers to the information it wants to convey. One way that groups have traditionally enhanced policymakers' receptivity to their arguments has been by developing long-term working relationships with them (Rosenthal 1993). For a policymaker to accept a group's argument on an issue, the group must have both access to and credibility with that policy-maker. The general lobbying strategy, then, is to use professional advo-cates (lobbyists)—whether employed full-time by the group or on a con-tractual basis—to meet policymakers, help them with their policy and political concerns, and develop ongoing professional relationships with them, unrelated to any specific policy question. Developing such a rela-tionship enhances both access and credibility and therefore makes it more likely that the policymakers will believe the group's argument when it is presented to them.

Term limits may affect the development of such lobbyist-policymaker relationships in a variety of ways. New legislators may suffer some of the same negative predispositions toward lobbyists and interest groups that the average citizen has (Hibbing and Theiss-Morse 1995, 105–7). The public tends to view lobbyists as manipulating policymakers, biasing pub-lic policy away from the public interest toward special interests. Thus, new legislators, perhaps especially those elected in the antigovernment political environment that term limits represent, may be more suspicious of lobbyists than are veteran legislators. Of course, such mistrusting fresh-men may not be unique to term-limited states, but their impact is greater in these states, since high turnover leads to more freshmen serving each term and to the absence of long-serving members to teach these freshmen how to develop productive working relationships with lobbyists. Thus, in term-limited states, legislators as a group will likely be more suspicious of lobbyists than will be legislators in non-term-limited states. Such suspi-cion will make it more difficult for lobbyists to develop relationships with legislators.

While the level of suspicion that legislators have for lobbyists is difficult to measure systematically, the qualitative evidence from the JPTL case studies clearly supports this hypothesis. While the relationship between lobbyists and lawmakers in the non-term-limited states was reported as being stable, "well developed, understood, and valued by legislators and staff" (Wright and Ogle 2004, 18), the story was quite different in the term-limited states. For example, in 2001, many freshmen members of the term-limited Ohio House mistrusted lobbyists so much that they flatly refused to meet with any of them for the first several months of the session. One observer in Maine said that "new legislators . . . are afraid to even talk with lobbyists because they view them as corrupt" (Powell and Jones 2004, 45). In Arizona and Colorado, too, new members were suspicious of lobbyists. The effect on legislators' suspicion that lobbyists were systematically eliminating long-serving members was demonstrated in the Colorado JPTL case study, in which Straayer and Bowser (2004, 17) conclude that before term limits, "old-timers served as coaches on the culture and behavioral norms of the institution, and could relate policy history information and help new ones figure out the interest group and lobbyist landscape."

If more legislators in term-limited states are suspicious of lobbyists and if long-term relationships are continually disrupted by term-limits-induced turnover, lobbyists will likely have to work harder to make their cases to legislators in these states (Moncrief and Thompson 2001a). Support for this hypothesis is found throughout the JPTL case studies. Veteran lobbyists who had developed good relationships with committee chairs and leaders over the years found themselves scrambling to meet and persuade a large cohort of freshman after each election. Under term limits, lobbyists were found to be "working harder to maintain their influence" (Farmer and Little 2004, 12) and "working harder to establish contact with the parade of new legislators" (Berman 2004, 12), because "more time is needed" to explain bills and the background of issues and for "generally educating members" (Straayer and Bowser 2004, 58). According to veteran Ohio political reporter Lee Leonard, speaking at a University of Akron conference on term limits in 2004, lobbyists in term-limited states were "seeing a lot more of the state," as they headed out to meet new members even before they were initially sworn in. At the same conference, a former Ohio Senate leader, Leigh Herrington, quoted a veteran lobbyist as saying, "[W]e are doing 300% more education than we ever did before." In Maine, one JPTL observer noted that lobbyists had gained less power from term limits than had been expected, because "it is harder for them to keep up with and get to know legislators" (Powell and Jones 2004, 45). Indeed, veteran lobbyists in term-limited states have been frustrated with this state of affairs, with several reportedly considering retirement because of it. At the 2004 term limits conference, Chuck Perricone, former speaker of the

Michigan House, said that all this extra work has made lobbyists the only group he knows of that wants to repeal term limits.

Regardless of the difficulty of lobbying term-limited legislators, groups wishing to influence public policy must still make their best effort to do so. Lobbyists must make personal contacts with legislators to make their cases, and they must develop their credibility with and access to them. Under term limits, with more new and suspicious legislators to contact, groups will need to expend more resources developing the necessary relationships with and communicating their information to lawmakers. The main resource in doing this is simply people—lobbyists to knock on doors, make telephone calls, wait in hallways, and otherwise do the groundwork of lobbying. Therefore, under term limits, interest groups may need to hire more lobbyists.

The JPTL case studies gave only scattered and conflicting reports about changes in the number of lobbyists after term limits and in non-term-limited states in recent years. So I gathered data on the number of registered lobbyists in most states from 1993 to 2002, to make a systematic assessment of this hypothesis. While lobbyist registration requirements and record keeping vary dramatically among the states (Newmark 2005), most states collected these data in an internally consistent manner during this period. Using the number of registered lobbyists in each of between thirty-three and forty states (depending on data availability) in the five bienniums in the study period (1993/94 to 2001/2), I compared the average percentage change in them from one biennium to the next for term-limited and non-term-limited states (table 8.3).

While there is a good deal of cross-state variation in the growth rates of lobbyist registration, the pattern of their averages supports the hypothesis that term limits lead to more lobbyists working in a state. Table 8.3 shows that before term limits, there was no major difference in the average increase in lobbyists in future term-limited and non-term-limited states, with both groups gaining an average of about 4 to 5 percent more lobbyists from 1993/94 to 1995/96. Indeed, the increase in lobbyist registration in future term-limited states was actually lower than that in non-term-limited states. But from 1995/96 to 1997/98, the two states that implemented term limits in the 1996 election, California and Maine, continued to gain close to 5 percent more lobbyists, while the other states averaged almost no change. Term-limited states continued to have a higher lobbyist growth rate in the next two periods. Moreover, in any given period, those states that will implement term limits in the future tend to have lobbyist growth rates like those of the non-term-limited states; this is further evidence that groups react to the extra work caused by term limits (i.e., that the correlation between term limits and differences in lobbyist growth rates is not spurious). Finally, since this comparison is of growth rates, the fact that the lobbyist growth rate in term-limited states continues to be positive year after year suggests that once the process of adjustment to this reform is completed, term-limited states will have many more lobbyists roaming their statehouses than they would have had absent this reform.

Another difference we might expect between lobbying in term-limited and non-term-limited states has to do with the distinction between contract and in-house lobbyists (Thomas and Hrebenar 2004). Contract lobbyists specialize in knowing the policymaking process and having relationships that open doors to the powerful people in the system. They are often former legislators or legislative staff whose services are available to any group for a fee. In-house lobbyists, by contrast, are typically full-time employees of the group for which they are lobbying. Their stock-in-trade is the technical policy knowledge that their groups' members often have to

TABLE 8.3.   Average Percentage Change in the Number of Registered Lobbyists in the States

Time Period	All States[a]	Non-Term-Limited States	Term-Limited States[b]	Future Term-Limited States[c]
Before term limits	4.60	n.a.	n.a.	3.87
(1993/94–1995/96)	($N = 33$)			($N = 9$)
First term limits period	n.a.	−0.66	4.86	2.48
(1995/96–1997/98)		($N = 37$)	($N = 2$)	($N = 8$)
Second term limits period	n.a.	1.73	2.54	1.73
(1997/98–1999/2000)		($N = 37$)	($N = 3$)	($N = 7$)
Third term limits period	n.a.	0.83	5.91	−0.14
(1999/2000–2001)		($N = 33$)	($N = 7$)	($N = 3$)

Source: Author's survey (with the assistance of Bill Davidson and Pam Schallhorn) of Web sites and offices of secretaries of states and ethics commissions.

Note: Includes all states except Arizona, Louisiana, Missouri, New Hampshire, and Vermont, for which data were unavailable.

[a]Values are the average percentage change in the number of registered lobbyists from the first to the second biennium in each period for each category (with the number of states for each cell in parentheses beneath). The number of states is less than fifty and varies between periods, based on the availability of the lobbyist data in each state in each year.

[b]A state was considered to have term limits in a given period if at least some of its members were forced from office in the election in the middle of the period. For example, in the first term limits period (1995/96–1997/98), California and Maine were the two term-limited states because they had members forced from office in the 1996 election.

[c]A state was considered to be a future term-limited state if it was scheduled to implement term limits after the given period.

a greater degree than any other actors in the system, possibly excepting career officials in administrative agencies.

Which of these types of lobbyists would be more effective with term-limited legislators? While in-house lobbyists may be the embodiment of the narrow, special interests that worry the public, these lobbyists have the solid substantive information that policymakers need to make decisions. Indeed, with higher turnover and shorter tenure, term-limited legislators are in great need of the policy information that in-house lobbyists can provide (Moncrief and Thompson 2001b; Cain and Levin 1999; Carey, Niemi, and Powell 2000; Sarbaugh-Thompson et al. 2004). In-house lobbyists also have the political support of their groups' members, to enhance their credibility. It may be more difficult for new legislators to appreciate the credibility or knowledge of contract lobbyists, those ultimate insiders whose image is not even burnished by the support of a group's membership. Moreover, with term limits, the ability to open the doors of the powerful may be more evenly distributed around the interest community (Moncrief and Thompson 2001a). For example, the personal relationships that a contract lobbyist may have developed when he or she was in the Senate will be valuable only as long as those people the lobbyist served with are still in office. In non-term-limited legislatures, these relationships gain value as they mature, as an ex-legislator's former colleagues rise in seniority and power in that body. With term limits, the shelf life of such relationships is very limited. Thus, since the value of contract lobbyists' wares decreases under term limits, strategic interest groups will rely on them less often, and contract lobbyists will be used less often in term-limited than in non-term-limited states.

While hard data to test this hypothesis do not exist, some indirect qualitative evidence supports it. Typically, the respondents in the JPTL case studies did not distinguish explicitly between contract and in-house lobbyists. The exception was in Illinois, a non-term-limited state, where several respondents noted that lobbying power had been increasingly concentrated in the hands of a few contract lobbyists throughout the 1993–2003 study period. But the term-limited states' case studies contained much discussion of "insiders," "old veteran" lobbyists, and "power brokers," whose "clout rested upon the personal tie" to top policymakers. If such lobbyists tend to be contract lobbyists, my hypothesis is supported by the many observations that term limits reduced their influence. One observer said, "[T]erm limits have helped break with a past in which the Arizona legislature was run by a small circle of legislative leaders and key lobbyists who were insulated from the public" (Berman 2004, 6). Term limits were seen as leveling the playing field, moving "the one time powerhouses [into] the same boat as everyone else as they scramble to introduce themselves to the new legislators" (Berman 2004, 12).

Finally, one of the positive impacts that the lobbyist-legislator relationship has on the political system is that it helps hold lobbyists accountable for their actions (Rosenthal 1993). Traditionally, lobbyists have known that if they lie to or mislead a legislator even once, their credibility will be lost permanently. As a result, they do their best to present factually correct information to legislators and to relate all sides of a policy debate. Given legislators' limited fact-checking ability and the speed at which the legislative process occasionally moves, legislators must be able to trust lobbyists in order to do their own job efficiently and effectively. The reciprocal benefits legislators and groups garner from the information flow in lobbying require mutual credibility (Milbrath 1960; Wright 1996). But term limits break up the long-term lobbyist-legislator relationship, making such mutual credibility harder to achieve. Perhaps even more important in the long run, term limits change the lobbyist-legislator interaction from an unlimited repeating process to a time-limited set of interactions. As a result of these changes, lobbyists may no longer be so scrupulous about guarding their credibility, and this situation may lead to less-ethical lobbying behavior (Capell 1996). In fact, Sarbaugh-Thompson et al. (2004, 64) observed, "[I]n situations where there is a known endpoint to the relationship between parties, it is 'rational' for the actors to behave deviously toward each other" (see also Axelrod 1984). Since the "endpoint" of the lobbyist-legislator relationship is known (at least for the individual legislator) under term limits, this reform may lead to more "devious" and unethical behavior by lobbyists.

Qualitative evidence from the JPTL case studies supports this hypothesis. After term limits, lobbyists reportedly worry less about keeping their long-term credibility if it conflicts with a short-term lobbying goal. An official in the executive branch in Colorado saw "less candor, less respect for legislators, [and] more revisionist history" from lobbyists after term limits (Straayer and Bowser 2004, 84). Lobbyists are thought to bias their narratives of a policy's history more often under term limits "because there are fewer veteran [legislators] around to keep them in check" (Berman 2004, 13). Lobbyists were said to be more disrespectful to legislators (especially to lame-duck members) and even to legislative leaders. In short, many JPTL observers agreed that term limits had led to "more shady, nasty, rude, pushy lobbyists" (Straayer and Bowser 2004, 88).

Conclusion

How have legislative term limits affected lobbyists and interest groups in state capitals? Given that much of the early debate over the adoption of term limits hinged on conflicting predictions about these effects, this is an important question, both for theory and practical politics. Certainly, this chapter only begins to shed light on this question. Time is needed for all the political actors in the term-limited states to adjust to this radical reform and for new patterns of behavior, relationships, and influence to stabilize. More theoretical and empirical research is needed to clarify the picture of how interest groups and lobbyists work within a policymaking process where legislators serve limited terms. But we can draw some lessons from the states' early experiences with this reform.

Term limits appear to have had considerable effect on lobbyists' behavior and the practice of lobbying. In term-limited state legislatures, the higher turnover and lack of veteran legislators have made legislators more suspicious of lobbyists, even as lobbyists are relied on more for policy information. As the states adjust to this reform, how this tension plays out between the disdain term-limited legislators feel toward lobbyists, on the one hand, and these legislators' special need for them, on the other, will have important implications for public policy and the tenor of politics in the states.

Perhaps most important, new legislators' mistrust of lobbyists and the continuous disruption of legislator-lobbyist relationships have made lobbying just plain harder work in term-limited legislatures. Lobbyists have to meet, educate, and establish relationships with many new members every two years. These lobbyists can no longer afford to ignore freshmen legislators, since some of the latter will very soon hold significant power in the body, becoming committee chairs, speakers, and presidents within a few years. Groups appear to be adjusting by hiring more and more people to help do the extra work of lobbying under term limits. At the same time, fewer contract lobbyists—or at least fewer established power-brokering lobbyists—dominate lawmaking in term-limited legislatures, as power shifts quickly with legislative turnover. The playing field is more level for lobbyists under term limits. On the negative side, the lack of incentives to develop and maintain long-term, trusting relationships with legislators has increased less-than-ethical behavior among some lobbyists in term-limited states. Overall, these effects on lobbying may be helping change term-limited legislatures into policymaking environments that are not just more hectic and less congenial but fairer and more open than they were before term limits.

The impact of term limits on interest groups' macrolevel influence in state policymaking is less clear. While term limits do not yet appear to have affected interest groups' overall influence in the states, they have caused lobbyists to become more prominent actors in policymaking. Why is the evidence of the impact of term limits on lobbyists and their behavior clearer than that of their impact on interest group influence? Term limits are still a relatively new reform, so it should not be surprising that their microlevel effects on the concrete behavior of political actors in the process would be apparent before their macrolevel effects. Systemic effects will likely take more time both to evolve and to be perceived. Term limits are already having an important microlevel impact on the behavior of lobbyists, and these behavioral changes will likely eventually manifest themselves in macrolevel changes in the political environment. Tracking these macrolevel changes over the coming decade should be a priority for scholars of term limits and interest groups.

Term limit advocates—both reformers and scholars (Will 1992; Mitchell 1991; Daniel and Lott 1997; Tabarrok 1994; Kroszner and Stratmann 1998; Struble and Jahre 1991)—initially predicted that this reform would reduce the influence that lobbyists and interest groups have in the legislative process. Even from this early analysis, it is clear that these predictions have not been fulfilled. At the very least, term limits have caused no loss of power for groups and lobbyists, and there is evidence that this reform has actually increased their influence, as some term limit opponents had feared (Cain and Levin 1999; Corwin 1991; Polsby 1990; Cohen and Spitzer 1996). This assessment of the impact of term limits on interest groups and lobbyists shows the need to consider major institutional changes very carefully before undertaking them. Such reforms always lead to unintended consequences, and the more fundamental the reform is, the more significant such consequences will likely be.

CHAPTER 9

Executive-Legislative Relations

Richard J. Powell

THE DRAMATIC CHANGES taking place in the composition and internal dynamics of state legislatures with term limits, described extensively elsewhere in this volume, have also altered relations between the legislative and executive branches of state governments. For the most part, these changes represent important, but unintended, consequences of term limits. Term limits were viewed by their advocates primarily as a way to restructure the relationship between legislators and their constituents as well as the internal dynamics of legislatures. In other words, term limits were designed to combat the perception that long-serving members were acquiring too much power and becoming unresponsive to citizens (Moen, Palmer, and Powell 2004). Notably, term limit advocates said almost nothing about potential changes in the institutional relationship between the legislative and executive branches of state governments. It was assumed that by removing entrenched members, power would devolve to citizens. However, as discussed in this chapter, research reveals that one of the clearest effects of term limits has been to weaken legislatures at the expense of executives. This shift in institutional power represents a significant restructuring of the representative nature of state government.

Term limit advocates failed to give much attention to issues related to separation of powers at the state level. But political scientists predicted some of the patterns that have emerged in term-limited state legislatures. For example, Benjamin and Malbin (1992) and Jewell and Whicker (1994) foresaw that term limits would likely lead to an increase in gubernatorial influence because of decreased levels of legislative experience.

This chapter begins by taking a general look at the changing relationship between legislatures and executives under term limits and explores the causes of such changes. It then examines an area of legislative activity—oversight—in which these changes have been particularly evident. In short, the ability of legislatures to exercise effective oversight has waned considerably. The chapter concludes with a discussion of the broader implications that the shifting institutional relationships hold for political representation.

The Changing Balance of Power

Term limits have brought about significant changes in executive-legislative relations. The root of all these changes is in the fact that term limits increase turnover in state legislatures and reduce the collective experience of legislators themselves. Of course, as observed in the introduction to this volume, there are a variety of different term limit laws in the states that have adopted them. Moreover, prior to the implementation of term limits, states had a range of different political environments in such key areas as professionalization, turnover, and the executive-legislative balance of power. In general, the Joint Project on Term Limits (JPTL) has found that term limits have had the greatest impact in those states where they had the potential to bring the greatest amount of change—states with relatively strong, professionalized legislatures and low legislative turnover. This is not surprising, since term limits were designed to reverse the trend toward increasingly professionalized legislatures around the country and to return power to citizens through the model of citizen legislatures. Thus, it makes sense that term limits would have less effect on the political systems of states with less-professionalized legislatures. Even so, term limits have been associated with increases in executive influence in almost every state in the JPTL study.

The turnover created by term limits creates the conditions for a weakening of the legislature in three major ways. First, term limits decrease the level of experience possessed by the typical legislator. Second, even in states that already have high turnover, term limits remove cadres of long-serving members who have been able to amass considerable personal influence; these long-serving members often served as powerful counterweights to the executive branch. This latter phenomenon has had a particularly devastating effect on legislative power. Third, term limits alter the internal relationships within legislatures by changing the behavioral incentive structures for legislators. On balance, these internal changes work to the disadvantage of the legislature in their interactions with the executive branch.

In Chapter 2 in this volume, we saw that term limits have created increased turnover, which is not surprising, since that is the primary intention of these reforms. With large numbers of new members, state legislatures have collectively lost hundreds of years of experience that would not have been lost in the absence of term limits. Overall, this has led to a sharp decrease in the amount of political and policy experience found in legislatures. Of course, not all new members are political neophytes; many of them bring valuable experience from careers in other government positions or from their nonpolitical careers. In Maine, for example, a new state legislator in 2003 had previously served as the state's budget director during a severe economic crisis. Upon entering the legislature, he took an active role on the appropriations committee. Nevertheless, state legislatures have suffered a very real decline in their aggregate experience levels.

Not only have legislatures seen increased turnover, but term limits have also removed from office a smaller number of members with extensive service—in some cases removing legislators with decades of experience. The ousting of Assembly Speaker Willie Brown of California is perhaps the most notable example of this development. Brown, a Democrat, had served in the assembly for thirty-two years—sixteen of those as Speaker—and had amassed so much political influence that he even managed to get himself elected Speaker when the Republicans narrowly won control of the Assembly following the 1994 elections. During his years in the Assembly, Brown and several of his experienced Democratic colleagues served as powerful counterweights to several successive Republican governors. Brown's experience was similar to long-serving legislative leaders in other states, such as John Martin in Maine and Vern Riffe in Ohio. Term limits removed from office or disrupted the careers of these and many other powerful legislators.

In looking at the various data collected for this project, it is clear that term limits have been perceived to decrease the influence of legislatures relative to their respective executive branches. Table 9.1 displays the mean responses from the JPTL 2002 National Survey of State Legislators for the questions that asked about the influence of governors and bureaucrats/civil servants on legislative outcomes, broken down by term-limited and non-term-limited states. On a scale ranging from 1 ("No Influence") to 7 ("Dictates Policy"), the mean response for gubernatorial influence was 4.5 in term-limited states and 4.1 in non-term-limited states, a difference that is statistically significant at the .01 level. Civil servants were also perceived to be more influential in term-limited states at a statistically significant level. Using a more sophisticated multivariate analysis of the same data set, Carey et al. (2006) found that governors and bureaucrats/civil servants are perceived as more influential in term-limited states than in non-term-limited states, at a statistically significant level.

The results from the JPTL 2003 Survey of Knowledgeable Observers are consistent with those just mentioned. Table 9.2 displays the mean responses broken down by state when observers were asked to assess changes in the influence of governors and administrative agencies relative to a decade ago, on a scale ranging from 1 ("Decreased a Great Deal") to 5 ("Increased a Great Deal"). Although the differences in means between term-limited and non-term-limited states are not statistically significant for gubernatorial influence, the means in five of the six term-limited states exceeded those of all the non-term-limited states. Looking at the data, one sees that the responses from Ohio were very atypical of term-limited states (Ohio's outlier status is discussed later in this section). In sum, the lack of statistical significance between term-limited and non-term-limited states is driven by Ohio's respondents, which comprise 38 percent of the total sample; the difference between term-limited and non-term-limited states is statistically significant when Ohio is excluded from the analysis.

The interviews in the various states generally confirmed the survey results and provided a more detailed account of why term limits increase the influence of the executive branch. Most important, interviewees noted repeatedly that the greater turnover generated by term limits puts legislatures at an informational disadvantage relative to executives. Quite simply,

TABLE 9.1   Relative Influence of the Executive Branch on Legislative Outcomes

	Governor	Bureaucrats/ Civil Servants
Term-limited states (mean)	4.5*	3.5*
Non-term-limited states (mean)	4.1	3.3

Source: 2002 National Survey of State Legislators.

Note: The survey asked, "What do you think is the relative influence of the following actors in determining legislative outcomes in your chamber?" Response categories ranged from "No Influence" (1) to "Dictates Policy" (7). $N = 2{,}910$.

*$p < .01$

legislatures possess significantly less policy expertise under term limits. When pitted against experienced officials in the executive branch, the disadvantage becomes readily apparent. A legislative observer in Maine reported: "Committees are deferential to the executive branch. More new people are accepting of the bureaucracy. There is not enough healthy skepticism. In the past committee chairs were more aggressive with the executive" (Powell and Jones 2004, 58). Under term limits, legislators have become much more deferential to officials from executive agencies because they do not have the background knowledge of complex state programs to ask the necessary questions. Moreover, legislators recognize that the expertise of agency officials is generally greater than their own. Similarly, executive officials now find that they have a greater ability to get their way with the legislature. For example, a Senate chair in California noted: "The bureaucracies know they can wait us out. They stall or don't implement what we tell them to do because they know we won't be around" (Cain and Kousser 2004, 79).

The decrease in legislative power relative to state executive branches is due not only to a decline in legislative experience but to the changing institutional incentives under term limits. Since members are now faced with shorter legislative careers, they have fewer incentives to defend the legislature as an institution. The survey of observers asked whether legislators were now more or less willing to support and defend the institution of the legislature. As shown in table 9.3, knowledgeable observers in all six term-limited states believed that legislators were now less supportive of their institution. Moreover, the difference between term-limited and non-term-limited states was statistically significant. A Colorado legislator observed, "Members are less understanding of the importance of separa-

TABLE 9.2.   Influence of the Executive Branch Relative to the Legislature in 2003 Compared to a Decade Before, by State

Actor	AZ	AR	CA	CO	ME	OH	IL	IN	KS	Total
The governor	3.2	3.5	3.4	3.9	3.9	2.1	2.6	2.6	3.1	2.9
Administrative agencies	3.0	3.9	2.9	3.5	4.0	2.9	2.8	2.9	2.8	3.1*
N	39	62	35	38	53	510	22	33	59	551

Source: 2003 Survey of Knowledgeable Observers.
Note: Questions asked respondents about "influence" of actors "relative to the legislature a decade ago." Response categories ranged from "Decreased a Great Deal" (1) to "Increased a Great Deal" (5).
Significance = level of confidence that results from term-limited states are different from those of non-term-limited states.
*$p < .01$

tion of powers, less inclined to defend the legislature versus the governor" (Straayer and Bowser 2004, 108).

In the past, members understood that an erosion of legislative authority would ultimately lead to a lessening of their own individual influence. Under term limits, members no longer feel the same degree of institutional loyalty to the legislature, because they do not have a personal stake in its long-term standing. Thus, even if it were possible to replace term-limited members with new legislators that possessed the same levels of substantive expertise, legislatures might still see their influence wane over time, as members shun the time-consuming task of institutional maintenance in order to focus more time on their own personal goals. Moreover, in many of the term-limited states, members face incentives to be more loyal to the executive branch, since it has become increasingly common for term-limited legislators to be appointed to executive positions upon leaving the legislature. This also has the effect of stocking the executive branch with politically experienced former legislators, even further exacerbating the informational advantage owned by the governor. A Colorado legislator explained: "You cross [the governor] at your own peril. Any member of the legislature who crosses him can kiss any future job in the state goodbye" (Straayer and Bowser 2004, 96).

Internal changes within term-limited legislatures also contribute to the shift in power from legislatures to executives, especially the weakening of leaders and committee chairs. In many states with term limits, leaders now occupy their positions for just one or two terms. This significantly weakens their ability to exercise their leadership role, because they are viewed by their colleagues as lame ducks from the day they take office. In Arkansas, for instance, 91 percent of respondents to the survey of legislators thought

TABLE 9.3 Legislators' Support for the Legislature as an Institution in 2003 Compared to a Decade Before, by State

Survey Item	AZ	AR	CA	CO	ME	OH	IL	IN	KS	Total
Support and defend the institution of the legislature	2.0	2.1	2.0	2.0	2.3	2.0	2.5	3.3	2.0	2.1*
N	39	62	35	38	53	210	22	33	59	551

Source: 2003 Survey of Knowledgeable Observers.

Note: The question asked respondents about "legislators compared to a decade ago." Responses categories ranged from "Quite a Bit Less" (1) to "Quite a Bit More" (5).

Significance = level of confidence that results from term-limited states are different from those of non-term-limited states.

*p < .01

that leadership had been weakened by term limits (English and Weberg 2004).

Rank-and-file legislators are less likely to follow their term-limited leaders, because these leaders have little influence over the legislators' long-term careers. In the past, state legislatures contained many powerful, entrenched leaders who were able to muster considerable influence over their fellow legislators. Members knew that crossing their leaders was fraught with peril if the legislators wanted to achieve their own legislative and career goals. Moreover, many of these long-serving leaders were respected for the significant political and policy expertise they had developed over time. With increased leadership turnover, leaders are less knowledgeable and less able to get their political party—let alone the entire legislature—to act in a coordinated way. Typical of the comments from the interviews in the JPTL study, an observer in Colorado noted that term limits give the governor a significant advantage in terms of experience and expertise (Straayer and Bowser 2004, 108). Even though the governors of many states are term-limited as well, they are generally interacting with leaders who are spending at most one or two terms in their positions.

Ironically, officials of the executive branch frequently complain about the diminished leadership capacity in the legislatures. Because of the legislatures' reduced capacity for action, executives often find it hard to advance significant legislative proposals. Moreover, a fragmentation of power in the legislatures can make it more difficult for executive officials to build support for their programs, because leaders can no longer be counted on to deliver their party's votes on key issues. A Maine legislator noted: "Leaders cannot control the members. Committee chairs disregard the deadlines set by the leaders and the members disregard the directives from the committee chairs. This has resulted in more chaos" (Powell and Jones 2004, 21). As a result, governors must increasingly build coalitions on an ad hoc, issue-by-issue basis, by courting rank-and-file legislators individually, a time-consuming and difficult process.

The changing nature of leadership under term limits complicates things for legislative power in one other significant way. In general, leaders with limited tenures in office are much less interested in the often mundane, but critical, tasks of institutional maintenance. Such issues as staff organization, preserving institutional memory, and other institutional needs take a backseat to the immediate policy concerns of leaders. Upon entering office, leaders know their time in office is limited, often to just one term. In that time, it is natural for leaders to want to accomplish their policy goals as a way of building their legacy and perhaps setting the stage for a run for another political office. With an abbreviated tenure, there is very little incentive for leaders to devote their energies to the institutional needs of the legislature. These functions are now more commonly filled by staff members, if at all (see chap. 6 in this volume). Without term limits, leaders have greater incentive to build the institutional strength of the legislature, since doing so increases their influence over time. In term-limited legislatures, leaders are less willing to devote their time to these duties.

The weakened status of committees and their chairs under term limits (discussed at length in chap. 5 in this volume) has had a similarly damaging effect on legislative power. In the past, committee chairs were often very influential players in their areas of policy expertise. Now, executive officials, legislative leaders, and rank-and-file legislators are much less likely to follow committee recommendations. A committee's influence depends mainly on two factors: (1) the perception that it has an informational advantage in its area of jurisdiction and (2) unwritten norms of legislative specialization. Both factors are weakened by term limits. That committees and their chairs are no longer viewed as having the same degree of expertise in their areas has further contributed to the shift in influence to executive officials.

Having examined the evidence that state executives have gained influence in states with term limits, we need to be sure that such changes are not part of some larger trend affecting states around the country, even those without term limits. To address this question, I turn to evidence from the control states in the JPTL study: Kansas, Indiana, and Illinois. In none of these states did research uncover any significant changes in the balance of power between the executive and legislative branches. In Kansas, interviewees suggested that the executive-legislative relationship was complex and heavily dependent on the personality and style of whomever happened to be governor at the time. None of the interviewees in Kansas perceived any significant institutional changes over the past decade (Smith and Erickson 2004). Indiana generally has a relatively weak governor in relation to the legislature. The JPTL study found that there has been little change in executive-legislative relations in Indiana in recent years, with governors continuing to defer to the legislature in agenda setting and policy-making (Wright and Ogle 2004, 17).

The lack of change in executive-legislative relations in non-term-limited states was also evident in Illinois. Under the 1970 Illinois Constitution, the governor is given very strong institutional powers to wield considerable influence over the legislature. For example, Illinois governors have one of the strongest veto authorities in the nation. In addition to simply vetoing a bill in total, governors can also exercise line-item vetoes by eliminating or reducing appropriations, and they can amend spending bills. The formal powers of the Illinois governor are supported by a strong individualistic political culture that enables governors to build considerable power through the spoils system, control over district projects, and the use of public appearances and fund-raising on behalf of individual legislators. Research in Illinois concluded that the broad outlines of executive-legislative relations have held constant despite personnel changes in key political positions. This finding was supported further by data gathered on legislative oversight functions. In the Illinois Assembly, the Joint Committee on Administrative Rules (JCAR) is charged with the task of reviewing rules made among executive agencies. However, interviewees stated that the JCAR generally held little power in dealing with executive agencies. Since 1992, JCAR challenges to executive rules have been relatively uncommon, with no discernible increase over time. In fact, from 1992 to 2003, the JCAR voiced concerns about less than 7 percent of proposed executive rules and formally blocked less than 1 percent of them (Mooney and Storey 2004, 73).

Among legislators from term-limited states across the nation, there is widespread agreement that term limit reform affects executive-legislative relations. The experience of the Ohio legislature, however, appears to represent a curious exception to the overall trend. Of the states we examined, Ohio was the only term-limited state in which the mean response from respondents to the survey of observers indicated that governors were actually less influential under term limits. When questioned in the JPTL study's interviews, Ohioans attributed this trend to the unique blend of personalities in key political positions since term limits took effect. Most notably, interviewees suggested that recent legislative leaders were unusually skillful in recruiting candidates and raising money on their behalf, thus strengthening their leadership positions. Also, Ohio's legislators have taken particular advantage of the state's term limit provision that allows term-limited members to run immediately for the other chamber. Although migrating from the House to the Senate has become fairly common in several term-limited states, Ohio's senators have shown an atypical enthusiasm for migrating to the lower chamber. This has helped Ohio's legislature maintain its influence in the executive-legislative relationship. Interestingly, however, interviewees in Ohio generally felt that term limits would eventually benefit the executive branch at the expense of the legislature, despite the short-term experience to the contrary (Farmer and Little 2004, 14).

In summary, the totality of the JPTL data suggests that term limits are having a significant effect on executive-legislative relations in a way that works to the disadvantage of legislatures. This is especially evident when comparing the experience of the term-limited states in the study with that of the non-term-limited, control states. In the next section, I will briefly examine the nature of these shifts in influence in a critical area of executive-legislative politics, legislative oversight.

Oversight

Thus far, this chapter has discussed the general trend in the direction of increased executive power at the expense of legislatures. As we have seen, the impact of the weakened status of leaders, committees, and legislators in general on executive-legislative relations is evident in several areas of the legislative process. However, questions of the executive-legislative power balance are relevant at many stages beyond the legislative process as well. For example, even after laws are passed, legislatures must exercise effective oversight functions to make sure they are implemented in the intended manner by executive officials.

Most notably, observers stated that committee oversight of executive agencies is much less rigorous under term limits. The JPTL study yielded numerous accounts of committee hearings at which executive officials were treated much more deferentially after than before term limits. Unfortunately, the basis for this change is not a general increase in civility but, rather, a diminished capacity for committee members to ask relevant questions. According to Berman (2004, 15), legislators in Arizona "saw term limits giving agency heads an advantage in dealing with legislators on budgeting matters and, by default, greater responsibility for coping with long term and complex problems." Similarly, Farmer and Little (2004, 14) report for Ohio: "[I]nterviews revealed concern that members were paying less attention to the actions of executive agencies. Generally, they felt that less oversight was taking place." In short, inexperienced committee members are more likely to view agency officials as privileged experts. In the past, long-serving committee members and chairs often had a more detailed understanding of policy than had agency officials. Term limits have dramatically altered this relationship.

The difficulties term limits caused for state legislatures in their interactions with their respective executive branches are especially evident in the area of oversight. Oversight, as commonly defined, entails a legislature's responsibilities in monitoring, scrutinizing, and sometimes challenging the actions of executive departments and agencies. Such activities are a crucial responsibility for legislative bodies in governmental systems relying on institutional separation of powers. A veteran Senate committee consultant in California explained: "In many ways, oversight is more significant than passing laws. . . . The passing of the law is an important event, but the implementation is vastly more important. Politicians don't get credit for oversight. It's the harder and less rewarding aspect of the work but it is a much more important function in terms of changing the world out there" (Cain and Kousser 2004, 85). Without the ability to effectively oversee the bureaucracy, legislatures are greatly weakened. Effective legislative oversight depends on many things, such as appropriate institutional structures, experienced legislators and staff, and a developed sense of institutional loyalty that leads legislators to defend legislative prerogatives. One of the central pillars of the American system of government, at both the national and state levels, is that government performs best when separated institutions struggle for influence.

The JPTL research indicates that term limits have undermined legislatures' oversight functions for a variety of reasons. Perhaps the most significant impediment to effective oversight is the dramatic loss of experience in term-limited legislatures. It takes a great deal of time for legislators to learn about the scores of policy areas on which they are asked to make decisions and to understand the bureaucracies that implement those decisions. With the dramatic loss of experience and institutional memory induced by term limits, especially from the departure of long-term members, oversight becomes more difficult. In an observation typical of the JPTL interviewees, a Maine legislator noted that "the short time horizon of the members elected under term limits and their inexperience contribute to make the oversight function less effective" (Powell and Jones 2004, 52–53).

In California, the decline of oversight under term limits is most evident in looking at the number of supplemental budget requests made by the legislature. Overall, the number of such requests has declined considerably. The average number of requests before term limits was 199, compared with an average of 120 requests after term limits. Similarly, the number of agencies covered by such requests declined from sixty-one to fifty-one (Cain and Kousser 2004, 87–88). After term limits took effect, there was a significant decrease in the number of the legislature's requests for reports from the Bureau of State Audits. However, in recent years, the frequency of these requests has begun to rebound (although not yet to the levels before term limits), suggesting that legislators are beginning to understand the process of using the Bureau of State Audits (Cain and Kousser 2004, 88).

These same patterns in oversight are evident in other states as well. For example, the dominant point of view expressed by legislators and observers in Colorado and Ohio indicated that legislative oversight functions have become weaker under term limits (Farmer and Little 2004; Straayer and Bowser 2004). Similarly, in Maine, numerous interviewees bemoaned the lack of effective oversight under term limits. One Maine legislator lamented: "Committees used to do more oversight and would meet once a month. Committees should direct the activities of government and spend more time on oversight. They are not doing enough now" (Powell and Jones 2004, 56). As in California, legislators in Maine have begun to understand the difficulty term limits cause for oversight. In 2002, to address its need for more-effective oversight, the Maine legislature created the Office of Program Evaluation and Government Accountability (OPEGA), a professionally staffed, nonpartisan oversight agency housed within the legislature itself. Modeled after similar offices in more than forty other states, OPEGA was designed specifically to counteract the reduced policy expertise and institutional memory of the legislature under term limits.

Ironically, the politics surrounding the creation of OPEGA in Maine underscored the difficulties term-limited legislatures face in working with executives. Although it was created in 2002—during the last year of independent governor Angus King's term in office—full funding and implementation was delayed for over two years by the new, Democratic governor John Baldacci and his allies. Publicly, Baldacci questioned the fiscal prudence of creating a new agency during a time of severe financial strain in the state, although many observers expressed the opinion that he was merely acting to maintain the executive branch's position of advantage. At one point, the governor even attempted to get the new agency moved to the executive branch, a move that would have undercut the legislature's goal of strengthening its oversight function. Although OPEGA was eventually funded and implemented in 2005, the legislature's difficulty in breathing life into the new agency served as a reminder of the difficulties it faces in dealing with the executive branch under term limits.

Under term limits, oversight functions have suffered greatly. As time passes and institutional memory declines, the danger is that legislatures will no longer appreciate what has been lost. However, as the experience of the California and Maine legislatures demonstrates, state legislatures are adaptive institutions that generally find ways to adjust to new realities as best they can. These adaptations are discussed in much greater detail in chapter 10 in this volume.

Conclusion

Like many political reforms, term limits have had a host of unintended consequences. One of the most significant changes brought about by term limits has been an increase in the influence of governors and executive agencies at the expense of the legislatures. Although term limit advocates had hoped term limits would weaken legislatures and their leaders, they expected power to devolve to citizens rather than to officials in the executive branch. Clearly, the experience of U.S. state governments shows that executive-legislative relations can take a wide variety of forms, with some states favoring stronger legislatures and others favoring stronger executives. Nevertheless, all states depend to some extent on a formal separation of powers. The first decade of experience in American states with term limits shows that these reforms have reshaped executive-legislative relations in a significant way.

Whether one finds these changes to be positive or negative on the whole depends on one's perspective about key issues of political representation. Generally, the American constitutional system—at the national level and, in varying extents, in the states—has sought to construct a careful separation and balance of executive, legislative, and judicial powers. This constitutional scheme also creates a balance among different political constituencies. For example, legislators represent relatively small districts, with localized concerns, while governors represent a state as a whole, with generally more-heterogeneous constituencies. In general, term-limited states have seen a fracturing of political influence, with a migration of influence from legislatures to executives.

Perhaps more important, term limits contribute to a migration of power from elected representatives to nonelected officials, such as partisan legislative staffers (see chap. 6 in this volume) and bureaucrats in executive agencies. Under term limits, unelected careerist officials are at an informational advantage over relatively inexperienced legislators in terms of both policy expertise and institutional memory. This unintended consequence appears to be strongly contrary to the expectations of term limit support-ers, who generally touted term limits as a way to strengthen political responsiveness to majoritarian impulses. By transferring power to non-elected officials, term limits may actually reduce the relative weight given to the preferences of citizen majorities.

CHAPTER 10

Budgets and the Policy Process

Thad Kousser & John Straayer

LEGISLATURES ARE THE centerpieces in the American arrangement for the separation of powers. They are the policy bodies, representative in nature and entrusted with the responsibility of converting public preferences into public policies. At the heart of legislative power is control of the purse strings—the constitutional authority to tax and spend.

In this chapter, we examine the impact that term limits have had on state legislatures, specifically on their processes, policies, and budgets. While term limit advocates had high hopes for their reform with respect to changed legislative demographics and electoral competition, critics worried that the orderliness and integrity of legislative processes and the institutions themselves might suffer and that an interbranch shift in power would weaken the power of legislatures, including, most critically, their control over the public purse. Our analysis in this chapter rests on case studies in nine states, the 2003 Survey of Knowledgeable Observers conducted in those states by the Joint Project on Term Limits (JPTL), and the JPTL 2002 National Survey of State Legislators.

Public Policy

As other chapters in this book demonstrate, term limits have had a wide range of impacts on the legislative process. Member experience and knowledge has shrunk, as has their inclination and capacity to deal with complex, long-term issues (see chaps. 2 and 7). Leaders are weaker, often functioning as lame ducks from the moment they assume their leadership positions (see chap. 4). Committees generally screen bills less well, making their handiwork more susceptible to floor amendments (see chap. 5). The entire process is more partisan and less orderly, less civil (see chap. 7). But what impact have term limits had on the results of that process, the public's policies?

In their report on term limits in California, Bruce Cain and Thad Kousser observe, "Perhaps the most important question we can ask is whether or not term limits have affected the quality of bills produced." They are correct, of course, and they are also on target with their follow-up comment that "it is also the most difficult question we seek to answer" (Cain and Kousser 2004, 52). The difficulty, as always, lies in the purely normative problem of determining the components of quality. But while we cannot assess the impact of term limits against some purely objective measure of quality, we can say something about how the limits have impacted the types of bills and legislation and the policy orientation of legislators. We can also speculate about the effects term limits might have generated if they had produced all the changes that advocates sought.

Judging from the comments of legislators, lobbyists, staffers, and others in and around term-limited legislatures, one result has been increases in bills that are "goofy," "dumb," "smaller," "crappier," trivial, narrow in scope, and lacking in vision. These characterizations come from comments heard from participants and observers by the case study investigators. Pretty much across the board, observers contend that with term limits, more members are ideological and conservative and bring with them more of a social agenda. The new members often operate with a sense of urgency, concerned to introduce and enact what an insider from the Colorado executive branch termed "brochure bills," designed to build a member's résumé for the next election (Straayer and Bowser 2004, 38). A California staffer put it this way: "You get people wanting to have something to put on their campaign brochure so they can run for the next office" (Cain and Kousser 2004, 51). Reporting on his case study of Arizona, David Berman wrote, "Term limits, interviewees felt, encourages legislators to concentrate on 'littler' issues and short term problems for which there is an immediate payoff and to ignore the long term consequences of their decisions" (Berman 2004, 14).

Many bills rehash old ideas. An influential, longtime legislator in Colorado commented: "In the old days our issues were schools, taxes, and roads. Now they're education, revenues, and transportation." This view was shared and repeated, over and over, by observers in other states as well. The new members may not always know it, but what they think of as new and important is often old and, at least in the eyes of the old hands in the Capitol, not so important.

Among the most potentially consequential impacts of term limits is the forced exodus, in state after state, of what a veteran Colorado legislator characterized as "policy champions" (Straayer and Bowser 2004, 24). These are legislators who, after some initial years in the institution, come to specialize in an issue—perhaps mental health, transportation, or tax policy. They may spend years studying the problem, crafting and promoting legislation but losing, slowly refining their proposals, educating colleagues, and eventually building a winning coalition. Processes of this nature may take years, but then, many observers contend, the result is well thought out, well designed, remedial public policy. Good policy of this sort, many of the old-time legislative watchers lament, is proving to be a casualty of term limits.

The survey of observers confirms that many legislative insiders have noticed a decline in the levels of expertise that are necessary to make good policy. Table 10.1 summarizes responses to three questions about policy and process knowledge. The first asked observers whether legislators' knowledge about statewide issues had declined over the past ten years. In six states with term limits, the average response of 1.94 indicates that observers typically said that legislators were somewhat less knowledgeable about statewide issues than legislators were ten years before. In the three states without limits, the 2.82 average response indicates that observers typically judged knowledge levels to be about the same as they were ten years before. The difference between states with and without term limits is strong and statistically significant, showing that the observed decline is not caused by any nationwide trend toward less informed legislators. Similar responses to the other questions demonstrate that legislators in term-limited states have also become less knowledgeable about the legislative process and about issues before committees. Finally, the survey showed that knowledgeable observers viewed legislators under term limits as less concerned about clarity and precision in legislation and less apt to specialize in issue areas (see chap. 7).

These conclusions about expertise and policy content derive from perceptions of persons very familiar with the term-limited legislatures. The most extensive effort to nail down hard data on any change that term limits generated in policy was done in California. Cain and Kousser attempted to compare the breadth and complexity of law produced by the California legislature before and after term limits, by counting such items as bill lengths, the number of bill sections, and the range of code chapters affected. Based on the sorts of insider observations cited earlier in this chapter, they expected to find policy to be both narrower and less complex after term limits: "We expected to find that the scope of successful legislation had become narrower after term limits and that chaptered bills were now shorter and simpler" (Cain and Kousser 2004, 56). But the results produced a surprise; bills after term limits were both broader and more complex. This may be because California's large legislative staffs have enabled term-limited members to keep pace with increasingly complex policy questions, because interest groups have replaced the role of veterans and staff in bill drafting, or because term limits have simply not diminished the capacity of legislators to craft major bills.

In another attempt at empirical determination of the impact term limits have on policy, Straayer compared the policy orientations of the Colorado legislators first tossed out by the limits in 1998 to those of their replacements. Using the ratings of Colorado's environmental lobby and the National Federation of Independent Business, he compared the scores of both departing and entering members to the average scores of their party caucus colleagues. While the numbers for each of the four party caucuses were insufficient to produce a high level of confidence in the results,

TABLE 10.1.   Changes in Expertise over the Past Ten Years, as Reported in 2003 Survey of Knowledgeable Observers

Type of Expertise	Average Response in States with Term Limits (AZ, AR, CA, CO, ME, OH)	Average Response in States without Term Limits (IL, IN, KS)
Legislator knowledge about statewide issues	1.94*	2.82
Legislator knowledge about how the legislature operates	1.80*	2.70
Committee member knowledge about issues before the committee	1.96*	2.71

Note: Entries report the average change in legislators' levels of expertise over the past ten years, on a five-point scale. The ratings of current knowledge ranged from "Quite a Bit Less" (1) to "About the Same" (3) to "Quite a Bit More" (5).

*$p < .001$ (states with term limits vs. states without term limits)

they suggested that precious little had changed. At least for the cases examined in that exercise, it appears that voters sent to the legislature new members who voted pretty much like those they replaced (Straayer and Bowser 2004, 98–102).

These efforts to assess the impact term limits have on the substance of public policy—whether based on personal interview responses, the JPTL survey of observers, direct observation, or empirical analysis (with all its limitations)—bring us back to the earlier observation by Cain and Kousser. The most important question may well be the most difficult to answer. Indeed, in some ways, it is impossible to answer, for what constitutes good public policy is, in substantial measure, in the eyes of the beholder. Still, with a longtime horizon, it should be possible to come to some judgments as to consequences.

Beyond seeking to assess the impact term limits have on policy, it is interesting to speculate about impacts that did not occur, given the failure of the reform to produce some of the results anticipated by the promoters. Recall that various supportive groups envisioned more-diverse legislatures and greater electoral competition—perhaps even some changes in party balance and control. We know that both the political styles and the policy preferences of women legislators differ from those of their male counterparts. Democrats and Republicans differ on issues ranging from taxation to regulation to social controls. The policy orientations of nonwhite members often differ from those of whites, and nonwhite legislators are more likely to be Democrats than Republicans. Moreover, there is a widespread assumption that legislators representing competitive districts are more moderate than are members from lopsided, one-party districts. It would be reasonable to assume, then, that increased gender, ethnic, and party diversity and greater electoral competition would make a difference in the public policies enacted by state legislatures.

But for the most part, no increase in diversity or competition has materialized (see chap. 2). In California, there has been some increase in the number of nonwhite legislators since the introduction of term limits, but in all the other term-limited states, almost nothing has changed. The numbers of both female and nonwhite members have gone both up and down, revealing no clear pattern that we could tie to term limits. No widespread shifts in party control have paralleled the introduction of term limits. If more diversity and more competition held some promise of changes in public policy, it simply has not happened.

The Budget Process: Varied but Profound Effects

The effect of term limits on the process through which legislatures review and rewrite the governor's proposed budget varies across the six term-limited states in the case study. In Colorado, California, and Ohio, budgeting power has become increasingly concentrated in the hands of top legislative leaders as well as in their staffs. By contrast, frequent revolts on the floor have decentralized influence over the budget in Maine, Arizona, and Arkansas. One possible interpretation of the lack of uniformity in the perceived effects of term limits is that limits exert no causal influence at all. Since they do not push the budget process in the same direction everywhere, it could be argued that limits have no true effect anywhere and that observers are simply giving them credit for unrelated fluctuations in each state's budget process.

We argue for a different explanation. At the onset of term limits, state budget processes varied considerably. As limits began to shift the incentives and resources of legislators in complex ways, they moved houses that began at different starting points in different directions. The institutional arrangements in a legislature conditioned the effects of term limits. The diffusion of budget-writing power in Arizona was no less profound than the centralization of authority in Colorado, and both can be logically linked to the implementation of term limits in legislatures that began their transformations from very different places. We begin our analysis here by describing the broad structure of the budget process in each case study state. We then use the testimony of Capitol observers to show how term limits have altered the dynamics of influence within this general outline. We conclude by proposing a set of conditions that may predict whether term limits will lead to centralization or decentralization of power over the budget process.

Even though power over the budget was never equitably dispersed across their rank-and-file memberships, the legislatures of Colorado, Ohio, and California have seen budgeting authority become increasingly consolidated into the hands of a few members since the implementation of term limits. This effect has been especially strong in Colorado. In that state's hybrid between a full-time and a part-time legislature, the Joint Budget Committee (JBC) has consistently stood out as a strong and united committee with a professional staff supporting a citizen legislature. While the rest of the legislative body meets only until May in most years, the JBC holds meetings on and off all year and full-time throughout the legislative session. Although staff assistance is scarce in Colorado's General Assembly overall, the JBC is staffed by fifteen veteran analysts. The state's budget plan is contained in the "Long Bill," initially drafted by the JBC, which, as the official conference committee for the budget, also possesses an ex post veto. Because of these advantages, the six members of the JBC—which consists of the chairs of the Senate and House appropriations committees, as well as one majority and one minority member each from the House and Senate—have traditionally wielded great power over the budget process (Straayer and Bowser 2004, 90–91).

After term limits went into effect in Colorado's 1998 elections, the JBC's influence increased further. Prior to term limits, experienced members who were not on the JBC could challenge the committee's recommendations in their party caucuses and on the floor. When these veterans were forced out of the General Assembly, their replacements did not know enough about state agencies or the Long Bill to dispute the committee's recommendations. "On the budget," according to an official in the executive branch, "most of the other 94 members who are not on the JBC haven't a clue." Term limits also reduced the experience level of committee members, from an aggregate of fifty-seven years in the legislature in the 1997–98 session to twenty-eight years in 1999–2000, but the JBC's staff and full-time schedule gave it a huge informational advantage. Almost every Colorado observer noted that this always-powerful committee has become even more dominant since term limits, with many observers noting that the influence of its staffers has grown as well. "Budget control is slipping to the JBC, then to the JBC staff," remarked one observer. "That's where the budget knowledge is and knowledge is key" (Straayer and Bowser 2004, 104).

The hands that held budget power before term limits in Ohio and California have grabbed more and more control in both states, in the manner that the JBC did in Colorado. The majority caucus and its leaders have traditionally wielded great authority in the Buckeye state, dating from Vern Riffe's reign as House Speaker from 1975 to 1994 and Stan Aronoff's leadership of the Senate from 1989 to 1996 (Farmer and Little 2004, 7). These powerful leaders, in consultation with their party caucuses, made the key budget decisions before term limits. When limits brought 55 percent turnover in the House after the 2000 elections, there emerged a new leader, who had recruited, trained, and funded most of the rookie members. Speaker Larry Householder held the allegiance of these members and was able, over four years, to demand their loyalty on budget votes as on most other matters (Farmer and Little 2004, 7).

Even though none of California's five Speakers after term limits has rivaled the power once held by Willie Brown, leaders in that state have grown even more central to the budget process than they were before limits went into effect in 1996. Budget negotiations in Sacramento often come down to summerlong staring contests between the "Big Five," the governor and the majority and minority leaders in each house. These leaders—often the most experienced of those left in California's legislature—are advised by cadres of veteran staffers, while rank-and-file members usually employ former campaign workers who are unacquainted with the intricacies of the state's budget of over one hundred billion dollars. Since term limits, the budget subcommittees that include many members in each house have become less influential. The leadership-selected Budget Conference Committee that reviews their proposals can now open up any budget line, even if both the Senate and the Assembly were in agreement on it. Neither of these changes are entirely the result of term limits. But because the institutional prerogatives of the Big Five and the conference committee are so strong now, term limits have left inexperienced and inexpertly staffed new members with little influence over the state's spending plan (Cain and Kousser 2004).

That pattern has been reversed in Maine, Arizona, and Arkansas, where rank-and-file members are now arguably more powerful in the budgeting process than they were before term limits. Formal budgeting powers in all of these states were already relatively dispersed when limits first came into effect. In the wake of stalled legislative-executive negotiations that led to a government shutdown in 1991, Maine opened up its budgeting process. The Joint Standing Committee on Appropriations and Financial Affairs, which used to work with top leaders to write the budget, began to work with the relevant policy committees to review each agency's requests. The nonpartisan staff of the Legislative Fiscal Office started to produce background reports and train all members on the budget process and became less involved in behind-the-scenes budget negotiations (Powell and Jones 2004, 49–50). When term limits were implemented in 1996, these diffusions of institutional power left the new, less experienced leaders without as much power over the budget. In 2001, veteran senators used their knowledge to rewrite the budget passed out of the appropriations committee, a break from tradition that would not have been tolerated in the days when the powerful Speaker John Martin led the House (Powell and Jones

2004, 51). One observer noted that term limits have accelerated a process already in motion: "In the past there was more of the 'smoke-filled' rooms and now it is more open. Policy committees have more say in the budget process. This is both related to term limits and is a natural progression of where the process was heading" (Powell and Jones 2004, 54).

While experienced senators led the revolt against centralized budget power in Maine, rookie House members took on their leaders over the direction of state spending in Arizona. In 1999, on the eve of term limit implementation, sixteen moderate Republicans in the House formed a "Mushroom Coalition" to protest the way that they had been "kept in the dark and covered with bull" (Berman 2004, 4). Many were first-term members, and they focused their demands on obtaining greater inclusion in the budget process. Legislative leaders were forced to give in because they possessed no formal mechanisms to keep the rank-and-file in line on the budget. Their informal source of power—the ability to punish and reward members in the future—was about to be taken away by term limits. One member of the Mushroom Coalition proclaimed that term limits "have liberated us," adding: "The Speaker will be gone in a year. He can't put me in the doghouse for the next ten years." The 2003 budget negotiations also brought a rebellion by twenty rank-and-file members who felt that term limits gave them an incentive to change policy quickly. "This group is more in a hurry," said one member about the uprising of newcomers, "and is not willing to blindly follow leaders" (Berman 2004, 5). Without a mechanism like Colorado's JBC or California's Big Five to control the flow of information and power, Arizona's leaders left themselves open to a mutiny on the floor.

In Arkansas, the budgeting power in the citizen legislature has traditionally been derived from the knowledge of a core of veteran members who served on the Joint Budget Committee. In the old days, English and Weberg report, "it was not unusual for legislators to simply overrule a contract or a program that they didn't like and it was not a complete surprise for a senior legislator to eliminate a personnel item in the budget to issue revenge" (Joint Project on Term Limits 2002, 18). Budgeting power was centralized in the hands of the senior members, a situation that resulted from their experience levels rather than from a large committee staff or from parliamentary prerogatives. After term limits removed these veterans in 1998, the joint committee lost much of its power.

The three states in which budget-writing power became decentralized after term limits have much in common, as do the states in which small groups have consolidated their authority. Maine, Arizona, and Arkansas are all part-time bodies. When term limits came into effect, the budgeting power of leaders or a top committee was not guaranteed by any firm rules or the control of any key resources. Floor leaders or budget committee members may have been powerful, but their powers rested on their experience (as in Arkansas and Maine) or on their threats of future punishments (as in Arizona). After term limits repopulated legislatures and shortened the time horizons of their members, these informal advantages disappeared. As power dissipated, budget authority became dispersed across the bodies.

By contrast, the parliamentary privileges and staffing resources possessed by the budget writers in Colorado and California insulated them against a similar loss in power. Because they were able to control knowledge, term limits made them even more powerful, as limits stripped rank-and-file legislators and their staffs of the experience levels necessary to challenge budget recommendations. In Ohio, the centralization of budgeting power appears a bit more precarious. It relies on the overall power of leaders—especially Speaker Householder—who have used the turnover created by term limits to their advantage. Unless the Speaker enshrines budgeting powers in a permanent institution, they may spread out across the legislature.

Even if the future of Ohio politics remains cloudy, it is clear that past budget-writing arrangements and patterns have conditioned the effects of term limits on legislatures today. Where institutions helped a small set of leaders lock in their power at the outset of term limits, their power has grown as limits have come into effect. But legislatures without these formal arrangements were set on a different path and have seen their budgeting power decentralized. The varied effects of term limits on the centralization of budgeting power should be taken not as evidence against the causal impact of limits but as further confirmation of the path-dependent nature of political processes.

Budget Outcomes: Power Slips to the Executive Branch

No matter what conditions were present in a state on the eve of term limits, the limits shifted control over the broad direction and narrow minutiae of state spending toward the executive branch. This effect has been significant and measurable. Whether a legislature traditionally exerted strong influence over the budget—as Colorado's General Assembly did over its Long Bill—or whether it has customarily followed the governor's lead in crafting a state spending plan, its influence declined with the implementation of term limits. Over the same time period, the legislative-executive balance of budgeting power remained fairly constant in our control states. The effect of term limits is made clear and its causal pathways are explained in the interviews conducted by case study researchers. Statistically significant trends in the survey of observers provide numerical backing for this finding, as do archival records of the battles over budget lines. This section of this chapter lays out the qualitative and quantitative evidence for one of term limits' most troubling effects (from the standpoint of legislative institution advocates): each legislature's grip on its state's purse strings is slipping ever farther into the hands of the governor and executive officials. Our findings here are consistent with those presented by Richard Powell in chapter 9 of this volume.

Interviewees across the country report that when term limits remove veteran members, legislatures lose the expertise in the intricacies of budgeting that is needed to exert meaningful control over state agencies. "The executive branch is clearly driving the budget process," said one observer of Maine politics. "It was like this before, but much more so now because of lack of legislative experience." Another Augusta expert, who pointed out that the governor was becoming more powerful, noted "hesitancy on the part of legislators to challenge the budget," as they "are fine tuning around the edges." A third Mainer stated, "Bureaucrats become empowered on issues because of a loss of institutional knowledge" (Powell and Jones 2004, 57–62). One staffer in California offered a different rationale for that state's increase in executive power: "On the budget, members will be much more interested in their pork after term limits, because they don't have time there to do something tangible on the bigger scale. They are much more susceptible to getting picked off with pork" (Cain and Kousser 2004, 78).

The power shift toward the executive branch has been more gradual—but present nonetheless—in the citizen legislatures of Arizona and Arkansas. Some interviewees in Arizona felt that the increasing power of governors might be due to the individual characteristics of some chief executives. Others, though, "saw term limits giving agency heads an advantage in dealing with legislators on budgeting matters" (Berman 2004, 15). In Arkansas, those who had participated in budget hearings reported that "inexperienced legislators did not know what questions to ask administrators" and that "agency heads were able to pull the wool over the eyes of novice legislators very easily." They added, "This apparently is not like the old days when the powerful senior-dominated Joint Budget Committee could and did intimidate agency heads" (Joint Project on Term Limits 2002, 18).

In Colorado, the Joint Budget Committee previously kept the legislature strong in the budgeting process, but today's high levels of turnover have eroded some of this power. "The budget is the biggest example of the downside of term limits," one observer asserted. "Virtually all members haven't a clue as to the contents of the budget. It is complicated and they are uneducated, inexperienced." The JBC's veteran staff has compensated to some extent for this loss of knowledge. "The JBC staff is more influential," noted an eyewitness to Denver's budget battles, but overall "the legislature has lost power to the governor" (Straayer and Bowser 2004, 104). Some in Colorado attribute this trend to Governor Bill Owens's urge to control information flows and budget outcomes, just as Ohio experts note the difficulty of separating the effects of term limits from the impact of the powerful Speaker Larry Householder. Due to Householder's tight control over his Republican caucus in the House, Ohio is the one exception to the rule that term limits have compromised legislative power. A survey revealed that 72 percent of insiders from Columbus, Ohio, judged that the governor had lost power to the legislature since the implementation of term limits. This may be a permanent trend or simply a reflection of current personalities. Case study researchers reported that "many of those interviewed believe that eventually the executive branch will dominate because it speaks with one voice and has a very large staff" (Farmer and Little 2004, 14).

There is less uncertainty in the case study's non-term-limited states, where none of the researchers noted a decline in legislative control over the budget. Increasing partisan strife in Indiana has ended the tradition in which both parties' members on the budget committee would get together over the summer and then present a consensus budget, but case study researchers did not note that this harmed the legislature's power (Wright and Ogle 2004, 7). The governor of Illinois has long been and has remained dominant in that state's budget negotiations (Mooney and Storey 2004, 12–13). Finally, researchers in Kansas, where the budget is written in a frenzy during the closing nights of session, found no systematic changes in the legislative-executive balance of budgeting power.

The survey of observers, conducted in all of these states, backs up the testimony provided in case studies. It asked respondents to report how power relationships had changed in state capitols over the past decade, comparing the influence of legislators to other players, such as the governor, administrative agencies, lobbyists, and staffers. Although it did not specifically prompt the observers to comment on budget outcomes, this is the primary realm in which legislatures annually clash with governors and agency heads. Comparing power shifts since term limits with reported shifts in control states over the same time period provides a quantitative test of the proposition that term limits have shifted budgeting power to the executive branch. Figure 10.1 confirms this proposition.

Setting aside the relationship between Ohio's General Assembly and its governor, figure 10.1 reveals that a growth of the power of governors and agency officials in term-limited states has occurred contemporaneously with a decline in executive authority in control states. On average, survey respondents reported an increase in the governor's influence in five of the six term-limited states, but only a weak rise in one of the three control states. Ohio's legislature has grown in power with the strong speakership of Larry Householder, but we have already noted that this may be a temporary phenomenon. Excluding Ohio, the difference between these sets of states was statistically significant, with a confidence level of 95 percent. Respondents in term-limited states were also significantly more likely to note an increase in the power of administrative agencies.

Another quantitative measure of the effects of term limits looks at budget records to see how much legislatures altered the line-by-line proposals of governors. This measure of the legislative-executive balance of power comes from archival research first presented and more fully described elsewhere by Kousser (2005, chap. 6). It focuses on two budget areas (health care and higher education) over which states exert considerable discretion and that are not fully determined by caseload shifts or other demographic factors. For each state, Kousser (2005) reports legislative adjustments to executive budgets, compiled from line-by-line comparisons of the governors' initial proposals to the final spending plans. To test the effects of term limits, he looks at the size of legislative adjustments made in comparable sessions—matched up by the state's party balance and its fiscal condition—held before and after term limits in four states. To make sure that term limits were responsible for any observed shifts, he conducts the same comparison over time for two states that never enacted term limits.

The central finding, which holds in all four term-limited states and does not depend on the state's level of legislative professionalism, is that

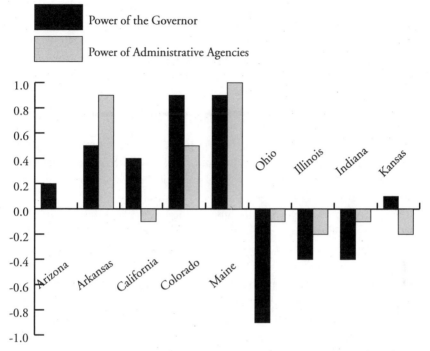

Fig. 10.1.   Power shifts reported in 2003 Survey of Knowledgeable Observers. *Note:* Bars represent average reported shifts over the past decade in the influence of the governor or administrative agencies, relative to the influence of the legislature. The power ratings ranged from "Stayed about the Same" (0) to "Increased Some" (1) to "Increased a Great Deal" (2). Negative scores represent an increase in legislative power. No measured change for administrative agencies in Arizona.

term limits have led to a decline in legislative budgeting power. Legislatures that have been stripped of their veteran leadership make far fewer amendments to the governor's budget proposals. This effect is largest in Colorado, where legislative adjustments declined from changes totaling 10.3 percent of the budget before the implementation of term limits to changes totaling 2.1 percent afterward. The extent to which the legislature rewrote the governor's budget also declined in California (from 16.2 to 6.7 percent), in Oregon (from 6.1 to 4.0 percent), and in Maine (from 26.5 to 19.2 percent). As a check on the finding that implementation of term limits diminishes a legislature's bargaining power, Kousser (2005) provides parallel numbers for control states with professional (Illinois) and citizen (New Mexico) legislatures. Instead of declining, legislative power over budget outcomes increased in these states over the period that limits were being imposed elsewhere. Combined with data from the survey of observers and the testimony of Capitol insiders, these budget records clearly demonstrate that term limits have led to a significant erosion of legislative independence in the state budgeting process.

Generalizing Our Findings to Other States

Are the trends that we observe by comparing six term-limited states to three control cases specific to our sample, or can they be generalized across the country? As a check on the universality of our conclusions, we compared the lessons from our case studies to the findings of the JPTL survey of legislators. The survey results support the finding that term limits have brought a significant power shift toward the executive branch all across the country.

Respondents in states that had already implemented term limits reported higher levels of power for both governors and bureaucrats/civil servants than did legislators in non-term-limited states. On a seven-point scale running from "No Influence" to "Dictates Policy," term-limited legislators scored governors about half a point higher than their colleagues did and rated bureaucrats 0.36 points higher. Neither of these differences existed for legislators in states that adopted but had not yet implemented limits. Even with their time horizons shortened, members of these houses retained the experience and expertise necessary to stand up to the executive branch (Carey et al. 2006). These survey results confirm our findings that term limits shift power to the executive and suggest that the steep drop in legislative experience brought by the implementation of limits is the causal pathway that this effect follows.

Adaptations

Many of the most purposeful and consequential legislative adaptations to term limits have been made to enrich orientation and training programs for new members. These efforts receive in-depth treatment by Alan Rosenthal in chapter 11 of this volume. We confine our treatment here to other types of changes specifically related to policy and budgeting.

Most adaptations have taken the form of developing material or making institutional adjustments designed to quickly bring new members up to speed on budget and policy issues. In most of the term-limited states, there have been additional budget briefings by staff members. In Ohio, the Speaker led an effort to recruit and train candidates and then provide training in floor and committee work. The party caucus was used for policy deliberations, and the caucus staff provided policy advice.

In Colorado, both leaders and staffers made several early moves aimed at keeping the policy and budgetary processes moving along smoothly. Russell George, the first Speaker after term limits, asked the chief clerk of the House to develop a timeline, a listing of dates and deadlines that leaders would have to meet with respect to signatures, reports, appointments, and the like. Staff of both the Legislative Council and the Joint Budget Committee assembled notebooks containing significant constitutional, statutory, and case law information for new members and their new leaders. The JBC invited members to meet with them to ask budget questions and provide input, though as it turned out, few members took advantage of such opportunities.

Other common adaptations have been changes in committee appointment practices, especially concerning appointments to important fiscal bodies. Since term limits, leaders in Colorado have made appointments to the JBC with an eye toward ensuring some continuity in that powerful body's membership. In California, some members who were selected to serve on Senate and Assembly budget committees in the next session "shadowed" current members to learn the process and its politics. Leaders in California also appointed members to prestigious fiscal committees earlier in their careers than in the past, in order to give them more years of service. Ohio's Senate president Dick Finan adapted to term limits by putting a mixture of old and new members on the Finance Committee to provide for policy continuity (Kousser 2005, epilogue).

Another strategy, not unique to term-limited states but perhaps particularly valuable to them, has been to use technology to help new members after term limits quickly get up to speed on policies. The Arkansas General Assembly provides its members with laptop computers so that they can access background information during committee hearings. The online reports supplied by Florida's Office of Program and Policy Analysis and Government Accountability and by the Colorado Legislative Information and Communications System help to compensate for lost institutional knowledge. Finally, after term limits, the members of the professional staffs who write these reports spend more time describing their roles to new members.

Conclusion

Term limits have loosened legislatures' control over the purse strings of state spending, made their policy-making processes more chaotic and confrontational, and eroded their already-weak capacity to oversee the implementation of their policies. The testimony of observers of all partisan stripes from across the nation confirms the findings of quantitative analyses of budget records and surveys. Inexperienced legislators, even those who serve on powerful fiscal committees, simply do not have the knowledge of state government or the politics of budget negotiations to write their house's will into their state's final spending plan. The policy process has been reshaped by the drop in experience levels, the election in some states of more ideologically polarized members, and the decline (except in the case of Ohio) of the power of leaders. This has sometimes led to frenzy and rancor, with legislative traditions and deadlines often cast aside, old policy debates recycled, and compromise harder to reach. When legislators do settle on decisions, members have diminished incentives and resources to watch the executive branch closely as it implements their policy choices.

It is important to note the areas in which term limits have brought no measurable change or where its effects have varied across states. We found no concrete evidence that the legislation produced by term-limited states was systematically different; in fact, a California study showed that limits brought no slowing in the state's long-term trend toward writing broader and more complex bills. While term limits shifted the budget-writing power within all of our case study legislatures, it centralized authority in three of those states but dispersed it in three others. The level of district-specific pork spending did not appear to be strongly affected by term limits.

Still, in two important legislative functions, control over the budget and control over the policy process, the worst fears of term limit critics have been realized. By altering legislatures in these ways, term limits have shifted the overall balance in power between the branches of state government. Term-limited legislatures are less capable of checking executive power over the budget than they were before limits. Many observers noted that because of the chaos of the policy-making process in these legislatures, major issues are now resolved outside of them—by governors, interest groups, or initiatives. In these concrete and troubling ways, term limits have reduced the role of the legislative branch of state governments.

Education and Training of Legislators

Alan Rosenthal

LEGISLATIVE ADAPTATION IS for the most part an unconscious process and is ongoing. Legislatures face constant change in their environments. As political institutions, they try to be responsive to the public, to the media, to interest groups, to trends, to exemplary practices, to many things. Rarely, however, are legislatures faced with as fundamental a change to the institution and process as has been wrought by term limits. Rarely, too, do they consciously try to adapt to minimize the negative effects of change that has largely been imposed from outside.

Why Legislatures Need to Adapt

There is no mistaking the effects of term limits on the states that, in every case but one, had limits imposed on them by the statewide electorate. It was obvious from the beginning that the immediate effects would be to increase turnover and reduce experience in state legislatures. Other effects were also projected by commentators and scholars (Benjamin and Malbin 1992). Undeniably, term limits promise to cut short the legislative careers of members elected to serve.

In chapter 2 of this volume, Gary Moncrief, Lynda W. Powell, and Tim Storey explore the effects of term limits on legislator turnover. Although term limits generally affect Houses more than Senates, both bodies experience higher turnover with term limits. Higher turnover, of course, means more new members in the legislature. Higher turnover also means fewer years of legislative experience and the complete removal of the most senior members from legislative ranks.

As far as the legislature is concerned, these changes in membership have two major drawbacks: first, because legislators are less experienced, they have less knowledge and less skill in working the legislative process; and second, because legislators are less experienced, they have less knowledge of and expertise with regard to policy issues with which the legislature deals. In the 2003 Survey of Knowledgeable Observers conducted by the Joint Project on Term Limits (JPTL) in six term-limited and three non-term-limited states, respondents were asked whether "in comparison to their counterparts a decade or more ago," current legislators were "more or less likely" to "be knowledgeable about statewide issues" and to "be knowledgeable about how the legislature operates." Respondents generally found current legislators to be less knowledgeable on both counts, with knowledge being rated less in the term-limited than in the non-term-limited states. Adaptation, therefore, could usefully be directed toward providing legislators knowledge about the issues and both knowledge and skill with respect to the lawmaking process itself.

What Adaptation Entails

Different actors in the process adapt differently to term limits. For example, legislators have to adjust their political careers in light of the certainty of having to leave the office they hold by a specified time. No longer can they pursue a career of indefinite length in one house or the other, while preparing themselves to run for higher office if the prospects for such a race appear promising. The eviction notice is part and parcel of the lease; they have it as soon as they move in. This means that term-limited legislators have to plan quickly for their postlegislative service. Lobbyists also have to adapt to term limits. They no longer can conduct business the old-fashioned way, relying heavily on a network of relationships that are already in place. Relationships in term-limited legislatures are more difficult to cultivate, because time, which relationships take to build, is limited. Lobbyists therefore have to put greater effort into relationship building or have to devise other approaches to maintain their influence.

The focus here is how the legislature as an institution, rather than the legislator as an individual, adapts. Many possible adaptation strategies exist; most remain theoretical possibilities, without having been put into practice. One way to increase the time available to members and supplement their experience would be to expand the number of days the legislature is in session. Even the so-called full-time legislatures (e.g., in California, Michigan, and Ohio) could become somewhat more full-time than they are now. Part-time legislatures (e.g., in Arizona, Colorado, Louisiana, Maine, and Oregon) could certainly become less part-time. But there is little likelihood that the days legislatures spend in session will increase in order for members to gain experience.

Alternative ways of affording members knowledge and skill have been put into practice. For example, caucus staffs in Oregon and Colorado were expanded to compensate for legislators' lack of experience (Kousser 2005, 214–20). A few meritorious programs were devised. Colorado adopted a "buddy system," in which a senior member of the nonpartisan staff paired up with a legislator through the latter's tenure in the legislature. In Maine, veteran legislators were paired up with newly elected colleagues. In a few states, such as Arkansas, the House restructured its standing committee system so that newly elected members could take on leadership responsibility right away. By creating subcommittees, the Arkansas House managed to appoint forty out of the one hundred members to positions as chair or vice-chair.

The amount of information furnished legislators in term-limited states was expanded. Nonpartisan staffs in legislative service agencies quickly realized that they would have to demonstrate their value to new legislators. Nearly everywhere, they made efforts to provide additional information, of a timely nature and artfully packaged. The fiscal staff in Maine began to produce more summary documents for members of the appropriations committees, and the staff of the Joint Budget Committee in Colorado started to provide more materials for members. Meanwhile, the clerk of the House in Colorado saw the need for distributing more information to members on legislative policies, procedures, and process. In adapting, Colorado also hastened the establishment of a computerized information and communication system to provide legislators what they needed to do their jobs better.

The Special Role of Education and Training

On-the-job training used to be the dominant mode of learning for legislators. It is still dominant, but now it is supplemented by classroom-type training that is delivered to new members. According to two senior members of the staff of the National Conference of State Legislatures (NCSL), "legislatures today no longer have the luxury of time for members to learn through observation and osmosis" (Feustel and Jones 2001). Jump-starting the learning process through an orientation program for new members is a feature in just about every legislature nowadays; it is an especially vital one in the term-limited states.

The Legislative Effectiveness Committee of NCSL surveyed the state of legislative training programs late in 2001, almost a decade after the initial enactment of term limits. In a 2002 report titled "New Member Orientation Survey Results," NCSL suggested that a nationwide effort was to bring legislators up to speed even before they began their actual work. The curriculum varied, but most legislatures appeared to be covering the bill enactment process, leadership powers and duties, the roles of caucuses, legislative staff, committees, rules and procedures, media and lobbyist relations, and a plethora of administrative details. Half the Senates and Houses reporting in the survey indicated that they also used mock floor sessions, and one-quarter indicated that they used mock committee hearings. A large number also included an ethical component in their training. In most cases, the orientations ran for one or two days, although in a few states, it resumed from time to time during the course of the legislative session.

Legislative orientations have been a staple for years. If not already in existence, they were recommended by legislative committees, citizens commissions, and consultants who were engaged in the legislative modernization movement of the late 1960s, 1970s, and early 1980s. By the time term limits swept initiative states, orientations for new members were being offered just about everywhere, more often by Houses, which had to manage substantial turnover, than by Senates, which had relatively few new members every two years (a number of them not new to the legislature, in that they had served previously in the House). The seriousness with which the states approached the training and the resources they committed to it ranged widely, but on the whole, the training of new members seldom was legislative leadership's top priority. Indeed, it was not unusual for orientation sessions to be scheduled at the same time as party caucuses, committee meetings, or other functions. In such circumstances, members would be inclined to miss the training session in order to attend the session where they would be engaged in their immediate work. When push comes to shove, training accommodates more pressing legislative concerns.

Term limits brought a heightened sense of urgency to the states that were being affected by higher turnover and shorter tenure. New members, it was thought, would have to be brought up to speed much more rapidly than before. They no longer would have enough time on the job to learn on the job; they would have to learn earlier. Speaker Larry Householder of Ohio explained that in term-limited states, "freshmen are players from day one, carrying major bills and handling major assignments" (Householder 2001). The result was the expansion of training programs, among other steps, to minimize negative consequences (Little 2001). NCSL's survey indicates that orientation sessions are longer than they used to be in each of eleven term-limited states reporting and that training takes place throughout the year in eight of these states .

There is no doubt that the states impacted by term limits responded with greater effort to train newly elected House members. California went the farthest. Under Speaker Robert Herzberg, it established the California Assembly Program for Innovative Training and Orientation for the Legislature (CAPITOL) Institute. The program was designed to be comprehensive and to extend over ten days. Colorado also took orientation more seriously. Before term limits, Colorado's orientation for new members was two and one-half days. By 1996, it had been expanded to four days: a half day in November; two half days in December; and one and one-half days in January, before the start of the session. In 1998, when term limits took effect in Colorado, the orientation was expanded to eight days: one and one-half days in early November; three days in mid-November; two days in early December; and one and one-half days in January, before the session.

In Missouri, the legislature's orientation increased to five days, in addition to a two-week bus trip in which new members visited state institutions, facilities, and programs. The Arkansas House, under Speaker Shane Broadway, began to offer periodic sessions of continuing education, and Arizona held a three-day orientation, followed by other meetings. Florida's House held four three-day sessions for new members, while Maine added sessions on policy issues and continued its statewide bus tour and mentoring programs. In Ohio, Householder began to offer sessions on policy issues for prospective new members even before the ongoing orientation conducted by the Ohio Legislative Service Commission was expanded and moved from Capitol Square to a retreat setting outside the city. However, the amount and nature of the training in term-limited states has not been steady. It has varied from biennium to biennium, depending largely on the degree of support furnished by legislative leaders.

Training has sometimes been designed for all new legislators, but it has sometimes been conducted separately by the Senate and House. Training has also been done by the legislative party for its own members, with objectives that are not the same as those of bipartisan training programs. Partisan training is not new; in New Jersey, the legislative parties and their staffs have been using the partisan approach to training for years. In term-limited states, the trend toward the legislative parties and their leaders taking responsibility for orienting new members appears to be on the rise.

The increase in partisan training may be part of the general rise in partisanship in state legislatures, especially term-limited ones. Majority leaders tend to allocate more decision-making authority to their caucuses, in part perhaps because committees have been losing expertise and influence in the lawmaking process. One scholar reports that leaders in six of the term-limited states have increased the number of their caucus meetings and that leaders in several states have stepped up their activity in the recruitment of party candidates (Little 2001). Such efforts are often accompanied by partisan training of one sort or another. For example, in Ohio, Speaker Householder focused (more than his predecessors) on bringing along new Republican House members. He helped recruit them and then offered them training at a special retreat. Then, after the standing committee had made its budget recommendations, Householder presented them to the majority caucus for deliberation. As a consequence, according to the Speaker, the budget contained the fingerprints of every member of the Republican caucus, which then voted unanimously for it (Householder 2001). Training Republican House members was simply part of a larger partisan-oriented enterprise, which appears, to some extent, to have been an unanticipated product of term limits.

The creation of partisan staff in legislative bodies predated term limits. Partisan staff did not cause partisanship, but it did strengthen it (Rosenthal 1970). Similarly, training by the legislative parties—especially if it supplants, rather then supplements, training of a nonpartisan nature—will not in itself cause partisanship where none would otherwise exist. But it can be expected to make partisan views and considerations more salient and hence to increase partisanship. An important question is how partisan and nonpartisan elements can be combined and balanced in the training of new members. In the following examination of training and how it helps legislatures adapt to term limits, our focus is on the nonpartisan elements (while we recognize, of course, that partisan ones may be operating as well).

How Training Can Be Assessed

Members of the legislative community believe that training efforts are of benefit to new members and, by extension, to the legislature itself. In the national survey undertaken by the Joint Project on Term Limits, legislators were asked to rate the importance of the formal training program they took when first elected. In term-limited states, 25 percent of the respondents rated them very important, while in the non-term-limited states, 18 percent rated them likewise, suggesting that it made slightly more of a difference to those whose terms were limited. The JPTL survey of observers produced similar results. According to them, more frequent and important training for legislators was considered to be somewhat helpful (but not, it should be noted, very helpful). Still, as far as these observers were concerned, there was nothing they thought more helpful than training. Overall, however, these knowledgeable observers did not perceive that training for legislators was much improved compared to ten years earlier.

As could be predicted, these results varied among the states. In Colorado, where a significant effort had been made, John Straayer and Jennie Bowser (2004, 118) concluded that "the enhanced orientation appears to have been an important and somewhat effective antidote to the diminishment of legislative experience brought about by term limits." By contrast, in Arizona, David Berman (2004) reported that members were aware of an increase in training but that they doubted it did much; in their judgment, it was of marginal value only.

It is difficult to know what standards legislators and knowledgeable observers have in mind when they rate the training. Most of them probably make use of no particular standards but, instead, are predisposed to believe that training ought to and therefore probably does produce better legislators. What can we expect from legislator training? Can we really expect an improvement in the "quality" of members themselves and hence in the quality of the legislative process?

Figuring out whether legislator training has beneficial effects on individuals and on processes is a challenge, to say the least. To meet such a challenge, we would initially have to be able to specify what a "good" legislator is, so that we could recognize a "better" one after training. Similarly, we would need some idea of what "good" and "better" processes are. It would be necessary to be able to measure qualities of goodness in both legislators and the legislature. Then, even more difficult, our measurement procedure would have to demonstrate that enhancements of training, independent of other factors, had produced improvements in the quality of members and of processes.

These challenges are well beyond the resources of the current project. Political scientists have yet to agree on what a "good" legislator or a "good" process is, let alone a method of measuring each. They are even further away from being able to control for diverse factors that could cause changes that might at first be attributed to training. Yet initial steps can be taken in devising standards that ought to be met for training to be considered effective.

Our approach to setting out such standards here is to examine what might be considered a model training program, one that can be compared to programs in other states, particularly states with term limits. Georgia provides such a model, with a training program that is widely regarded as effective. To study this model, I conducted interviews in February 2005 with legislators in the state capitol, Atlanta, and with staff at the Carl Vinson Institute of Government (CVIG) at the University of Georgia, in Athens.

Georgia does not have a term-limited legislature, and its turnover rates have not been particularly high, although they rose in 2004 because of the Republican surge in the state. Georgia has a citizen legislature, with relatively little professional staff at its disposal, even though it is one of the most populous states in the nation. The legislature meets for a compressed time of forty legislative days each year, so there is not much leeway for on-the-job training during the session. It is significant, however, that the Georgia General Assembly enhances its lawmaking capacity by contracting with CVIG for research, training, and other services.

Legislators in Georgia are extraordinarily positive in the evaluations of the training they have been receiving for almost half a century at CVIG's Biennial Institute for Georgia Legislators, held just after each biennial election and before the beginning of the following session. An examination of training in Georgia suggests a number of standards, ones that ought also to apply to other states—whether term-limited or not. Programs for training need not measure up to each and every standard, but if they fall too far short on a number of them, we ought to question how effective the training can be in overcoming the disabilities inflicted by term limits.

1.   *For training to have a chance of achieving positive results, members must at the very least attend.*
Woody Allen was not just kidding when he said that showing up is 90

percent of life. There is never a guarantee that members will attend or participate in a training program put on for their benefit. Attendance varies, among members in non-term-limited as well as term-limited states. At the initiation of a program, such as the California Assembly's CAPITOL Institute, legislators did attend. They learned specifics about how to set up their staffs and deal with travel, as well as general information about the process and legislative ethics. At subsequent sessions, however, legislators failed to show up, preferring to learn about bill writing and the budget informally, from colleagues. According to Bruce Cain and Thad Kousser (2004, 106), who investigated California for this project, "the appetite for legislator training is probably limited." So since its early days, CAPITOL has focused more on training staff than on training legislators; staff are more inclined to attend training. In Colorado, training attendance also fell off when the legislative staff tried, after the initial orientation, to deliver an additional education program to members. By then, the Colorado legislators confronted the day-to-day pressures of the session and became absorbed in their representational and lawmaking tasks. Continuing education was no longer among their priorities.

By contrast, the Biennial Institute in Georgia has had a remarkable attendance record over a long period of time. Biennium after biennium, virtually every new legislator shows up for the institute—even though, until recently, those who had just been elected had to pay their own expenses, because they had not yet been sworn in. The unique feature of the training here is that not only new members but returning members are expected to attend. A number of returning members are on the program, and all of them receive both training in common with and different from that of their new colleagues. All told, anywhere from 210 to 220 out of the total 236 senators and representatives in Georgia turn out for the Biennial Institute. That attendance record is tough to match.

The advantages of training new and returning members together in one place and at one time are obvious. First, training in Georgia is not intended simply for those who have yet to serve; it is intended also for those in their early, middle, and later careers. The assumption is that legislators with experience can benefit as much as those without experience. Second, the training treats the legislature as a whole: new and returning House and Senate members all attend. At the institute, members not only see themselves as in, say, the Class of 2004 or as Senate Republicans or House Democrats; they also see themselves as members of the Georgia General Assembly.

The first training standard is not an easy one to meet. If training is to be effective in term-limited (as well as non-term-limited) legislatures, it must be universal, with high participation rates. It must involve not only new members or those who choose to attend but everyone.

2. *The formal content of training has to be of sufficient quantity and of high quality.*

According to member evaluations, the Georgia legislature does a good job as far as substance and delivery of training are concerned. Although the program is not without criticism from legislators (e.g., that too much is packed into too little time or that one policy issue or another is omitted), the evaluations are always excellent. Most recently, ten of the twelve 2004 sessions were rated by participants at 5 or above on a 6-point scale (with 6 as the highest rating). The other two sessions received ratings between 4 and 5. Over time, the program of the Biennial Institute has changed, from an early concentration on the nuts and bolts of serving in the legislature to a balance among discussions of policy issues, sessions on skill building, and simulations of the legislative process.

Take the 2004 Biennial Institute, for example, which was held for three days in Athens, in addition to a day at the Capitol and a lunch in Atlanta for new members and their spouses. New members had special training, but all members received training on negotiation and consensus building, strengthening the connection between legislators and citizens, and accountability in budgeting. All of them also had the opportunity to discuss issues that were affecting the state and were likely be taken up at the forthcoming session—such as education funding, Medicaid, and transportation. Only during programs like this do legislators get to view issues broadly, rather than as bills and amendments, which is what issues get translated into during the legislative session itself.

Georgia's legislature is not the only one that has done its job delivering the goods. Elsewhere, legislative leaders, special committees, and staff have been adept in formulating curricula. Much had to be learned, and those putting together orientation programs wanted to pack in a lot. In a number of places, as the 2001 NCSL survey suggested, participants were overwhelmed with information. Because of member feedback that too much came at them too fast, the Michigan legislature scaled back its program in 2000, only two years after it had expanded it.

Expansion and then contraction of legislative training programs occurred in a number of states. Several years ago, the Legislative Service

Commission's program in Ohio had lengthened its training of new members to five days and moved it to a retreat setting at a state park. Recently, with Ohio facing budgetary difficulties, the length of the orientation session was reduced, and it was moved back to a hotel in Columbus, across the street from the Capitol.

While orientating new legislative members has its ups and downs, the formal content standard for their training is probably the easiest one for legislatures to meet. It not only provides for sharing the necessary nuts-and-bolts information. Hands-on training, simulations, and issue analysis are being incorporated by more states.

3. *Whatever the formal content, extracurricular content and activity count heavily with legislators.*

In its 2001 report on orientation of new members, NCSL recommended that legislatures "give the participants time to get to know each other" (National Conference of State Legislatures 2002). This implies that the occasion must be viewed not only in strict educational terms but also through a political and social lens.

Georgia's Biennial Institute has never ignored the extracurricular. The gathering always seemed to offer something extraordinary that appealed to members. For example, at the second institute he attended, Jimmy Skipper, then a former member of the House, was invited to dinner by Speaker Tom Murphy. The car that was sent to pick him up was driven by the University of Georgia's head football coach, a state icon. "I was in heaven," recalls Skipper.

Legislators not only feel obligated to attend CVIG affairs; they want to do so. Returning members look forward to reconnecting with their colleagues after the biennial election. They use this opportunity to renew friendships and reestablish camaraderie before the legislative session begins and then quickly picks up its pace, leaving little time for socializing. The receptions that legislators mill around at in Atlanta during the course of the session are a poor substitute for being with colleagues in Athens before the session actually begins.

Older members have already been filled in on the newcomers; at the institutes, they can see them firsthand. In the words of Representative Kathy Ashe, the get-together gives experienced members a chance to "figure out who the new faces are." These "new faces" naturally will be able to furnish votes for bills returning members want to move. For their part, new members have a chance to interact with one another and to meet their more experienced colleagues. "Everything is a blur the first couple of years anyway," says Representative Terry Coleman. What helps new members ease in, he adds, is forging friendships as soon as possible.

It does not hurt, of course, that politics gets done. The governor is one player who always has a role, frequently using the Biennial Institute to give legislators advance notification of the administration's budget or policy priorities. The governor's department heads show up and make themselves available to legislators for their requests. "I always have a laundry list of things I want a commissioner to do," explains Senator George Hooks. Legislators also busy themselves rounding up support from one another. "A lot of legislative proposals," says Skipper, "are hatched here." Deals are cut; coalitions begin to form; business gets under way.

Ambiance matters. The Biennial Institute could probably not be done as well at any other time of the year or at any other place in the state. The scheduling may be fortuitous, but it works. Both the time that elapses and the election that intervenes after the even-year session ends in March or April prime members for reassembling in December. What Representative Jerry Keen calls the "first picnic" of the session occurs before the relentless pressure of the legislative session takes hold. It is a period when both returning and new members can and do feel relaxed. Moreover, the Biennial Institute takes place just before the holiday season, so everyone is in a festive mood. Of importance also is that most of the training is conducted in Athens, on the University of Georgia campus, a setting conducive to learning and away from the distractions of the Capitol and downtown Atlanta. The facilities are excellent, and enough free time is available between and after scheduled sessions for legislators to socialize and politick with one another.

The extracurricular standard for legislative training should be attainable for term-limited legislatures. But few locate their orientations for new members in retreat settings. One problem is that legislatures do not want to risk media and public criticism of funds expended on a meeting held outside the Capitol. Some manage to introduce legislators to the governor, and most offer an occasion for new members to get to know one another. Missing from most orientations, however, are experienced members. Other than the few who make presentations or serve on a panel and leave soon thereafter, experienced members normally are busy on other tasks. Without returning members, not only are opportunities for political relationships to form diminished, but less learning goes on.

4. *The people who conduct the training require substantial capacity to deliver the goods.*

It is difficult to imagine any organization having the capacity that CVIG has when it comes to working with the legislature and training legislators. The institutions engaged in legislator training that come nearest CVIG are the Institute of Government at the University of North Carolina, the Lyndon Baines Johnson School of Public Affairs at the University of Texas, and the University of Massachusetts at Amherst (each of which is working with a non-term-limited legislature).

Jim Ledbetter, CVIG's director, refers to the University of Georgia institute as a home for practitioners in academia. Most of the members of the CVIG professional staff have had experience in state and local government. These people believe in government; they respect and like it. This shows in the relationship they have had and continue to have with the legislature. The university and CVIG have taken their public service mission most seriously, and the state has in return been generous in its support. The institute's relationship with the legislature has been cemented over a period of many years, by its creation of a legislative research division that staffed legislative committees, by its furnishing of professional assistance on reapportionment, and by its provision of special research and advice on matters involving scientific questions. The institute also publishes a handbook for legislators, which members find valuable.

The dominant enterprise at CVIG is training—of county and local officials and of state executive officials, as well as of legislators. Thirty members of the staff deliver training to sixteen thousand persons through more than six hundred programs, at a cost of over four million dollars a year. The Biennial Institute amounts to only a small portion of the total, but an extremely important part. It requires a lot of time, with eight people starting to plan almost a year before the institute is scheduled to be held.

Other legislatures conduct training of a similar nature and rely on legislators, legislative staff, lobbyists, and other experts for delivery. With few exceptions, the training programs are planned and executed in-house, by legislative staff. Few staffers can be expected to have broad, professional experience in training; rather, they have knowledge and skills related more to the other assignments they have with the legislature. Training expertise matters, but it is in extremely short supply in legislatures across the country.

5. *The training has to be responsive to what legislators themselves think they need.*

When orientation of new members is the responsibility of legislative service agencies, responsiveness is almost assured. Legislative staff are accustomed to trying to discern the needs and desires of their employers. The problem, however, is that staff usually has difficulty getting much advice or input from legislators, although they do take into account the evaluations given by participants after a program is completed. In Georgia, the staff of CVIG, although independent of the General Assembly, is always checking on what legislators may think. The CVIG director literally runs back and forth to the leaders of the Senate and House and to other key legislators, asking what they need and think.

CVIG has to endure the almost inevitable tension between its educational goals, on the one hand, and legislators' political and personal goals, on the other. Representative Ashe explains, "[I]t is tough to get legislators to concentrate on issues when they want to socialize with one another." But somehow CVIG manages, and that vital balance between the more formal and the more informal parts of the Biennial Institute is achieved. One of CVIG's principal supporters, Representative Burke Day, sums up, "[T]hey have been able to maintain their mission without compromising it."

With the change from more than a century of Democratic control of the Georgia legislature to Republican control after the 2004 election, a new challenge has arisen. It is understandable that Republican leaders feel somewhat wary of an organization that has responded to a Democratic majority uninterruptedly for so many years. Now, the Republicans have the upper hand. Representative Keene, one of the Republican leaders, maintains that things may be a little difficult for a while because "there is no playbook on how to transition." A few misunderstandings have arisen, but CVIG has been paying special attention to cultivating the new leadership and to working things out. CVIG has no partisan or ideological agenda; yet Ledbetter acknowledges that the new majority party has "to grow comfortable with us."

The transition from Democratic to Republican majorities is a test of the Biennial Institute. In other states, especially in term-limited ones, a shift in majority control or even turnover in top leadership has had substantial effects on the course of legislative training. In the meantime, CVIG recently launched a new training program for the Georgia legislature's future leaders, with the help of a foundation grant it was awarded for leadership development.

6. *Legislative leadership has to make a genuine commitment to the training.*

In its 2001 report, NCSL notes that one requirement of a training program is "ownership by leadership" (National Conference of State Legislatures 2002). Achieving this is essential but difficult. It has been done in Georgia. A succession of legislative leaders have taken on ownership. The key, as Representative Keen puts it, is that "leaders have to want something, then they will make a commitment to it." Because it has suited their purposes, Georgia's leaders have endorsed training. Tom Murphy, a powerful leader who held the speakership for twenty-eight years, would have seemed to be a most unlikely advocate of legislator education. Yet he was one of the Biennial Institute's champions, because it offered him an occasion to build support. The new Republican leaders, much like their Democratic predecessors, also stand to benefit. They favor more-informed legislators, not less-informed ones. They recognize that knowledge facilitates work on issues and, particularly, on the budget and heightens a sense of loyalty to leadership.

The Biennial Institute accomplishes more than training, although training alone would be sufficient. The institute also enables leaders to hear face-to-face from members—veterans and freshmen alike. Legislators always want to meet with their leaders. At a recent institute, Representative Keen, as House Republican leader, sat in the cafeteria for six hours just meeting with members. Leaders also take advantage of the opportunity to bring members of their caucus together for dinner, where they and their colleagues get to know newly elected members (and vice versa) and where bonding as partisans continues or begins.

Both the curricular and the extracurricular activities afford leaders an opportunity to size up the newcomers and start figuring out what makes them tick. A perceptive leader can spot future leaders early on. Representative Ashe thinks leaders may learn even more by observing new members at the formal sessions of the institute. According to her, by listening to what is said and observing who is diligently taking notes, they can pick out the people who know what they are talking about. During the course of the institute, leaders engage in the most practical ways. Representative Coleman, who campaigned for Speaker at the institute, said, "[I]t gives leaders the opportunity to meet with specific legislators, vetting them for committee chairs, and figuring out committee organization and members' assignments."

Leaders in term-limited states could also commit themselves to training. The problem, however, is that they have less time and inclination to do so. Since they are swiftly passing through the House (or Senate) and even more swiftly passing through leadership positions, training is unlikely to be high on their agenda.

7. *To be most effective, training ought to be institutionalized.*

Georgia's former Senate leader Bill Stephens does not think that the legislature any longer has a choice about whether to put on the Biennial Institute. "It's what you do, it's institutionalized," he explains. For him, the institute effectively starts the legislative session off; indeed, it has become part of it. House leader Jerry Keen agrees completely: "It's institutionalized, and is now very much a part of the legislative experience."

When Morris W. H. Collins, at the University of Georgia, brought the idea of legislator training to Speaker George L. Smith almost a half century ago, no one could have expected that a strongly rooted, long-enduring program would result. Members of the first class, in 1958, included Tom Murphy, a future House Speaker, and Zell Miller, a future Senate president. Both became big supporters of the Biennial Institute. Early on, Speaker Smith initiated the practice of announcing his appointments of chairs and members of standing committees at the institute, ensuring that just about every legislator came. Even without this practice, receiving an invitation from the Speaker or the president probably would have compelled members of the House and Senate to attend. Although the announcement of committee assignments can no longer be counted on, the habit of going to the university campus every two years has become ingrained.

A few years ago, just to cement things, the Georgia legislature enacted the Ethics and Efficiency in Government Act. The act is based on the premise that "[i]t is in the fundamental interests of the citizens of Georgia and of the legislature as an equal branch of state government to foster the knowledge, professionalism, and standards of its membership." The act creates a board composed of the CVIG director ex officio and three members from each house. One duty of the board is to establish guidelines for the training to be given by CVIG. Thus, training is now in Georgia's statute books.

That the Biennial Institute has become such an integral part of the legislative process is remarkable. It took time and effort and required continued support by leaders and members alike. Institutionalization of such a training practice would be difficult to achieve elsewhere, particularly in term-limited states, where there is too little time and too little continuity. Because leaders come and go rapidly, each wants to make his or her own distinctive mark; thus, the commitment to the work of one's predecessors is not strong.

How Training Helps the Legislature

Orientation and training programs for members are designed to enhance the knowledge and skills of legislators as individuals. Depending on the specific legislatures and their programs, these objectives may be achieved at least to some degree. Whatever the effects on individual legislators, probably of more concern are the effects the educational efforts have on the legislature and on the manner in which it performs its job. In a recent book (Rosenthal 2004), I explore the three most important components of a legislature's job. Here, I shall add a fourth.

The first component is representing constituents and constituencies. Here is where legislators and legislatures probably do their best work. It is also where training makes little difference overall. When they arrive at the Capitol, legislators already have a pretty good idea of their constituency. What they need to know about communications, casework, and how best to keep in touch is high on their agendas, and they are strongly motivated to find out. They pick up the necessary information early on. In fairly short order, they are carrying out their representational tasks as skillfully as their more senior colleagues.

The second component of the legislature's job is lawmaking, which involves not only the issues—big and small—on the legislature's agenda but also the processes (e.g., study, deliberation, negotiation, and support building) according to which such issues are considered and decided. This is where training tends to be targeted and is likely to have impact both on members directly and on the legislature indirectly. Since the measurement of effects is so elusive, all we can do is assume that members become better informed and more adept and that the legislature does its lawmaking somewhat better as a consequence of training. If this assumption is correct, term-limited states are better off with training than they would be without it.

The third component of the legislature's job is balancing the power of the executive. This clearly is an institutional, rather than an individual, requirement. Yet members and, particularly, legislative leaders help determine how the legislature performs in a separation-of-powers/checks-and-balances political system. Important in this regard is the orientation of the legislature vis-à-vis the governor and whether leaders and members have the will and the wherewithal to ensure that the legislature acts as an independent and coequal branch of state government, in particular if the governor, Senate majority, and House majority are of the same party. Not much of the training that legislators receive has bearing on how the legislature balances the executive. One might assume that more knowledgeable and skillful legislators would develop greater self-confidence, which in turn would result in stronger legislative will. But that is quite a stretch. If, as chapter 9 of this volume indicates, the executive is advantaged by term limits, it is highly unlikely that anything short of training by indoctrination instilling a sense of legislative independence will do very much at all to redress the imbalance.

The fourth component of the legislature's job can be referred to as institutional maintenance. The legislature has to maintain itself; that is, it has to look out for its own well-being (Rosenthal 1996). For the legislature to maintain itself as an institution, support from outside and support from within are requisite. During the past thirty years, public support for the legislature has been in decline, while public cynicism and distrust of the legislature, its processes, and its members has been on the rise. During the past twenty years, member support for legislative institutions appears to have been eroding (Rosenthal 1998). For a number of reasons, fewer legislators identify with, show loyalty to, or have particular concern for their institutions.

The erosion of internal support appears to be greater in term-limited states than elsewhere. In the survey of observers in Arizona, Arkansas, California, Colorado, Maine, and Ohio (among the term-limited states) and Illinois, Indiana, and Kansas (among non-term-limited states), respondents were asked whether "in comparison to their counterparts a decade or more ago," current legislators were "more or less likely" to "support and defend the institution of the legislature." Respondents tended to find current legislators to be less likely to support the institution, particularly in the six term-limited states.

If institutional commitment is important to the functioning of legislatures (as I argue in this chapter) and is at greater risk in term-limited states (as indicated by the survey of observers), what can be done to strengthen it? Can member training make a difference? To address these questions, it is necessary to indicate how institutional commitment develops in the first place.

The likelihood is that not many members come to the legislature with much of an institutional sense. As a result of study, a few may have developed a sense of the legislature as an institution. But most have not. Legislators have career goals, constituency needs, electoral interests, and policy agendas, as well as job and family concerns. All of these are concrete and impending. By contrast, institutional commitment is abstract and remote. Moreover, there are no incentives or rewards that encourage its development. It does not arise spontaneously. It develops over time.

The longer legislators serve, the more institutional they tend to become. It takes a while for a member to begin to appreciate the legislature as an institution. Usually, what engenders institutional sensitivity and commitment is leadership responsibility. When legislators achieve leadership positions (as party leaders or committee and subcommittee chairs), they have to put their personal agendas somewhat aside and work to build consensus for and promote a chamber, caucus, committee, or subcommittee position on legislation. All of this is critical to the lawmaking process. With such leadership responsibility, legislators begin to get a different sense of the legislature and start seeing it more as a consensus-building mechanism. In addition, their leadership responsibilities increase their identification with and stake in the Senate, House, or legislature as a whole. Thus, it is from among the ranks of legislative leaders that a cadre of legislators with institutional loyalties emerges.

Can legislator training programs compensate for the diminished support legislators give their institutions? NCSL, an organization with a keen institutional commitment, hopes so. In discussing what needs to be done, two of its senior staff members wrote, "And last of all, training needs to give members a strong sense of the legislative institution and their role in serving in that institution" (Feustel and Jones 2001, 19). This is an especially tall order for legislative training, even training as effective as Georgia's.

How can commitment to the Senate, House, or legislature be engendered when division and conflict are at the core of the process? The minority party will criticize how the majority party runs things, and this may be understood as criticism of the institution itself. Individual legislators, in pursuing their individual objectives, also take issue with processes and procedures that get in their way, and their criticism also can undermine institutional support.

To expect legislator training to build institutional commitment is to expect much. There are strong arguments as to why it cannot be done. Legislative leaders and legislators have objectives that are more practical, especially in term-limited states. In any case, how can institutional commitment be taught—by exhortation, historical analysis, case studies, stories? It will not be simple, but there does not seem to be a good alternative to education and training, if institutional commitment and strengthening are important objectives. The Georgia model demonstrates that it is possible for a legislature to take the job seriously and do it well.

Term-limited legislatures are trying to adapt as best they can, but they still have a long way to go as far as preparing new and returning members is concerned. Even if they go as far as Georgia or further, they are not likely to overcome the adverse effects of term limits. The damage to the legislature's performance—in lawmaking, balancing the power of the executive, and maintaining the well-being of the institution—can be reduced by effective education and training programs but probably cannot be undone.

CHAPTER 12

Conclusion and Implications

Bruce Cain, Karl T. Kurtz, & Richard G. Niemi

AS WE SUGGESTED in the introduction to this book, the imposition of
term limits on fifteen state legislatures was the most significant—and some
would say drastic—institutional change in state government in the last two
decades. Between 1991 and 2000, twenty-one states adopted term limits.
But this number was winnowed—and the extension of term limits to new
legislatures abruptly halted—as states were blocked from applying term
limits to Congress by the Supreme Court's interpretation of the
qualifications clause, as state court decisions invalidated some state term
limit provisions, and as the movement ran its course through the states
with the initiative process. Contrasting the states that did not adopt and
retain term limits with the fifteen states that did provides a natural experiment on the effect of finite terms of office on representation, legislative
structure, the balance of power, and policy-making.

The preceding chapters discussed the findings from the Joint Project
on Term Limits—comprised of state studies and national surveys—on the
effects of term limits on the composition, representation, leadership, committee systems, lobbyists and interest groups, culture, staffing, legislative-
executive relations, and policy of state legislatures. In this chapter, we
return to the arguments of the proponents and opponents of term limits in
chapter 1 and discuss them in the context of the project's empirical results,
as a way of summarizing the project's findings.

An important preliminary point, discussed repeatedly in the preceding
chapters, is that some effects vary with the nature of the term limit and the

type of state legislature under consideration. It matters whether the term limit is shorter (e.g., six years in the House and eight years in the Senate in Arkansas, California, and Michigan) or longer (e.g., twelve years in each chamber in Louisiana and Nevada). In more subtle ways, it also matters whether there is a lifetime ban or a consecutive term limit.

Moreover, these variations in term limit law interact with the institutional differences present in legislatures before term limits were applied. Generally, the more professionalized the legislature was, the greater the impact of term limits has been. Because the greater resources (time, staff, facilities, and compensation) of the more professionalized legislatures make them more attractive places to serve, fewer incumbents leave these legislatures voluntarily. Those greater resources (particularly staff) also make incumbents more difficult to defeat. As a result, the more professionalized legislatures had lower rates of turnover before term limits were imposed and were more likely to be affected in measurable ways by the imposition of finite legislative terms. In the less professionalized legislatures, the rates of turnover did not change nearly as much as a result of term limits, except among leaders and committee chairs, who tended to come from a relatively small number of long-serving members.

Taking the restrictiveness of the limits together with the degree of professionalization, we can place the impact of term limits on states along a continuum. California, with its highly professionalized legislature and fourteen-year maximum lifetime limit, is at one end of the continuum. Louisiana, with its less professionalized legislature and twenty-four-year consecutive limit, is at the other.

Some states are farther along in their term limit cycles than others. Even so, it is possible to make some clear assessments of the questions we posed at the beginning of the book. In their chapter on the evolution of term limits (chap. 1), Jennie Drage Bowser and Gary Moncrief set out the terms of the debate as articulated in the initiative campaigns and court cases about term limits. In the following section, we review the results in that framework.

Arguments in Favor of Term Limits

1. *Term limits would allow more people to have the chance to serve in the legislature, thus retaining the notion of the citizen legislatures.*

Some proponents hoped that by increasing turnover, term limits would give more opportunities to previously underrepresented groups and restore the model of a citizen legislature. Turnover increased in all of the term-limited state legislatures we studied, more than in the control states. But the compositional effects were less definitive than the proponents had hoped.

The higher turnover helped some states to realize underlying demographic trends faster. For example, in states that experienced a rapid rise in Latino population (e.g., Arizona and California), there was some increase in Latino representation. Not all of that change can be attributed to term limits, as the Voting Rights Act and redistricting clearly mattered, but the turnover did open up seats more quickly, and many of the gains Latinos made came though open-seat opportunities. There is also some evidence that term limits contributed to the higher representation of African Americans in Michigan and Arkansas.

But term limits did not increase the number of women in the legislature and did not change significantly the age and occupational backgrounds of those elected to serve. More to the point of the proponents' hopes, term limits did not produce a less career-oriented politician. They did shape the direction of political careers in different ways, causing those who wanted politics as a career to run for higher offices sooner than they might otherwise have done and causing some to return to local government.

2. *Those who run for office knowing that their terms are limited are more likely to represent their constituents' interests and to seek policy changes that might be opposed by entrenched interest groups.*

Lynda Powell, Richard Niemi, and Michael Smith discuss this expectation extensively in chapter 3 of this volume. One part of the expectation is apparently true; representatives in term-limited states seem to be less linked to the particularistic interests of their districts. They spend less time talking with and solving the problems of their representatives, they place less emphasis on securing projects and pork for their districts, and they devote less time and effort to constituency issues. However, the other part of the expectation—that they, freed from particularistic pressures, might spend more time deliberating issues—does not seem to be true. In fact, the evidence from several of the chapters in this book indicates that term-limited members are less knowledgeable about both issues and process and are as preoccupied as ever with reelection and finding a postlegislative career. There is also evidence that they spend less time on lawmaking and being attentive to statewide needs.

3. *Term limits reduce the extraordinary power of incumbents during elections. As a result, a more diverse group of people will be elected to state legislatures.*

As we noted before, racial and ethnic diversity has increased marginally in a few term-limited states, but we could detect no other trend. Moreover, incumbency is still important despite increased turnover. Incumbents still have advantages in terms of name recognition, resources of their office, campaign money, and credit-claiming opportunities, though they cannot exploit those advantages for as long as they could before term limits. Furthermore, some evidence suggests that term limits may discourage challenges to incumbents that would otherwise have occurred: when an incumbent's tenure will end with certainty two or four years hence, there is less reason for potentially strong challengers to mount a costly campaign to unseat him or her. In other words, limiting terms is an effective way to offset incumbency advantages and increase legislative turnover (as compared to both non-term-limited states and Congress), but only when it creates open seats.

4. *Interest groups will be weakened under a system with term limits, because such groups would not be able to develop long-term relationships with legislators.*

This was one of the core claims by proponents of term limits. Many believed that the longer that members served in the legislature, the more infected they would become by lobbyists and special interests. Proponents of term limits hoped that by rotating members out of office before they got too cozy with the lobbyists and special interests, legislators would produce better deliberation and, ultimately, better laws. There is no question that term limits have had an effect on lobbyists and interest groups. Lobbyists report that their job has gotten harder because they cannot establish long-term working relationships with members. But has this lessened the lobbyists' influence on legislators?

The evidence is mixed. On the one hand, partly because there are more lobbyists now than before, there is a more level playing field, and it is less likely that a few established, power-brokering lobbyists dominate the scene. On the other hand, because term-limited members are less knowledgeable than in the past, they are more dependent on lobbyists for information and institutional knowledge. In addition, because there are more open seats (which generally make for more expensive elections) and hence less overall incumbency advantage, lobbyists and interest groups are as important as ever in the funding of elections.

5. *Most states already limit the number of terms that governors can serve. Term limits on legislators are just an extension of this policy and level the playing field for all officeholders.*

The impact of term limits on legislators and governors seems to be different. Governors have a mixture of permanent and political appointees to help them. Legislatures depend on the division of labor into committees and the experience of staff and legislative leaders for expertise. By limiting the experience levels of members and especially of their leaders, term-limited legislatures have lost a key element of organizational capacity. Term-limited members are learning faster and assuming more responsibility than in the past, but the evidence indicates that, on average, they are still less knowledgeable than their counterparts in non-term-limited legislatures. Moreover, because term-limited members are less secure and need to position themselves to run for another office, the balance between partisan and nonpartisan staff has shifted. Partisan staff has become more important (see chap. 6 of this volume), and nonpartisan staff has a bigger educational job than in the past. Instead of leveling the playing field between the legislative and executive branches, term limits have weakened the legislative branch and strengthened executive power (see chaps. 9 and 10).

Arguments against Term Limits

1. *Term limits interfere with the fundamental right of voters to elect their representatives. If voters do not want a person to represent them, they can vote him or her out of office.*

This is predominantly an argument of principle rather than fact and is therefore difficult to assess empirically. However, it is important to note that voters have not taken the opportunity to overturn term limits to date. As Bowser and Moncrief point out in chapter 1 of this volume, it was state supreme courts that invalidated term limits in four states, and the legislatures repealed the term limit statute in two other states, Utah and Idaho. For their part, voters have rejected attempts by two states (Arkansas and Montana) to extend the length of the legislative term limits to twelve years, and California voters rejected a March 2002 measure that would have allowed termed-out members to petition their voters for an extended term. Repeated surveys of voters have also shown no diminution of support for term limits. In short, voters are not acting as though they have been deprived of a fundamental right.

Political science research long ago demonstrated the curious phenomenon that voters like their individual representatives more than their legislatures as collective bodies. So while it may be true that some voters will regret losing a good representative, it does not mean that they will vote to repeal or even substantially amend term limit laws. That term limits are likely here to stay is one reason we have chosen to emphasize adaptive strategies in response to them. Failing a change of heart on the part of voters, the challenge for legislatures is how to remain effective institutions under the constraints of term limits.

2.   *By removing experienced and knowledgeable legislators, term limits weaken the legislative branch of government. A weak legislature upsets the balance of power that is the basis of our form of government.*

This volume's chapters on committees, leadership, executive-legislative relations, and the budget and policy processes contain a fair amount of evidence that the legislature has declined in capacity relative to the executive branch. The impact seems to be greatest in the legislatures that, in the words of Richard Powell (in chap. 9 in this volume), "had the potential to bring about the greatest change—states with relatively strong, professionalized legislatures and low legislative turnover." California, the state with the largest potential by this definition, witnessed a decrease in oversight activities and a decline in legislative influence over the budget. The effects were less obvious in other states, such as Arkansas.

One problem that critics of term limits face is that the public tends to be interested less in procedural issues than in policy outcomes. That governors may have acquired more power at the expense of the legislature matters a great deal to legislators and political scientists, but it is not a burning concern for most voters. The argument about division of power concerns how precisely to divide the power, not whether to do away with the legislature. While their capacity to function has been weakened, legislatures still have considerable formal and informal powers over legislation, budgets, and appointments.

Power between the branches has ebbed and flowed over time. Executive power in state governments was very weak in many states until the early twentieth century. The Progressive Era built up the governor's office, and civil service reform established a less corrupt and more efficient bureaucracy. This was followed in the 1960s by the trend toward legislative professionalization in many states, an attempt to give the legislature more capacity to check the governors and executive agencies. Term limits represent a swing back in the direction of enhanced executive power. The term limits movement was most strongly supported by Republicans and advocates for smaller government. As Republicans have gained control in more state legislatures, their enthusiasm for term limit reform has lessened. But the general suspicion of legislatures, exemplified by their usually low job ratings, remains an obstacle for making the case for overturning term limits.

3.   *Term limits ignore the value of experience in crafting and managing public policy.*

The JPTL study provides no clear evidence that policy-making has gotten better or worse as a result of term limits. As Kousser and Straayer point out in chapter 10 of this volume, "better" or "worse" policy is in the eyes of the beholder: there is no objective way of measuring it. They found that there is no "evidence that the legislation produced by term-limited states was systematically different."

This raises the important point that most of the evidence in this book has to do with the inputs and processing of policy rather than the outputs or policies themselves. Should we care about the former? The authors of this book would argue that we should. Alan Rosenthal (2004, 7) has eloquently argued: "[T]he legislature is not primarily the means to another end [i.e., policy], but rather an end in itself. . . . Democracy is largely about process, and the legislature—not the executive or the judiciary—is the engine that drives democratic processes."

Several of the chapters in the present volume mention that term limits have been accompanied by a decline in civility and respect for the institution and for open government. Under term limits, there are more departures from standard processes of deliberation: for example, bills are gutted and changed at the last minute, in conference committees. This deprives the public, press, and interested groups from observing and voicing objection to bills as they work their way through the legislative process. Sometimes, such departures might occur for good reasons, such as overcoming troublesome members in the other house. But they also increase the odds of unreported mischief and deals that serve private, rather than public, interests.

4.   *Term limits encourage legislators to opt for short-term solutions or quick fixes, over more-difficult solutions that are best over the long term.*

To begin with, we did not find any systematic evidence that this is true.

Some legislators in some states testified that it was. But as we have said, the evidence about representation and procedural effects is stronger than the evidence about policy impacts.

There may be several reasons for this apparent absence of change in legislative output. First, even without term limits, legislators tend to have a short-term horizon. After all, the next election is never more than two or four years away.

Second, as David Berman points out in chapter 7, lack of experience may mean that term-limited legislators are less knowledgeable than legislators who can serve longer, but less knowledgeable does not mean dumb. Term-limited legislators are driven by the same commitment to public service and desire to solve state and community problems as their non-term-limited predecessors or counterparts in other states. They have to deal with the same conflicts and disagreements among the public, and they are still supported, advised, and cajoled by the same cadre of staff, executive officials, lobbyists, and constituents.

Third, a number of adaptations, both natural and planned, have eased the problems of lessened leadership and continuity in policy-making. An example of a natural adaptation is the bicameral career. In many of the states with chamber-specific term limits, the House of Representatives has become the entry point of a legislative career. The Senate has become the more experienced house, with members of the House moving to the Senate when their terms expire. So one reason the lack of experience has not been as debilitating as some expected is that the bicameral structure provides offsetting experience in Senates.

The final factor is planned adaptation. Several states have adopted training programs designed to educate legislators and staff in policy and process. Several states have also found ways to ease and regularize leadership transitions, by having members serve as vice-chairs or by bringing back experienced members in states that have consecutive (as opposed to lifetime) bans.

5.   *The power of lobbyists, legislative staff, and bureaucrats increases under a system with term limits, because they possess institutional knowledge about policy issues and what went on in the past.*

As we noted earlier, lobbyists and interest groups have had to work harder to establish relationships with term-limited members, but the evidence suggests that their power has continued unabated—neither increasing nor decreasing. Changes in the power of legislative staff are mixed, depending on preexisting staff structure, whether one refers to partisan or nonpartisan staff, how staff changes with the entrance of new legislators and new leadership, and the roles of staff before term limits. The studies in this volume do indicate that term-limited legislatures are at an informational disadvantage—more with respect to the executive branch than with respect to lobbyists.

The Future of Term Limits

In short, we conclude that term limits have weakened legislatures institutionally, especially in states with strict limits that had more professionalized legislatures with low turnover. However, due to natural and planned adaptations, the consequences have not been as dire as they might have been. So what is the future of term limits? Will more states adopt them, or will some repeal or alter them? Will legislatures that have them continue to adapt; if so, in what ways? Let us enter the realm of speculation.

As we have already pointed out, voters do not appear to have much of an appetite for repealing term limits. Moreover, the legislative, business, and labor leaders who would have to lead the fight to overturn term limits either do not appear to have the stomach for it or have better things on which to spend their time and money. In some future, more prosperous time in which levels of public trust in government return to those of an earlier generation, it might be possible for legislative advocates in states with the most restrictive limits to craft a package of legislative reforms that would include easing their term limits, but in today's atmosphere of cynicism and distrust toward elected officials and legislatures, even this seems like a stretch.

On the other side of the coin, advocacy of term limits has mostly run its course among the twenty-four states that allow voter initiatives. Since no legislature has yet imposed limits on its own terms (at least not without the threat of it being done for them by voter initiative), the number of states with term limits seems unlikely to grow significantly. It is conceivable that proponents of term limits could succeed in drawing up new term limit plans that would obtain voter approval and pass constitutional muster in a few of the states in which limits have previously passed but been invalidated by the courts.

So, for better or worse, term limits appear to be here to stay in somewhere between one-quarter and one-third of the states. Analysts who wish to generalize about state legislatures will continue to have to take the differences between term-limited and non-term-limited legislatures into account. The choice that legislatures face is whether to figure out ways to compensate for the informational disadvantage they find themselves in or to cede policy-making power to the executive branch.

As Alan Rosenthal commented in chapter 11 of this volume, institutional adaptation is often not a conscious process. Our project team found adaptations difficult to pinpoint and identify, in part because they are likely to occur over long periods of time, often by indirection. Nonetheless, we identified a series of adaptations to term limits that are present in at least a few states and may gradually spread to others in the future. These adaptations fall into four categories:

1. *Education and training.* In chapter 11 of this volume, Alan Rosenthal argues forcefully for legislatures to adapt to term limits through education and training. He points to the Georgia program at the Carl Vinson Institute for Government as a model program and outlines seven guidelines for success. There is no denying that term limits have deprived legislatures of the expertise they once had, but there is no reason why they cannot try to adapt to this problem with better methods of training and orientation. We found plenty of evidence that legislatures are doing this, but the problem is that none has had the same success as Georgia at getting new members to participate in and benefit from this training.

2. *Political careers.* In chapter 2 of this volume, Moncrief, Powell, and Storey report that ambitious officeholders who want a career in politics have adapted to term limits by moving on to other offices whenever they become open and available and not staying in the state legislature as long as they might have without limits. We have already commented on the pattern of bicameral careers that is occurring in most states with chamber-specific limits. These trends are already well established in virtually every state in which term limits have taken effect and are not likely to change.

3. *Apprenticeship.* A few state legislatures—or at least selected leaders in the states—have instituted plans to prepare new legislators to be leaders in the future. These apprentice-like programs include mentoring by older members for new ones and appointing likely future committee

chairs to be vice-chairs of those committees or to "shadow" experienced chairs. Also in this category is evidence of nascent leadership ladders in which future presiding officers normally follow a standard path to the top position, learning as they go. No state legislative chamber appears likely to go as far as the Florida House, which has a long-standing practice—predating term limits in that state—of selecting speakers, at least informally, five years in advance of their taking office (Hodson et al. 1995). But a few states have moved up their dates for selection or elevation of future legislative leaders, in order to lessen, at least for a time, the lame-duck status that term limits have built into the system. These apprenticeship adaptations are likely to spread to more states, although perhaps on a hit-or-miss basis, as they are heavily dependent on the willingness of leaders to adopt them.

4. *Staffing.* In chapter 6 of this volume, Brian Weberg and Karl Kurtz point to nonpartisan staff who, as a matter of self-preservation under term limits, are expanding their role as educators about the institution and repackaging, marketing, and expanding their services, to gain the confidence of legislators who know nothing about their work and may view them as "part of the problem" in the legislature. They found evidence that a few term-limited states have added caucus staff to provide more strategic, policy-oriented advice to legislators. They also reported that lawmakers in the more professionalized legislatures have increased their reliance on partisan staff under term limits. The downside of this is that in a few legislatures, such as the Michigan House and California Assembly, the partisan staff turn over nearly as fast as the legislators, resulting in an experience deficit among key staff. Under its system of rotating speakers every two years, the Florida House has dealt with this problem by maintaining a cadre of senior staff who continue as key advisers (perhaps in different roles) from one speaker to the next (Hodson et al. 1995). The California Senate similarly prohibits new committee chairs from replacing committee consultants until at least six months into the chair's term, and even then, consultants can be replaced only one at a time (Cain and Kousser 2004). Other legislatures that suffer from the problem of staff turnover may consider adopting similar measures to stabilize the support they receive from partisan staff.

Legislatures are enduring and flexible engines of American democracy. Their roles evolve and change over time. Just as the human body adjusts and copes with weakness or disability in a limb or organ by compensating or building strength in another, legislative bodies adapt to challenges imposed by new rules of the game. While they may not come out of such tests as strong as before, they emerge as durable institutions that represent their constituents' interests, make laws, and balance the power of the executive.

Appendix

STATE LEGISLATOR SURVEY

1. IMMEDIATELY PRIOR TO YOUR ELECTION TO THE LEGISLATURE, WHAT PUBLIC OFFICE DID YOU HOLD?

	None	Local/County Executive	Local/County Legislative	School District	Political Party Office	Other
Appointed	☐	☐	☐	☐	☐	☐
Elected	☐	☐	☐	☐	☐	☐

2. WHAT OTHER PUBLIC OFFICES HAVE YOU HELD? [CHECK **ALL** THAT APPLY]

	None	Local/County Executive	Local/County Legislative	School District	Political Party Office	Other
Appointed	☐	☐	☐	☐	☐	☐
Elected	☐	☐	☐	☐	☐	☐

3. HAVE YOU EVER SERVED AS A LEGISLATIVE STAFFER? ☐ No ☐ Yes

4. WERE YOU OPPOSED IN YOUR LAST CAMPAIGN?

   Primary Election ☐ No ☐ Yes   **General Election** ☐ No ☐ Yes

5. IF OPPOSED, WHAT PERCENT OF THE VOTE WAS WON BY:

   Primary _____ % You _____ % 2nd Place Candidate

   General _____ % You _____ % 2nd Place Candidate

6. IF OPPOSED, APPROXIMATELY HOW MUCH MONEY WAS SPENT IN THE:

   Primary $_____ By You $_____ By Your Main Opponent

   General $_____ By You $_____ By Your Main Opponent

7. IN ADDITION TO WHAT YOU REPORTED IN QUESTION 6, IN THE GENERAL ELECTION CAMPAIGN, ABOUT HOW MUCH DID PARTIES OR OTHER GROUPS SPEND TO ELECT:

   $_____ You $_____ Your Main Opponent

8. WHICH OF THE FOLLOWING DESCRIBE THE **2ND PLACE** CANDIDATE? [CHECK **ALL** THAT APPLY.]

	Incumbent	Had Held Other Public Elected Office	Had Held Appointed Public Office	Had Held Party Office	Unopposed
Primary	☐	☐	☐	☐	☐
General	☐	☐	☐	☐	☐

9. WHEN YOU WERE FIRST ELECTED TO THE LEGISLATURE, HOW IMPORTANT WERE EACH OF THE FOLLOWING IN TERMS OF LEARNING HOW TO DO YOUR JOB? [CHECK ONE BOX IN **EACH** ROW.]

	Not Important At All 1	2	3	4	Very Important 5
Formal training programs in the legislature	☐	☐	☐	☐	☐
Trial and error	☐	☐	☐	☐	☐
Working on a committee	☐	☐	☐	☐	☐
Listening to debate on the floor	☐	☐	☐	☐	☐
Senior colleagues	☐	☐	☐	☐	☐
Party leaders	☐	☐	☐	☐	☐
Legislative staff	☐	☐	☐	☐	☐

10. AS YOU CONSIDER THE VARIOUS SOURCES OF INFORMATION AVAILABLE TO YOU AS A LEGISLATOR, HOW IMPORTANT ARE EACH OF THE FOLLOWING? [CHECK ONE BOX IN **EACH** ROW.]

	Not Important At All 1	2	3	4	Very Important 5
Personal expertise	☐	☐	☐	☐	☐
Legislative staff	☐	☐	☐	☐	☐
Leadership	☐	☐	☐	☐	☐
Other members	☐	☐	☐	☐	☐
Lobbyists	☐	☐	☐	☐	☐
Governor	☐	☐	☐	☐	☐
State agency personnel	☐	☐	☐	☐	☐
National organizations (e.g. CSG, NCSL)	☐	☐	☐	☐	☐
Media	☐	☐	☐	☐	☐

11. WHAT PERCENT OF VOTERS IN YOUR DISTRICT (BOUNDARIES IN LAST ELECTION) DO YOU THINK FEEL CLOSER TO THE REPUBLICAN PARTY, TO THE DEMOCRATIC PARTY, OR ARE TRULY INDEPENDENT?

_____ %   _____ %   _____ %
Republican   Democrat   Independent

12. WHAT DO YOU THINK IS THE RELATIVE INFLUENCE OF THE FOLLOWING ACTORS IN DETERMINING LEGISLATIVE OUTCOMES IN YOUR CHAMBER? [CHECK ONE BOX IN **EACH** ROW.]

	No Influence 1	2	3	4	5	6	Dictates Policy 7
Majority party leadership	☐	☐	☐	☐	☐	☐	☐
Minority party leadership	☐	☐	☐	☐	☐	☐	☐
Committee chairs	☐	☐	☐	☐	☐	☐	☐
Governor	☐	☐	☐	☐	☐	☐	☐
Bureaucrats/Civil servants	☐	☐	☐	☐	☐	☐	☐
Interest groups	☐	☐	☐	☐	☐	☐	☐
Mass media	☐	☐	☐	☐	☐	☐	☐
Other chamber	☐	☐	☐	☐	☐	☐	☐
Legislative staff	☐	☐	☐	☐	☐	☐	☐

Could you further distinguish between:

Partisan legislative staff	☐	☐	☐	☐	☐	☐	☐
Non-Partisan legislative staff	☐	☐	☐	☐	☐	☐	☐

13. DO YOU FEEL YOU SHOULD BE PRIMARILY CONCERNED WITH LOOKING AFTER THE NEEDS OF YOUR DISTRICT, OR THE NEEDS OF THE STATE AS A WHOLE?

District 1	2	3	4	5	6	State as a Whole 7
☐	☐	☐	☐	☐	☐	☐

14. WHEN THERE IS A CONFLICT BETWEEN WHAT YOU FEEL IS BEST AND WHAT YOU THINK THE PEOPLE IN YOUR DISTRICT WANT, DO YOU THINK YOU SHOULD FOLLOW YOUR OWN CONSCIENCE OR FOLLOW WHAT THE PEOPLE IN YOUR DISTRICT WANT?

Always District 1	2	3	4	5	6	Always Conscience 7
☐	☐	☐	☐	☐	☐	☐

15. TO WHAT EXTENT IS THE CONTENT AND PASSAGE OF BILLS IN YOUR CHAMBER INFLUENCED BY THE FINANCIAL CONTRIBUTIONS OF INDIVIDUALS AND GROUPS TO CANDIDATES AND PARTIES?

Not at all Influenced						Completely Determined
1	2	3	4	5	6	7
☐	☐	☐	☐	☐	☐	☐

16. DO YOU SPECIALIZE IN A SINGLE POLICY AREA OR ARE YOU EQUALLY ACTIVE IN MANY AREAS?

Specialize In Single Policy Area						Equally Active In Many Areas
1	2	3	4	5	6	7
☐	☐	☐	☐	☐	☐	☐

17. IF THIS IS NOT YOUR FIRST TERM, WERE YOU THE PRIMARY AUTHOR OF ANY BILLS THAT BECAME LAW DURING YOUR LAST TERM?

☐ None   ☐ One or Two   ☐ Three or Four   ☐ Five or more

18. HOW MUCH TIME DO YOU ACTUALLY SPEND ON EACH OF THE FOLLOWING ACTIVITIES? [CHECK ONE BOX IN EACH ROW.]

	Hardly Any				A Great Deal
	1	2	3	4	5
Studying proposed legislation	☐	☐	☐	☐	☐
Developing new legislation	☐	☐	☐	☐	☐
Building coalitions within own party to pass legislation	☐	☐	☐	☐	☐
Building coalitions across parties to pass legislation	☐	☐	☐	☐	☐
Keeping in touch with constituents	☐	☐	☐	☐	☐
Helping constituents with problems with government	☐	☐	☐	☐	☐
Making sure your district gets a fair share of government money and projects	☐	☐	☐	☐	☐
Campaigning/Fundraising	☐	☐	☐	☐	☐
Could you further distinguish between:					
Fundraising for yourself	☐	☐	☐	☐	☐
Fundraising for your caucus	☐	☐	☐	☐	☐

19. HOW WOULD YOU DESCRIBE YOUR POLITICAL VIEWS AND THOSE OF OTHERS? (IF YOU ARE UNCERTAIN ABOUT A PLACEMENT, PLEASE LEAVE IT BLANK)

	Extremely Liberal	Liberal	Slightly Liberal	Moderate / Middle of the Road	Slightly Conservative	Conservative	Extremely Conservative
	1	2	3	4	5	6	7
Yourself	☐	☐	☐	☐	☐	☐	☐
Primary Election Main Opponent	☐	☐	☐	☐	☐	☐	☐
General Election Main Opponent	☐	☐	☐	☐	☐	☐	☐
Views of voters in your district:							
Average General Election Voter	☐	☐	☐	☐	☐	☐	☐
Average Democratic Primary Voter	☐	☐	☐	☐	☐	☐	☐
Average Republican Primary Voter	☐	☐	☐	☐	☐	☐	☐

20. WHAT GROUPS DO YOU REGARD AS AMONG YOUR STRONGEST SUPPORTERS? [CHECK **ALL** THAT APPLY]

☐ Labor/Union ☐ Business ☐ Women's Groups ☐ Christian Coalition
☐ Gun Owners ☐ Pro-Life ☐ Pro-Choice ☐ Tax Relief
☐ Environmentalists ☐ Teachers ☐ African Americans ☐ Latinos

21. AVERAGED OVER AN ENTIRE YEAR AND TAKING INTO ACCOUNT SESSION TIME, INTERIM WORK, CONSTITUENT SERVICE AND CAMPAIGNING, WHAT PROPORTION OF A FULL-TIME JOB IS YOUR LEGISLATIVE WORK?

☐ 90% or more ☐ 70-90% ☐ 50-70% ☐ 30-50% ☐ less than 30%

22. DO YOU PLAN TO RUN FOR REELECTION TO YOUR CURRENT CHAMBER WHEN YOUR PRESENT TERM EXPIRES?

☐ Definitely ☐ Probably ☐ Probably Not ☐ Definitely Not ☐ Definitely Not; Term-Limited

23. AFTER SERVICE IN THE PRESENT CHAMBER, WHAT ARE YOU LIKELY TO DO? [CHECK **ALL** THAT APPLY]

☐ Run for Other Chamber ☐ Run for Local Office ☐ Return to Previous Non-political career
☐ Run for Statewide Office ☐ Appointive Office ☐ Lobbying/Consulting
☐ Run for U.S. House or Senate ☐ No Further Office ☐ Retire

24. PLEASE INDICATE HOW MUCH ATTENTION YOU THINK YOUR LEGISLATIVE PARTY LEADER SHOULD GIVE TO EACH OF THE FOLLOWING ACTIVITIES:

	Hardly Any 1	2	3	4	A Great Deal 5
Agenda setting	☐	☐	☐	☐	☐
Working with Executive	☐	☐	☐	☐	☐
Working with other chamber	☐	☐	☐	☐	☐
Media relations	☐	☐	☐	☐	☐
Floor management	☐	☐	☐	☐	☐
Party fundraising and campaign activity	☐	☐	☐	☐	☐
Building legislative coalitions	☐	☐	☐	☐	☐
Candidate recruitment	☐	☐	☐	☐	☐
Assisting members with legislative problems	☐	☐	☐	☐	☐

25. DO YOU CURRENTLY WORK FOR PAY OUTSIDE POLITICS? ☐ No ☐ Yes

26. YEAR OF BIRTH: 19____ **27.** GENDER: ☐ Female ☐ Male

28. RACE/ETHNICITY:

☐ Asian ☐ Black ☐ Hispanic ☐ Native American ☐ Pacific Islander ☐ White

29. FAMILY INCOME:

☐ Below $25,000 ☐ $50,000-$74,999 ☐ $100,000-$249,999 ☐ Prefer Not To Answer
☐ $25,000-$49,999 ☐ $75,000-$99,999 ☐ Above $250,000

30. RELIGIOUS AFFILIATION:

☐ Roman Catholic ☐ Mainline Protestant ☐ None
☐ Jewish ☐ Fundamentalist Christian ☐ Other
(Specify) _____

Knowledgeable Observer Survey Questionnaire

1. This survey is intended to be filled out by people who have been observing or participating in the legislative process in your state for at least 10 years. If you haven't been involved with the legislature for at least 10 years or don't feel that you are able to answer the questions, please check the appropriate box below.

   ☐ I have not been involved with my state's legislature for at least 10 years.

   ☐ I have not observed the legislature closely enough to respond to your questions.

If you checked one of these boxes, you may either stop here or fill out the survey anyway. In either case, please return the survey to us.

For each of the statements below, please circle the number that most closely reflects your opinion:

2. In comparison to their counterparts a decade or more ago, today's legislators are more or less likely to:	Quite a bit More	Somewhat More	About the Same	Somewhat Less	Quite a bit less	No Opinion
A. Introduce bills.	5	4	3	2	1	0
B. Offer amendments to bills.	5	4	3	2	1	0
C. Rely on staff to draft legislation.	5	4	3	2	1	0
D. Sponsor interest group legislation.	5	4	3	2	1	0
E. Be knowledgeable about statewide issues.	5	4	3	2	1	0
F. Be knowledgeable about how the legislature operates.	5	4	3	2	1	0
G. Be concerned about clarity and precision in legislation.	5	4	3	2	1	0
H. Specialize on issues.	5	4	3	2	1	0
I. Support and defend the institution of the legislature	5	4	3	2	1	0

3. Compared to a decade ago, in committee legislators today are more or less:	Quite a bit More	Somewhat More	About the Same	Somewhat Less	Quite a bit Less	No Opinion
A. Willing to compromise in committee.	5	4	3	2	1	0
B. Collegial and courteous in committee.	5	4	3	2	1	0
C. Willing to amend / substitute bills in committee.	5	4	3	2	1	0
D. Knowledgeable about issues before the committee.	5	4	3	2	1	0
E. Likely to seek public input on legislation.	5	4	3	2	1	0

4. Compared to a decade ago, on the floor legislators today are more or less:	Quite a bit More	Somewhat More	About the Same	Somewhat Less	Quite a bit Less	No Opinion
A. Likely to follow parliamentary procedure.	5	4	3	2	1	0
B. Willing to follow floor leaders.	5	4	3	2	1	0
C. Likely to offer amendments.	5	4	3	2	1	0
D. Collegial and courteous to other members.	5	4	3	2	1	0

5. Relative to the legislature, the influence of (__) has increased/decreased compared to 10 years ago.	Increased a Great Deal	Increased Some	Stayed About the Same	Decreased Some	Decreased a Great Deal	No Opinion
A. The governor	5	4	3	2	1	0
B. Administrative agencies	5	4	3	2	1	0
C. Majority and minority party leaders	5	4	3	2	1	0
D. Nonpartisan staff	5	4	3	2	1	0
E. Partisan staff	5	4	3	2	1	0
F. Personal staff (skip, if no personal staff available to members)	5	4	3	2	1	0
G. Legislative committees	5	4	3	2	1	0
H. Legislative party caucuses	5	4	3	3	1	0
I. Lobbyists	5	4	3	2	1	0

6. Compared to a decade ago, legislators in their districts are more or less likely to:	Quite a bit More	Somewhat More	About the Same	Somewhat Less	Quite a bit Less	No Opinion
A. Spend time talking to their constituents.	5	4	3	2	1	0
B. Spend time solving constituents' problems.	5	4	3	2	1	0
C. Seek state funds for projects in their districts.	5	4	3	2	1	0
D. Send newsletters or other mailings to their constituents.	5	4	3	2	1	0

7. Compared to a decade ago, how much more or less:	A Great Deal more	Somewhat More	About the Same	Somewhat Less	A Great Deal Less	No Opinion
A. Successful are committee recommendations on the floor?	5	4	3	2	1	0
B. Control does the leadership have over committees?	5	4	3	2	1	0
C. Partisan is the legislature as a whole?	5	4	3	2	1	0
D. Attention do legislators give to statewide issues?	5	4	3	2	1	0
E. Deliberation (debate, negotiation and compromise) takes place in the legislative process?	5	4	3	2	1	0
F. Aggressive are legislators in seeking campaign funds?	5	4	3	2	1	0

8. Compared to a decade ago, legislative leaders (presiding officers, majority and minority leaders) are more or less likely to:	A Great Deal more	Somewhat More	About the Same	Somewhat Less	A Great Deal Less	No Opinion
A. Focus on election campaigns	5	4	3	2	1	0
B. Be selected on the basis of their fund raising capabilities	5	4	3	2	1	0
C. Move through an established ladder of leadership positions	5	4	3	2	1	0
D. Be involved in candidate recruitment	5	4	3	2	1	0
E. Sanction rebellious legislators	5	4	3	2	1	0
F. Plan their path to leadership positions early in their legislative careers	5	4	3	2	1	0

9. During the last 10 years, have any of the following changes in legislative procedures been implemented and have they been helpful in improving the legislative process?	To what extent has this been done?				If done, how helpful has it been?		
	Extensively	Somewhat	Not at all	Don't know	Very helpful	Somewhat helpful	Not helpful
A. More frequent or improved training for legislators.	3	2	1	0	3	2	1
B. Establishing regular patterns of leadership rotation and succession.	3	2	1	0	3	2	1
C. Planning for succession of committee chairs through committee placements of new members.	3	2	1	0	3	2	1
D. Increased staff support.	3	2	1	0	3	2	1
E. Increased reliance on formal rules in place of traditions and norms.	3	2	1	0	3	2	1

10. Do you have any other observations about institutional changes in your legislature over the last decade?

11. Finally, which of the following best describes your current position (circle all that apply)?

A. Lobbyist

B. Partisan legislative staff

C. Nonpartisan legislative staff

D. Executive agency

E. News media

F. Former Legislator

G. Other _____

Thank you very much for taking the time to respond to our survey!

Please return completed survey in the enclosed self-addressed, stamped envelope to:

State Services Department
National Conference of State Legislatures
7700 East First Place
Denver, Colorado 80230

Summary of Knowledgeable Observer Survey Results by State

Q1. What state are you from?

Responses	Count	Percent
AZ	39	7.1%
AR	62	11.3%
CA	35	6.4%
CO	38	6.9%
ME	53	9.6%
OH	210	38.1%
IL	22	4.0%
IN	33	6.0%
KS	59	10.7%

Legislators today compared to a decade ago

Questions	AZ	AR	CA	CO	ME	OH	IL	IN	KS	Total	Signif.
4. Introduce bills.	3.5	4.1	3.4	3.3	3.7	3.2	3.8	3.6	3.3	3.5	
5. Offer amendments to bills.	3.4	3.3	3.7	3.2	3.5	3.3	2.7	3.3	3.8	3.4	
6. Rely on staff to draft legislation.	3.7	4.0	3.7	3.7	4.0	3.7	3.8	3.7	3.3	3.7	**
7. Sponsor interest group legislation.	3.7	3.8	3.9	3.7	3.8	3.8	3.7	3.4	3.9	3.8	
8. Be knowledgeable about statewide issues.	2.2	1.7	2.0	1.9	2.3	1.9	3.1	3.3	2.4	2.1	***
9. Be knowledgeable about how the legislature operates.	2.0	1.5	2.0	1.8	1.9	1.8	2.7	3.1	2.5	2.0	***
10. Be concerned about clarity and precision in legislation.	2.2	2.1	1.9	2.2	2.2	1.9	2.7	2.7	2.2	2.1	***
11. Specialize on issues.	2.9	2.6	2.0	2.7	2.8	2.7	3.4	3.4	3.6	2.8	***
12. Support and defend the institution of the legislature.	2.0	2.1	2.0	2.0	2.3	2.0	2.5	3.3	2.0	2.1	***
Total	2.9	2.8	2.7	2.7	2.9	2.7	3.2	3.3	3.0	2.8	

Legislators in committee compared to a decade ago

Questions	AZ	AR	CA	CO	ME	OH	IL	IN	KS	Total	Signif.
13. Willing to compromise in committee.	2.5	2.5	2.4	2.6	2.4	2.4	2.5	2.9	2.2	2.4	
14. Collegial and courteous in committee.	2.1	2.5	2.4	2.0	2.6	2.2	2.9	3.0	2.1	2.3	*
15. Willing to amend/substitute bills in committee.	2.8	2.6	3.1	3.0	2.9	2.8	2.7	3.0	3.0	2.9	
16. Knowledgeable about issues before the committee.	2.1	1.7	1.9	2.1	2.3	1.9	2.8	3.1	2.5	2.1	***
17. Likely to seek public input on legislation.	2.6	2.8	2.5	2.7	2.9	2.5	3.1	3.2	2.8	2.7	**
Total	2.4	2.4	2.5	2.5	2.6	2.4	2.8	3.1	2.5	2.5	

Legislators on the floor compared to a decade ago

Questions	AZ	AR	CA	CO	ME	OH	IL	IN	KS	Total	Signif.
18. Likely to follow parliamentary procedure.	2.4	2.5	2.4	2.5	2.4	2.6	3.2	3.0	2.6	2.6	***
19. Willing to follow floor leaders.	2.3	2.6	3.2	2.6	2.5	2.6	3.9	3.2	2.0	2.6	
20. Likely to offer amendments.	3.1	2.5	3.1	3.2	3.2	2.9	2.4	3.1	3.8	3.0	**
21. Collegial and courteous to	2.1	2.6	2.3	2.0	2.7	2.4	2.6	3.0	2.1	2.4	

	AZ	AR	CA	CO	ME	OH	IL	IN	KS	Total	Signif.
other members.											
Total	2.5	2.6	2.7	2.6	2.7	2.6	3.0	3.1	2.6	2.7	

Influences of (_) relative to the legislature compared to a decade ago

Questions	AZ	AR	CA	CO	ME	OH	IL	IN	KS	Total	Signif.
22. The governor	3.2	3.5	3.4	3.9	3.9	2.1	2.6	2.6	3.1	2.9	
23. Administrative agencies	3.0	3.9	2.9	3.5	4.0	2.9	2.8	2.9	2.8	3.1	
24. Majority and minority party leaders	2.5	3.3	3.3	2.7	2.9	3.0	4.0	3.2	2.5	3.0	
25. Nonpartisan staff	3.3	3.5	2.6	3.4	3.4	2.9	2.8	3.1	3.0	3.1	
26. Partisan staff	3.8	3.4	3.8	3.8	3.6	3.9	3.9	3.5	3.4	3.7	**
27. Personal staff (skip, if no personal staff available to members)	3.4	3.3	3.7	3.7	3.3	3.6	3.1	3.2	3.3	3.5	**
28. Legislative committees	2.7	3.1	2.6	2.9	2.6	3.0	2.8	3.3	2.8	2.9	
29. Legislative party caucuses	2.8	3.6	3.6	2.8	2.9	3.6	3.5	3.5	2.7	3.3	*
30. Lobbyists	3.9	3.9	4.1	3.9	4.0	4.0	4.0	3.6	3.6	3.9	
Total	3.1	3.5	3.3	3.4	3.4	3.2	3.3	3.2	3.0	3.3	

Legislators in their districts compared to a decade ago

Questions	AZ	AR	CA	CO	ME	OH	IL	IN	KS	Total	Signif.
31. Spend time talking to their constituents.	2.9	3.0	2.7	3.0	2.9	3.0	3.1	3.5	2.9	3.0	
32. Spend time solving constituents' problems.	2.8	2.8	2.9	2.8	3.1	2.8	3.4	3.6	2.9	2.9	**
33. Seek state funds for projects in their districts.	2.8	3.6	3.5	3.0	3.1	3.2	4.0	3.9	3.1	3.3	**
34. Send newsletters or other mailings to their constituents.	2.9	3.0	3.3	3.4	3.2	3.2	3.6	4.1	3.6	3.3	***
Total	2.9	3.1	3.1	3.1	3.1	3.0	3.5	3.8	3.1	3.1	

Compared to a decade ago, how much more or less

Questions	AZ	AR	CA	CO	ME	OH	IL	IN	KS	Total	Signif.
35. Successful are committee recommendations on the floor?	2.9	3.1	2.9	3.2	2.5	2.8	3.0	3.2	2.8	2.9	
36. Control does the leadership have over committees?	2.8	2.9	3.2	3.0	2.5	3.3	4.1	3.4	2.6	3.1	
37. Partisan is the legislature as a whole?	3.9	3.9	4.4	4.1	3.5	4.2	4.1	3.6	3.9	4.0	
38. Attention do legislators give to statewide issues?	2.6	2.4	2.4	2.8	3.0	2.6	3.1	3.3	2.5	2.7	**
39. Deliberation (debate, negotiation and compromise) takes place in the legislative process?	2.4	2.5	2.0	2.5	2.6	2.4	2.6	2.8	2.4	2.4	
40. Aggressive are legislators in seeking campaign funds?	3.5	3.6	4.2	4.3	3.3	4.6	4.2	4.5	4.2	4.2	
Total	3.0	3.1	3.2	3.3	2.9	3.3	3.6	3.4	3.1	3.2	

Legislative leaders compared to a decade ago

Questions	AZ	AR	CA	CO	ME	OH	IL	IN	KS	Total	Signif.
41. Focus on election campaigns.	3.3	3.4	4.1	4.3	3.6	4.3	4.1	4.1	3.8	4.0	
42. Be selected on the basis of their fund raising capabilities.	2.5	3.1	4.1	3.5	3.3	4.4	3.7	3.6	3.3	3.8	**

	AZ	AR	CA	CO	ME	OH	IL	IN	KS	Total	Signif.
43. Move through an established ladder of leadership positions.	2.0	2.1	2.3	2.3	2.7	2.0	2.9	3.0	2.5	2.3	***
44. Be involved in candidate recruitment.	2.7	2.8	3.2	3.5	3.7	3.8	3.8	3.7	3.6	3.5	
45. Sanction rebellious legislators.	2.4	2.6	2.7	2.8	2.8	3.4	3.3	3.1	2.6	3.0	
46. Plan their path to leadership positions early in their legislative careers.	4.0	3.6	3.9	4.0	4.1	4.4	3.5	3.2	3.3	4.0	***
Total	2.8	2.9	3.4	3.4	3.3	3.7	3.6	3.5	3.2	3.4	

Legislative procedures implemented compared to a decade ago

Questions	AZ	AR	CA	CO	ME	OH	IL	IN	KS	Total	Signif.
47. More frequent or improved training for legislators.	2.1	2.3	2.1	2.5	2.0	2.0	1.8	2.0	1.6	2.0	***
48. Establishing regular patterns of leadership rotation and succession.	1.1	1.6	1.6	1.7	1.8	1.6	1.1	1.1	1.1	1.5	***
49. Planning for succession of committee chairs through committee placements of new members.	1.3	1.4	1.5	1.7	1.4	1.8	1.3	1.4	1.3	1.5	***
50. Increased staff support.	1.8	2.0	1.5	1.7	1.6	1.7	1.9	1.9	1.4	1.7	
51. Increased reliance on formal rules in place of traditions and norms.	1.4	1.8	1.3	1.7	1.7	1.5	1.6	1.5	1.4	1.6	
Total	1.5	1.8	1.6	1.9	1.7	1.7	1.5	1.6	1.4	1.7	

Legislative procedures helped improve leg. process compared to a decade ago

Questions	AZ	AR	CA	CO	ME	OH	IL	IN	KS	Total
52. More frequent or improved training for legislators.	2.0	2.0	2.1	2.3	2.1	1.9	2.1	2.0	1.9	2.0
53. Establishing regular patterns of leadership rotation and succession.	1.1	1.5	1.4	1.5	1.4	1.4	1.2	1.4	1.2	1.4
54. Planning for succession of committee chairs through committee placements of new members.	1.4	1.5	1.6	2.0	1.6	1.6	2.0	1.7	1.6	1.6
55. Increased staff support.	2.0	2.0	1.4	2.0	1.9	1.7	2.1	2.3	1.7	1.8
56. Increased reliance on formal rules in place of traditions and norms.	1.5	1.6	1.3	1.5	1.7	1.4	1.6	2.0	1.5	1.5
Total	1.7	1.8	1.6	1.9	1.8	1.6	1.8	2.0	1.6	1.7

Note: Significance=Level of confidence that results from term-limited states are different from those of non-term-limited states. *p>95%; **p>99%; ***p>99.9%

References

Allebaugh, Dalene, and Neil Pinney. 2003. "The Real Costs of Term Limits: Comparative Study of Competition and Electoral Costs." In *The Test of Time: Coping with Legislative Term Limits*, ed. Rick Farmer, John David Rausch Jr., and John C. Green. Lanham, MD: Lexington Books.

Axelrod, Robert. 1981. "The Emergence of Cooperation among Egoists." *American Political Science Review* 75:306–18.

Axelrod, Robert. 1984. *The Evolution of Cooperation*. New York: Basic Books.

Basehart, Harry. 1980. "The Effect of Membership Stability on Continuity and Experience in U.S. State Legislative Committees." *Legislative Studies Quarterly* 5:55–68.

Battista, James Coleman. 2006. "Jurisdiction, Institutional Structure, and Committee Representativeness." *Political Research Quarterly* 59:47–56.

Benjamin, Gerald, and Michael J. Malbin, eds. 1992. *Limiting Legislative Terms*. Washington, DC: CQ Press.

Benson, Clea. 2005. "Same-Sex Marriage Gets State Senate OK." *Sacramento Bee*, September 2, A1.

Berman, David R. 2004. *Effects of Legislative Term Limits in Arizona*. Final Report for the Joint Project on Term Limits. http://www.ncsl.org/jptl/casestudies/CaseContents.htm.

Beyle, Thad. 2003. "The Governors." In *Politics in the American States*, ed. Virginia Gray and Russell L. Hanson, 8th ed. Washington, DC: CQ Press.

Bowser, Jennifer Drage, Rich Jones, Karl T. Kurtz, Nancy Rhyme, and Brian Weberg. 2003. "The Impact of Term Limits on Legislative Leadership." In *The Test of Time: Coping with Legislative Term Limits*, ed. Rick Farmer, John David Rausch Jr., and John C. Green. Lanham, MD: Lexington Books.

Burke, Edmund. 1774. *The Works of the Right Honourable Edmund Burke*. London: Henry G. Bohn.

Burns, John. 1971. *The Sometime Governments: A Critical Study of the 50 American Legislatures*. New York: Bantam Books.

Cain, Bruce. 1996. "The Varying Impact of Legislative Term Limits." In *Legislative Term Limits: Public Choice Perspectives*, ed. Bernard Grofman. Boston, MA: Kluwer Academic Publishers.

Cain, Bruce, and Thad Kousser. 2004. *Adapting to Term Limits in California: Recent Experiences and New Directions*. Final Report for the Joint Project on Term Limits. http://www.ncsl.org/jptl/casestudies/CaseContents.htm.

Cain, Bruce, and Marc A. Levin. 1999. "Term Limits." *Annual Review of Political Science* 2:163–88.

Capell, Elizabeth A. 1996. "The Impact of Term Limits on the California Legislatures: An Interest Group Perspective." In *Legislative Term Limits: Public Choice Perspectives*, ed. Bernard Grofman. Boston, MA: Kluwer Academic Publishers.

Caress, Stanley. 1999. "The Influence of Term Limits on the Electoral Success of Women." *Women and Politics* 20:45–63.

Caress, Stanley, Charles D. Elder, Richard Elling, J.-P. Faletta, S. Orr, E. Rader, Marjorie Sarbaugh-Thompson, John Strate, and Lyke Thompson. 2003. "Effect of Term Limits on the Election of Minority State Legislators." *State and Local Government Review* 35:183–95.

Carey, John M. 1998. *Term Limits and Legislative Representation*. New York: Cambridge University Press.

Carey, John M., Richard G. Niemi, and Lynda W. Powell. 2000. *Term Limits in State Legislatures*. Ann Arbor: University of Michigan Press.

Carey, John M., Richard G. Niemi, Lynda W. Powell, and Gary Moncrief. 2006. "The Effects of Term Limits on State Legislatures: Results from a New Survey of the 50 States." *Legislative Studies Quarterly* 30:105–34.

Carroll, Susan, and Krista Jenkins. 2001. "Do Term Limits Help Women Get Elected?" *Social Science Quarterly* 82:197–201.

Clucas, Richard A. 2001. "Principle-Agent Theory and the Power of State House Speakers." *Legislative Studies Quarterly* 26:319–38.

Clucas, Richard A. 2003. "California: The New Amateur Politics." In *The Test of Time: Coping with Legislative Term Limits*, ed. Rick Farmer, John David Rausch Jr., and John C. Green. Lanham, MD: Lexington Books.

Cohen, Linda R., and Matthew L. Spitzer. 1996. "Term Limits and Representation." In *Legislative Term Limits: Public Choice Perspectives*, ed. Bernard Grofman. Boston, MA: Kluwer Academic Publishers.

Cooper, Christopher A., and Lilliard E. Richardson Jr. 2006. "Institutions and Representational Roles in American State Legislatures." *State Politics and Policy Quarterly* 6: 174–94.

Corwin, Erik H. 1991. "Limits on Legislative Terms: Legal and Policy Implications." *Harvard Journal on Legislation* 28:569–608.

Cox, Gary W., and Mathew D. McCubbins. 1993. *Legislative Leviathan: Party Government in the House*. Berkeley: University of California Press.

Cox, Gary W., and Matthew D. McCubbins. 2005. *Setting the Agenda: Responsible Party Government in the U.S. House of Representatives*. Cambridge: Cambridge University Press.

Crane, Edward H., and Roger Pilon, eds. 1994. *The Politics and Law of Term Limits.* Washington, DC: Cato Institute.

Daniel, Kermit, and John R. Lott. 1997. "Term Limits and Electoral Competitiveness: Evidence from California's State Legislative Races." *Public Choice* 90:165–84.

English, Art, and Brian Weberg. 2004. *Term Limits in the Arkansas General Assembly: A Citizen Legislature Responds.* Final Report for the Joint Project on Term Limits. http://www.ncsl.org/jptl/casestudies/CaseContents.htm.

Erickson, Brenda. 1996. *Inside the Legislative Process.* Denver, CO: National Conference of State Legislatures.

Everson, David H. 1992. "The Impact of Term Limitations on States: Cutting the Underbrush or Chopping Down the Tall Timber?" In *Limiting Legislative Terms*, ed. Gerald Benjamin and Michael J. Malbin. Washington, DC: CQ Press.

Farmer, Rick, and Thomas H. Little. 2004. *Legislative Power in the Buckeye State: The Revenge of Term Limits.* Final Report for the Joint Project on Term Limits. http://www.ncsl.org/jptl/casestudies/CaseContents.htm.

Farmer, Rick, Christopher Z. Mooney, Richard J. Powell, and John C. Green, eds. Forthcoming. *Legislating without Experience: Case Studies in State Legislative Term Limits.* Lanham, MD: Lexington Books.

Farmer, Rick, John David Rausch Jr., and John C. Green, eds. 2003. *The Test of Time: Coping with Legislative Term Limits.* Lanham, MD: Lexington Books.

Feustel, Bruce, and Rich Jones. 2001. "Legislator Training 101." *State Legislatures* 27, no. 8: 16–19.

Francis, Wayne L. 1989. *The Legislative Committee Game: A Comparative Analysis of Fifty States.* Columbus: Ohio State University Press.

Francis, Wayne L., and Lawrence Kenney. 2000. *Up the Political Ladder.* Thousand Oaks, CA.: Sage Publications.

Fund, John H. 1992. "Term Limitation: An Idea Whose Time Has Come." In *Limiting Legislative Terms*, ed. Gerald Benjamin and Michael J. Malbin. Washington, DC: CQ Press.

Glazer, Amihai, and Martin P. Wattenberg. 1996. "How Will Term Limits Affect Legislative Work?" In *Legislative Term Limits: Public Choice Perspectives*, ed. Bernard Grofman. Boston, MA: Kluwer Academic Publishers.

Goldstein, Kenneth M. 1999. *Interest Groups, Lobbying, and Participation in America.* Cambridge: Cambridge University Press.

Gordon, Stacey B., and Cynthia L. Unmack. 2003. "The Effect of Term Limits on Corporate PAC Allocation Patterns: The More Things Change . . ." *State and Local Government Review* 35:26–37.

Grofman, Bernard. 1996. "Introduction to the Term Limits Debate. Hypotheses in Search of Data." In *Legislative Term Limits: Public Choice Perspectives*, ed. Bernard Grofman. Boston, MA: Kluwer Academic Publishers.

Hamm, Keith E., and Ronald D. Hedlund. 1990. "Accounting for Change in the Number of State Legislative Committee Positions." *Legislative Studies Quarterly* 15:201–26.

Hamm, Keith E., Ronald D. Hedlund, and Nancy Martorano. 2001. "Structuring

Committee Decision-Making: Rules and Procedures in U.S. State Legislatures." *Journal of Legislative Studies* 7:13–34.

Heaphey, James J., and Alan P. Balutis, eds. 1975. *Legislative Staffing: A Comparative Perspective.* Beverly Hills, CA: Sage Publications.

Hedlund, Ronald D., and Keith E. Hamm. 1996. "Political Parties as Vehicles for Organizing U.S. State Legislative Committees." *Legislative Studies Quarterly* 21:383–408.

Hibbing, John R., and Elizabeth Theiss-Morse. 1995. *Congress as Public Enemy.* Cambridge: Cambridge University Press.

Hinckley, Barbara. 1980. "House Re-elections and Senate Defeats: The Role of the Challenger." *British Journal of Political Science* 10:441–60.

Hird, John A. 2005. *Power, Knowledge, and Politics: Policy Analysis in the States.* Washington, DC: Georgetown University Press.

Hodson, Timothy, Rich Jones, Karl Kurtz, and Gary Moncrief. 1995. "Leaders and Limits: Changing Patterns of State Legislative Leadership under Term Limits." *Spectrum: The Journal of State Government* 68 (summer): 6–15.

Householder, Larry. 2001. "Term Limits and a Model for Governance." *Spectrum: The Journal of State Government* 74 (fall): 31.

Jewell, Malcolm E., and Marcia Lynn Whicker. 1994. *Legislative Leadership in the American States.* Ann Arbor: University of Michigan Press.

Joint Project on Term Limits. 2002. Project Reports for Arkansas, California, Colorado, Maine, Ohio. Working paper, National Conference of State Legislatures, Denver.

Kousser, Thad. 2005. *Term Limits and the Dismantling of State Legislative Professionalism.* Cambridge: Cambridge University Press.

Kousser, Thad, Gary Cox, and Mathew McCubbins. 2005. "What Polarizes Parties? Preferences and Agenda Control in American State Legislatures." Paper presented at the annual meeting of the American Political Science Association, Washington, DC.

Krehbiel, Keith. 1991. *Information and Legislative Organization.* Ann Arbor: University of Michigan Press.

Kroszner, Randall S., and Thomas Stratmann. 1998. "Interest-Group Competition and the Organization of Congress: Theory and Evidence from Financial Services' Political Action Committees." *American Economic Review* 88:1163–87.

Kurtz, Karl T. 1974. "The State Legislatures." In *The Book of the States.* Lexington, KY: Council of State Governments.

Kurtz, Karl T. 2006. "Custodians of American Democracy." *State Legislatures* 32, no. 7: 28–32.

Little, Thomas. 2001. "Lighting a Candle rather than Cursing the Darkness: Adapting to the Challenge of Legislative Term Limits." *Spectrum: The Journal of State Government* 74 (fall): 33–35.

Loftus, Tom. 1994. *The Art of Legislative Politics.* Washington, DC: CQ Press.

Luttbeg, Norman. 1992. "Legislative Careers in Six States: Are Some Legislatures More Likely to Be Responsive?" *Legislative Studies Quarterly* 17:49–68.

Malbin, Michael J., and Gerald Benjamin. 1992. "Legislatures after Term Limits."

In *Limiting Legislative Terms*, ed. Gerald Benjamin and Michael J. Malbin. Washington, DC: CQ Press.

Meinke, Scott, and Edward Hasecke. 2003. "Term Limits, Professionalization, and Partisan Control in U.S. State Legislatures." *Journal of Politics* 65:898–908.

Milbrath, Lester W. 1960. "Lobbying as a Communication Process." *Public Opinion Quarterly* 24:32–53.

Mitchell, Cleta Deatherage. 1991. "Limit Terms? Yes!" In *Extension of Remarks*. Norman, OK: Carl Albert Congressional Research and Studies Center.

Moen, Matthew C., Kenneth T. Palmer, and Richard J. Powell. 2004. *Changing Members: The Maine Legislature in the Era of Term Limits*. Lanham, MD: Lexington Books.

Moncrief, Gary, Richard G. Niemi, and Lynda Powell. 2004. "Time, Term Limits, and Turnover: Trends in Membership Stability in U.S. State Legislatures." *Legislative Studies Quarterly* 29:357–81.

Moncrief, Gary, and Joel A. Thompson. 2001a. "Lobbyists' Views on Term Limits." *Spectrum: The Journal of State Government* 74 (fall): 13–15.

Moncrief, Gary, and Joel A. Thompson. 2001b. "On the Outside Looking In: Lobbyists' Perceptions on the Effects of State Legislative Term Limits." *State Politics and Policy Quarterly* 1:394–411.

Moncrief, Gary, Joel A. Thompson, and William Cassie. 1996. "Revisiting the State of U.S. State Legislative Research." *Legislative Studies Quarterly* 21:301–35.

Moncrief, Gary, Joel Thompson, Michael Haddon, and Robert Hoyer. 1992. "For Whom the Bell Tolls: Term Limits and State Legislatures." *Legislative Studies Quarterly* 17:37–47.

Mooney, Christopher Z. 1991. "Peddling Information in the State Legislature: Closeness Counts." *Western Political Quarterly* 44:433–44.

Mooney, Christopher Z., and Tim Storey. 2004. *The Illinois General Assembly, 1992–2003: Leadership Control, Continuity, and Partisanship*. Final Report for the Joint Project on Term Limits. http://www.ncsl.org/jptl/casestudies/CaseContents.htm.

National Conference of State Legislatures. 2002. *New Member Orientation Survey Results*. http://www.ncsl.org/programs/legismgt/orientation.htm.

National Conference of State Legislatures. 2003. *50 State Staff Count, 1979, 1988, 1996, 2003*. http://www.ncsl.org/programs/legman/about/staffcount2003.htm.

National Conference of State Legislatures. 2004. *NCSL Backgrounder: Full- and Part-Time Legislatures*. http://www.ncsl.org/programs/press/2004/back grounder_fullandpart.htm.

Neal, Tommy. 1996. *Lawmaking and the Legislative Process: Committees, Connections, and Compromises*. Denver, CO: National Conference of State Legislatures.

Newmark, Adam J. 2005. "Measuring State Legislative Lobbying Regulation, 1990–2003." *State Politics and Policy Quarterly* 5:182–91.

Niemi, Richard G., and Lynda W. Powell. 2003. "Limited Citizenship? Knowing and Contacting State Legislators after Term Limits." In *The Test of Time: Coping with Legislative Term Limits*, ed. Rick Farmer, John David Rausch Jr., and John C. Green. Lanham, MD: Lexington Books.

Nownes, Anthony J. 2001. *Pressure and Politics: Organized Interest in American Politics.* Boston: Houghton Mifflin.

Nownes, Anthony J., and Patricia K. Freeman. 1998. "Interest Group Activity in the American States." *Journal of Politics* 60:86–112.

Olson, David J. 1992. "Term Limits Fail in Washington: The 1991 Battleground." In *Limiting Legislative Terms*, ed. Gerald Benjamin and Michael J. Malbin. Washington, DC: CQ Press.

Opheim, Cynthia. 1994. "The Effect of U.S. State Legislative Term Limits Revisited." *Legislative Studies Quarterly* 19:49–59.

Overby, L. Marvin, and Thomas A. Kazee. 2000. "Outlying Committees in the Statehouse: An Examination of the Prevalence of Committee Outliers in State Legislatures." *Journal of Politics* 62:701–28.

Payne, James L. 1991. "Limiting Government by Limiting Congressional Terms." *Public Interest* 103:106–17.

Peery, George, and Thomas H. Little. 2003. "Views from the Bridge: Legislative Leaders' Perceptions of Institutional Power in the Stormy Wake of Term Limits." In *The Test of Time: Coping with Legislative Term Limits*, ed. Rick Farmer, John David Rausch Jr., and John C. Green. Lanham, MD: Lexington Books.

Penning, James M. 2003. "Michigan: The End Is Near." In *The Test of Time: Coping with Legislative Term Limits*, ed. Rick Farmer, John David Rausch Jr., and John C. Green. Lanham, MD: Lexington Books.

Petracca, Mark P. 1991. *The Poison of Professional Politics.* Policy Analysis 151. Washington, DC: Cato Institute.

Petracca, Mark P. 1992. "Rotation in Office: The History of an Idea." In *Limiting Legislative Terms*, ed. Gerald Benjamin and Michael J. Malbin. Washington, DC: CQ Press.

Polsby, Nelson W. 1975. "Legislatures." In *The Handbook of Political Science*, vol. 5, ed. Fred I. Greenstein and Nelson W. Polsby. Reading, MA: Addison-Wesley.

Polsby, Nelson W. 1990. "Limiting Terms Won't Curb Special Interests, Improve the Legislature, or Enhance Democracy." *Public Affairs Report* 31 (spring): 9.

Polsby, Nelson W. 1997. "Term Limits." In *New Federalist Papers: Essays in Defense of the Constitution*, ed. Alan Brinkley, Nelson W. Polsby, and Kathleen M. Sullivan. New York: Norton.

Powell, Richard J., and Rich Jones. 2004. *First in the Nation: Term Limits and the Maine Legislature.* Final Report for the Joint Project on Term Limits. http://www.ncsl.org/jptl/casestudies/CaseContents.htm.

Price, Charles M. 1992. "The Guillotine Comes to California: Term-Limit Politics in the Golden State." In *Limiting Legislative Terms*, ed. Gerald Benjamin and Michael J. Malbin. Washington, DC: CQ Press.

Rausch, John David, Jr. 2003. "Understanding the Term Limit Movement." In *The Test of Time: Coping with Legislative Term Limits*, ed. Rick Farmer, John David Rausch Jr., and John C. Green. Lanham, MD: Lexington Books.

Rosenthal, Alan. 1970. "An Analysis of Institutional Effects: Staffing Legislative Parties in Wisconsin." *Journal of Politics* 32:531–62.

Rosenthal, Alan. 1974. *Legislative Performance in the States: Explorations of Committee Behavior.* New York: Free Press.

Rosenthal, Alan. 1981. *Legislative Life*. New York: Harper and Row.

Rosenthal, Alan. 1992. "The Effects of Term Limits on Legislatures: A Comment." In *Limiting Legislative Terms*, ed. Gerald Benjamin and Michael J. Malbin. Washington, DC: CQ Press.

Rosenthal, Alan. 1993. *The Third House: Lobbyists and Lobbying in the States*. Washington, DC: CQ Press.

Rosenthal, Alan. 1996. "State Legislative Development: Observations from Three Perspectives." *Legislative Studies Quarterly* 21:169–98.

Rosenthal, Alan. 1998. *The Decline of Representative Democracy: Process, Participation, and Power in State Legislatures*. Washington, DC: CQ Press.

Rosenthal, Alan. 2004. *Heavy Lifting: The Job of the American Legislature*. Washington, DC: CQ Press.

Rothenberg, Larry S., and Mitchell S. Sanders. 2000. "Severing the Electoral Connection: Shirking in the Contemporary Congress." *American Journal of Political Science* 44:316–25.

Sarbaugh-Thompson, Marjorie, Lyke Thompson, Charles D. Elder, John Strate, and Richard C. Elling. 2004. *Political and Institutional Effects of Term Limits*. New York: Palgrave Macmillan.

Schaffner, Brian, Michael Wagner, and Jonathan Winburn. 2004. "Incumbents Out, Party In? Term Limits and Partisan Redistricting in State Legislatures." *State Politics and Policy Quarterly* 4:396–414.

Smith, Michael A., and Brenda Erickson. 2004. *Kansas: A Retro Approach to Lawmaking*. Final Report for the Joint Project on Term Limits. http://www.ncsl.org/jptl/casestudies/CaseContents.htm.

Smyth, Julie Carr. 2004. "House Speaker Householder Exits under Cloud, Unmet Goals." *Cleveland Plain Dealer*, December 14, B5.

Squire, Peverill, and Keith E. Hamm. 2005. *101 Chambers: Congress, State Legislatures, and the Future of Legislative Studies*. Columbus: Ohio State University Press.

Squire, Peverill, Keith Hamm, Ronald Hedlund, and Gary Moncrief. 2005. "Electoral Reforms, Membership Stability, and the Existence of Committee Property Rights in American State Legislatures." *British Journal of Political Science* 35:169–81.

State Legislative Leaders Foundation. 2004. "Effective Leadership in the Face of Legislative Term Limits: Larry Householder's Legislative Team." Centerville, MA: State Legislative Leaders Foundation.

State Legislative Leaders Foundation. 2005. *What Have You Gotten Yourself Into? A Guide for New Legislative Leaders*. 2nd ed. Centerville, MA: State Legislative Leaders Foundation.

Straayer, John. 2003. "Colorado: Lots of Commotion, Limited Consequences." In *The Test of Time: Coping with Legislative Term Limits*, ed. Rick Farmer, John David Rausch Jr., and John C. Green. Lanham, MD: Lexington Books.

Straayer, John, and Jennie Drage Bowser. 2004. *Colorado's Legislative Term Limits*. Final Report for the Joint Project on Term Limits. http://www.ncsl.org/jptl/casestudies/CaseContents.htm.

Struble, Robert, Jr., and Z. W. Jahre. 1991. "Rotation in Office: Rapid but Restricted to the House." *PS: Political Science and Politics* 24:34–38.

Swain, John W., Stephen A. Borrelli, Brian C. Reed, and Sean F. Evans. 2000. "A New Look at Turnover in the U.S. House of Representatives, 1789–1998." *American Politics Quarterly* 23:435–57.

Tabarrok, Alexander. 1994. "A Survey, Critique, and New Defense of Term Limits." *CATO Journal* 14:333–50.

Thomas, Clive S., and Ronald J. Hrebenar. 1996. "Interest Groups in the States." In *Politics in the American States*, ed. Virginia Gray and Herbert Jacob, 6th ed. Washington, DC: CQ Press.

Thomas, Clive S., and Ronald J. Hrebenar. 2004. "Interest Groups in the States." In *Politics in the American States*, ed. Virginia Gray and Russell L. Hanson, 8th ed. Washington, DC: CQ Press.

Thompson, Joel A., Karl Kurtz, and Gary F. Moncrief. 1996. "We've Lost That Family Feeling: The Changing Norms of the New Breed of State Legislators." *Social Science Quarterly* 77:344–62.

Thompson, Joel A., and Gary Moncrief. 1993. "Implications of Term Limits for Women and Minorities." *Social Science Quarterly* 74:300–309.

Weberg, Brian. 1988. "Changes in Legislative Staff." *Journal of State Government* 64:190–97.

Weberg, Brian. 1997. "New Age Dawns for Legislative Staff." *State Legislatures* 23, no. 1: 26–31.

Will, George F. 1992. *Restoration: Congress, Term Limits, and the Recovery of Deliberative Democracy*. New York: Free Press.

Wright, Gerald C., and David Ogle. 2004. *The Indiana General Assembly*. Final Report for the Joint Project on Term Limits. http://www.ncsl.org/jptl/cases tudies/CaseContents.htm.

Wright, John. 1996. *Interest Groups and Congress: Lobbying, Contributions, and Influence*. Boston: Allyn and Bacon.

Contributors

DAVID R. BERMAN is a senior research fellow at the Morrison Institute for Public Policy and a professor emeritus of political science at Arizona State University. He is the author of *Local Government and the States; State and Local Politics; Arizona Government and Politics; Reformers, Corporations, and the Electorate;* and other works on state and local politics.

JENNIE DRAGE BOWSER is a program principal in the Legislative Management Program of the National Conference of State Legislatures. She specializes in the issues of term limits, initiative and referendum, campaign finance reform, and elections.

BRUCE CAIN is a Robson professor of political science and the director of the Institute of Governmental Studies at the University of California, Berkeley. He is the coauthor or coeditor of *The Reapportionment Puzzle, The Personal Vote, Congressional Redistricting,* and *Voting at the Political Fault Line: California's Experiment with the Blanket Primary.* He has served widely as a redistricting consultant.

RICK FARMER is the director of committee staff at the Oklahoma House of Representatives and a fellow at the Ray C. Bliss Institute of Applied Politics at the University of Akron. He is a coeditor of *The Test of Time: Coping with Legislative Term Limits.*

THAD KOUSSER is an assistant professor of political science at the University of California, San Diego. He is the author of *Term Limits and the Dismantling of State Legislative Professionalism* and has published research on the initiative process, reapportionment, recall elections, campaign finance laws, the blanket primary, health care policy, and European Parliament elections.

KARL T. KURTZ is the director of the Trust for Representative Democracy of the National Conference of State Legislatures and has been working with and studying American legislatures for over thirty years. He is a coauthor of *Republic on Trial: The Case for Representative Democracy.*

THOMAS H. LITTLE is the director of curriculum development and research for the State Legislative Leaders Foundation and an adjunct professor at the University of North Carolina at Greensboro. He is the author of several articles on leadership, state legislatures, and political parties and the coauthor of an upcoming reference book on state legislatures.

GARY MONCRIEF is a University Foundation research scholar and professor of political science at Boise State University. His publications include three books and over fifty book chapters and research articles on various aspects of state politics and state legislatures.

CHRISTOPHER Z. MOONEY is a professor of political studies at the University of Illinois at Springfield and a research fellow at the university's Institute of Government and Public Affairs. He is also the founding editor of *State Politics and Policy Quarterly*.

RICHARD G. NIEMI is Don Alonzo Watson professor of political science at the University of Rochester. He is the coauthor or coeditor of *Vital Statistics on American Politics, 2007–2008; Comparing Democracies 2; Term Limits in the State Legislatures;* and *Civic Education: What Makes Students Learn.*

LYNDA W. POWELL is a professor of political science at the University of Rochester. She is the coauthor of *Serious Money: Fundraising and Contributing in Presidential Nomination Campaigns, Term Limits in the State Legislatures,* and *The Financiers of Congressional Elections.*

RICHARD J. POWELL is an associate professor of political science at the University of Maine. He is the author of journal articles and book chapters on the presidency, Congress, elections, and state politics and is a coauthor of *Changing Members: The Maine Legislature in the Era of Term Limits.*

ALAN ROSENTHAL is a professor of public policy at the Eagleton Institute of Politics at Rutgers University. His research and writing have focused on state politics and state legislatures. His latest book is *Heavy Lifting: The Job of the American Legislature.*

MICHAEL SMITH is an assistant professor of political science at Emporia State University. He is the author of *Bringing Representation Home: State Legislators among Their Constituencies.* He has also published in *Perspectives in American Politics* and *Politics and Policy.*

TIM STOREY is a senior fellow with the National Conference of State Legislatures and specializes in the study of redistricting and legislative elections. He frequently consults with legislatures on staff organization and legislative institutional issues.

JOHN STRAAYER is a professor of political science at Colorado State University. He is the author of a number of books, including *The Colorado General Assembly.* Straayer directed an internship program in the Colorado legislature for over two decades.

BRIAN WEBERG is the director of the Legislative Management Program of the National Conference of State Legislatures. He specializes in legislative staff organization and management issues. He has written numerous articles on state legislative staffing and consults with legislatures on organizational and staff management issues.

GERALD WRIGHT is a professor of political science at Indiana University. He is a coauthor of *Statehouse Democracy* and has written numerous articles on legislative elections, public opinion, and representation at both the state and national level.

Index

Note: Page numbers in italic indicate tables and figures.